At last, a wine guid[e]
outstanding and a[ll]
all tasted by the 'p[...]

- The top 250 wines of the year – how
  much they cost, where to buy them
  and what they taste like

- An A-Z of invaluable advice on matching
  food and wine

- A global gazetteer of the best wine
  estates in the world

- A complete list of all the UK's best
  wine merchants

Whether you're a keen glugger or an
experienced oenophile, THE WINE LIST
is the only guide you'll ever need

'Buy this and you'll *never* drink
                    another bad bottle'
                    Mirror magazine

'An easy, *quick* guide' **Guardian**

'The *ideal* stocking filler...
A terrific read' **Woman & Home**

'This deserves to become an annual
must for anyone
who *loves* wine' **Bookseller**

'For all those people
who are slightly baffled
by the food and wine critics'
Joanne Harris, author of *Chocolat*

'A *must* for wine drinkers –
small, fun and *very* useful'
Alessandro Tome, Harpers & Queen

'Little *corker* – no snobbery here'
Real

THE WINE LIST 2005

THE TOP 250 WINES OF THE YEAR MATTHEW JUKES

headline

To Tom

www.thewinelist2005.com
www.expertwine.com

The right of Matthew Jukes to be identified as the Author of the Work has
been asserted by him in accordance with the Copyright, Designs and Patents
Act 1988.

First published in 2004 by
HEADLINE BOOK PUBLISHING

10 9 8 7 6 5 4 3 2 1

A CIP catalogue record for this title is available from the British Library

ISBN 0 7553 1250 3

Printed and bound in France by Pollina L93549
Designed by Fiona Pike, Pike Design

Headline Book Publishing
A division of Hodder Headline
338 Euston Road
London NW1 3BH

www.headline.co.uk
www.hodderheadline.com

CONTENTS

Three years in a row as the number one wine guide in the UK – thank you so much! The Top 250 has clearly hit the spot with your palates.

The book is split into four main sections:

The **A-Z of Food and Wine** will help you find which styles of wine go with any ingredient in a food lover's wish list. It will help you choose wine when you are eating out or entertaining at home. The **Gazetteer** is *the* comprehensive list of the finest wineries in the world – it is the ultimate vinous who's who. Add this priceless information to my Top 250 and you've cracked it! And the **Directory** is an essential compendium of the top independent wine merchants in the UK, plus their home town or postcode, telephone number and, if they have one, e-mail address. I have also included the HQ hot lines for each of the major supermarket and specialist wine retail chains.

The **Top 250** is the beating heart of **THE WINE LIST**, though. It is a distillation of over 25,000 of my tasting notes, into a final hard core 250. Fifty-one and a half week's worth of non-stop tasting ends and a few days' frantic writing begins. But how do I decide if a wine is worth listing? Every one of these bottles is the proud possessor of a knockout flavour and they all represent fantastic value for money – whether the price tag says a fiver or fifty quid. Also, I have made sure that each of the 250 wines is ready to drink now. Some of these bottles are in short supply and others will last all year round. If you like the sound of a wine, then get on the blower and reserve yourself some stock, as each year some wines sell out extremely quickly. Six months into the life of each edition of the book, I check out how many of the wines are still on the shelves – this number has never been less than two hundred and twenty so The Wine List is a true annual guide that works for the full twelve-month period. In many cases, I have tasted wines that are not even bottled in an effort to make this selection as cutting edge as possible. This means you'll be reading about some wines before anyone else in the UK (even the other wine journos) has even tasted them!

Bearing in mind I write every word of this book myself and don't use other people's tasting notes or refer to any industry databases, all of the research is mine. The prices and stockists of the wines are checked and rechecked, over and over, but things do change. Each year, after The Top 250 is published, more wine merchants understandably try to source these wines to sell to their own clientele. Clearly it is too late to list these shops as stockists so, come October, many of these wines will have much wider distribution. Price-wise, some shops may sell a little over my rrp (which I get from the UK agent), equally others can be under – I note the 'official' list price, so shop around and ask if merchants offer case discounts. Remember, if a shop is not on your doorstep, don't let it stop you buying their wines, as every merchant in this book delivers nationwide.

So, what trends appeared in the Top 250 this year? Last year the Old World had 150 wines exactly. This year the New World reigns supreme with 142. Australia and South Africa combined have a staggering 107 wines. If Australia is the mightiest power in the UK wine scene, then South Africa is the highest new entry. With 37 wines, this is a first-class year for the Cape. New Zealand, South America and California all held their form or increased their market share, but Spain, Italy and France all dropped the ball. The New World is working hard at the lower price points and, with generally better weather conditions, it is here where they have stolen the places from the Europeans. France and Spain, in particular, must do better next year.

Author's Note There are thousands of ordinary, dull or downright poor bottles out there – it is nothing short of a lottery if you go into a wine shop unprepared. This got me thinking – I probably write up about a total of 2,000 or so wines throughout the year between my website www.expertwine.com, the *Daily Mail* and, of course, The Wine List. But I taste well over 25,000 during the course of the year. That means that only one in twelve bottles is of a standard that I deem recommendable. Three or four others from the dozen might be OK – drinkable – but certainly not worthy of particular remark. It follows that seven or eight bottles are substandard and, in plenty of cases, actively unpalatable. Buyers are cutting corners and customers are either not sufficiently aware of the vast sliding scale of quality on the shelves, or they simply don't care. I travel the country lecturing about wine and I have never come across anyone who can't tell the difference between a poor bottle of wine and a first-class one, regardless of their supposed level of wine knowledge (even when these bottles are the exact same price). They just simply haven't had the choice of decent enough bottles, or the opportunity to taste a range and pick out their favourite. This is depressing. Most people buy on price and often they'll think the lower the better (the average price of a bottle of wine sold in the UK is around the £3.85 mark), but this is a disastrous way to pick out a bottle of wine.

This year there are only 21 wines under a fiver in the Top 250. This is because truly brilliant wines start around the six-pound mark. Allow me to explain. If you take the average cost of a cork, label, capsule and bottle, and add in transport, handling and the colossal duty charge, then mark this up by around 35% for gross profit (the average margin a retailer expects to make) and add VAT, you get a figure of £2.96. If you buy a bottle of wine for £3.49, clearly only 53p of that accounts for the cost of the wine itself – less VAT and margin and it's only 29p (less than 10% of the overall cost of the bottle). If you spend more, the base cost of the bottle, cork, duty etc. doesn't change, but the wine cost goes up exponentially. A £6.99er has around £2.23 worth of wine in it – seven times the wine at double the money! Which one would you rather be drinking this evening? The sub-fiver wines in this book are rare beauties – try these, by all means, for everyday drinking but, in general, it is time to trade up or go without!

THE TOP 250

£5.49 **Prosecco La Marca**, **NV**, Veneto, Italy (**Wai**). This epic little sparkler has made the Top 250 three years in a row – a remarkable achievement. In the world of five-pound fizzies this is the undisputed titleholder. Not much competition, you might say? Well, there is. La Marca is not only an effortlessly delicious wine to drink straight, it is also perfectly prickly and mightily refreshing when blended with peach juice to make a Bellini.

£6.49 **Hardy's Stamp Pinot Noir/Chardonnay**, **NV**, Australia (**Saf**, **Sai** and **Tes**). I tasted this wine 'blind' the other day and was amazed to discover that it was Stamp fizz (I thought it was around the tenner mark). This wine made the Top 250 last year because it is one of the best value party wines you can find. But it is more than that – it is a truly impressive sparkler that just happens to sport a teeny price tag.

£6.49 **Marqués de Monistrol Cava Selección Especial Rosé**, **NV**, Penedès, Spain (**Odd** and **Wai**). I am an unrepentant Cava snob. In other words, I don't choose to drink it very much, preferring to spend my time in the company of the other sparklers in this chapter. But very occasionally a cracker comes along and, like buses, very, very occasionally two. If I told you they were both rosés I am sure you'd fall over laughing. Well, here they are. Firstly, this stunner – it is my favourite sparkling pink in the world under a tenner – and, secondly, its big sister the 1997/8 Gran Reserva Rosé (£9.99, **Sai**). You will not believe how bright, ripe, smooth, delicious, dry, strawberry-kissed, well made and effervescent these wines are.

unadulterated *joy*

£7.99 **Jacob's Creek, Sparkling Chardonnay/Pinot Noir, NV**, Australia (**Mor**, **Saf**, **Sai**, **Som**, **Tes** and **Thr**). With a little more weight and a drier finish than Hardy's Stamp, this grown-up sparkler falls into my 'lunchtime' fizz category. When I am not in the mood for blockbuster Champagne, JC fills the gap without having to drop my standards. It has gone up a quid from last year but still looks phenomenally good value.

£8.49 **Pruno Nero Lambrusco, 2003**, Chiarli, Emilia Romagna, Italy (**Luvian's**, **Winecellars** and **Noel Young**). This is the smartest Lambrusco I have ever tasted. (OK, so there's not much competition.) Made from the Grasparossa grape variety it is bursting with wild strawberry and black cherry fruit, and it is, importantly, DRY! If you are eating crispy duck, rogan ghosh, oxtail, wild boar, venison bangers or even a dark chocolate pithivier, this is the wine to pop.

£8.60 **Blanquette de Limoux, Cuvée Princesse, 2001**, Sieur d'Arques, Limoux, France (**Jeroboams & Laytons**). I must admit, I let out a stifled giggle when the guys at Laytons opened this wine with its prissy label for me to taste. Blanquette has always been a bit naff, but they said, 'Wait for it. Taste it first!' I should have known better than to snigger because this wine is an unadulterated joy. It is bursting with fruit, and when they told me the price I was completely amazed. If you are organising a party and want to drink Champagne, stop and think. You could save five or more pounds on every bottle (add it up), so at least taste this first – it is a great wine. Just keep the label covered and everyone will praise your palate.

£9.99 **Greenpoint by Chandon**, NV, Brut, Australia (**Sai** and **Wai**). Greenpoint took a time out from the Top 250 last year as it was having some work done. It has emerged with its original name (it spent some time as Chandon Australia) and it has also tightened up the acidity and focused on a little more elegance and length. So, what's it like? It is finer than ever and still only a tenner.

£9.99 **Chapel Down Century Extra Dry**, NV, England (**English Wine Group at Tenterden Vineyard tel. 01580 763033** and **Sai**). The 'straight NV' Chapel Down (ex Top 250 twice) is one of my favourite sparklers for large parties (£7.99, **Boo**, **Saf**, **Selfridges**). This special 'Century Extra Dry' cuvée is a completely different kettle of fish. It is a bottle for true sparkling wine devotees. The palate is linear with an excellent, lifted attack on the nose, and a long, lingering, palate-cleansing finish. Lime, gooseberry and elderflower jostle for position on the palate, with elegant patisserie sauntering around in the background. At a tenner, this is sublime fizz. And now, for the first time these guys have cracked rosé – NV Chapel Down Brut Rosé (£13.99, **EWG** and **Philglas & Swiggot**) is made from a daring 100% Pinot Noir and it certainly hits the target.

£9.99 **Prosecco Santo Stefano**, NV, Ruggeri, Valdobbiadene, Veneto, Italy (**Bacchanalia**, **Boo**, **Harvey Nichols**, **Henderson**, **Sommelier**, **Valvona & Crolla**, **Villeneuve**, **Winecellars** and **Noel Young**). Top flight Prosecco must be drunk 'straight up' and not mixed. This single vineyard wine is as good as it gets, with surprising richness, tingly acidity, superb fruit and a lust for life.

£10.99 **Graham Beck Blanc de Blancs**, **1998**, Robertson, South Africa (**Bibendum**, **D. Byrne**, **Excecllars** and **Magnum**). This estate makes the best sparkling wines in the Cape. My chosen vintage Blanc de Blancs (100% Chardonnay) is extremely classy, with a white flower and faint citrus nose, a long, linear palate and crisp, cleansing finish. This is a very elegant wine indeed. If you want a truly great sparkling wine for a little over a tenner, this is a worthy bottle. Just to prove it's not a fluke, taste the NV Graham Beck Rosé (£10.99, stockists as above plus **Bintwo**) to see how competent Pieter Ferreira's winemaking is.

£12.99 **Jansz**, **1999**, Tasmania, Australia (**Bennett's**, **Thos. Peatling**, **Veritas**, **Vin du Van**, **Wine Library** and **Noel Young**). Vintage Jansz is luxurious, mouth filling, stunningly complex and it's also phenomenal value. This is one of my favourite sparkling wines in the world and when I opened this alongside two bottles of well-known, Grande Marque, vintage Champagne (£35 and £45) and served them blind to some pals, they unanimously chose Jansz.

£13.95 **Layton's Brut**, **NV**, Champagne, France (**Jeroboams & Laytons**). This wine still holds the 'best value Champs' in the country accolade for me, despite tasting loads of others in an effort to try and knock it off its spot – what a chore (hee hee). Wedding planners take note.

£14.95 **Camel Valley Cornwall Brut**, **2001**, Cornwall, England (**Wai** south west stores only and **Camel Valley Vineyard tel. 01208 77959**). Camel Valley makes a superb range of wines and this elegant sparkler is no exception.

It is smooth, charming, modern and, like Chapel Down's offerings, is at the vanguard of English sparkling winemaking. For some reason the old-timer estates (Nyetimber, Three Choirs etc.) seem to get the plaudits every year and these guys miss out. It is disappointing and this error of judgement is seriously slowing the industry down. Anyway, do your bit to support the perfectionists and dive into this ripe, lush, crowd-pleasing wine. If, however, you prefer stern, tight, racy, acidic fizzies, then head to another of Camel Valley's epic wines – 2001 Cornwall Pinot Noir Rosé (£19.95). It is a classy rosé sparkler that would give most rosé Champagnes a run for their money.

£17.50 **Larmandier-Bernier, Blanc de Blancs Premier Cru, NV**, Champagne, France (**Vine Trail**). Made from 100% Chardonnay, this is a striking and memorable wine. The flavour is profound – rich, lingering, intense and all enveloping. The finish is ever so long and very dry, and for that reason this is a foody style of Champagne. Fish and chips would be spot on but, if you really want to set this wine off well, get down to your fishmongers because a Dover sole and Dauphinoise potatoes would be perfect with a wine of this class.

£17.75 **Fleury Père et Fils, NV**, Champagne, France (**Vintage Roots** and **Wai**). There are not many organically grown grapes in Champagne. There are also not many sub-twenty-pound Champagnes (the important ones are in this list!). So when both bases are covered by one wine, it is worth taking note. Fleury is a balanced, bright, lively brew, with a frothy disposition and a long, even finish.

£17.99 **Théophile Roederer Brut**, **NV**, Champagne, France (**Fortnum & Mason**). Everyone has heard of Louis Roederer but nobody knows about the power behind the throne, Théophile, the holding company of Louis R! This is a stunning Champagne, with every flavour facet that you'd expect from such a Grand Vin but without the hefty price tag! Check it out.

£19.95 **Pierre Vaudon Brut Premier Cru**, **1996**, Champagne, France (**Haynes, Hanson & Clark**). You may not have heard of Pierre Vaudon but don't worry, because he flies under the radar. If you want to turn on some serious style, look no further than this spectacular bottle. Made from 75% Pinot Noir and 25% Chardonnay, it is terrifically rich and full on the palate, and it has superb revitalising acidity on the finish. Jim Eustace, wine buyer and all-round top geezer at HHC, reckons this is his favourite 1996 vintage Champagne, and that includes wines that retail for three times the price. He is not far wrong!

£19.95 **Berrys' United Kingdom Cuvée Rosé**, **NV**, Brut, Théophile Roederer, Champagne, France (**Berry Bros. & Rudd**). I rarely write up rosé Champagne, not because I don't love the style but because there are very few truly first-class versions out there. My regular TWL readers know I love Billecart-Salmon's gorgeous rosé (£34.99, **Berry Bros.**, **Lea & Sandeman**, **Odd**, **Peckham & Rye**, **Uncorked**, **Valvona & Crolla**, **Noel Young**), but at thirty-five quid this is a special occasion wine in the Jukesy household. Try Berry Bros. own label rosé instead. Made by the fabulous Théophile Roederer team, this is one of the best-value rosé Champagnes I have ever tasted. It is fine, elegant and classy, with good intensity and a luscious, ripe finish. It is, in one word, a stunner.

£19.95 **The Wine Society's Champagne**, **Brut**, **NV**, France (**Wine Society**). Made by the esteemed Champagne house Alfred Gratien, this is one of the finest own label Champagnes I have seen this year. The Wine Society recently celebrated their 250,000th share (or member) and they opened cases and cases of this wine for their thirsty audience – everyone loved it. The flavour is very grand and complex, with layers of flavour. I savoured every drop.

£20.30 **Gatinois**, **Grand Cru Brut Rosé**, **NV**, Aÿ, Champagne, France (**Haynes Hanson & Clark**). HHC again, and not a moment too soon! These guys really know how to sniff out exceptional wines. Gatinois is an old favourite in TWL, but I have not written about this cuvée before. With 100% Grand Cru Pinot Noir vines from the finest red grape village in the whole of Champagne, Aÿ, this is bound to be pretty smart. But nothing prepares you for the impact of this wine. It is spectacular, breathtaking, shocking almost, in its broad brushstrokes of flavour. A core of ripe, wild strawberry fruit is spiked with lightning strikes of tart mulberries and underpinned with warm, crunchy, almond cookie nuances. If you like this then pick up a few bottles of the white counterpart NV Gatinois Grand Cru Brut Reserve as well (£18.10, **HHC**), it is also a 100% Pinot Noir and is truly magnificent.

£23.75 **Dumagnin**, **Brut Vintage**, **1997**, Champagne, France (**Yapp Bros.**). This is a very small price to pay for a full-on vintage brew. It is sleek, cleansing and toasty on the palate, and the finish is light-years long. Well played – a new name to me, and one that I will be watching very closely.

£26.00 **Jacquesson**, **Cuvée No.728**, **NV**, Champagne, France (**Bintwo**, **Inspired Wines**, **Mayfair Cellars**, **La Réserve**, **Theatre of Wine** and **Wine in Cornwall**). Balanced, ripe and with great integrity and energy, this is an intellectual Champagne with a multi-layered palate and a smooth, lingering finish. Jacquesson is a house to look out for since they are really making waves in the wine trade and are sure to break on to the market in a big way at any moment.

£39.99 **Pol Roger**, **Brut Vintage**, **1996**, Champagne, France (**Bibendum**, **Corney & Barrow**, **Goedhuis & Co.**, **Haynes, Hanson & Clark**, **Lay & Wheeler**, **Maj**, **Odd**, **La Réserve**, **Tanners** and **Wine Society**). This is youthful and explosive in the glass, and the palate needs a few more months to settle down, but this might very well be Pol Roger's finest Brut Vintage since 1990. As prices creep up for this calibre of wine, it is nice to see Pol clinging like a limpet to the £40 barrier.

£49.99 **Billecart-Salmon**, **Cuvée Nicolas-François**, **1996**, Champagne, France (**Berry Bros.**, **Fortnum & Mason**, **Harrods**, **Lay & Wheeler**, **James Nicholson**, **Odd**, **Selfridges** and **Uncorked**). Billecart is regarded as one of the finest Champagne houses on the planet. I must admit that I drink more NV Billecart at home than any other label – it is nothing short of heavenly. My chosen vintage cuvée, Nicolas-François, has always been spectacular – the 1959 won the title of best Champagne of the 20th century. I fully expect this 1996 to follow in its footsteps, as it is staggeringly precise on the nose and extraordinarily long, dazzling and keen on the palate. Watch out for the hypnotic and glittering 1996 Blanc de Blancs (£56.99, **Harrods** and **Uncorked**) – it is yet another mind-blowing offering from this never-ending cellar of surprises.

£49.99 **Louis Roederer**, **Brut Vintage**, **1997**, Champagne, France (**Averys**, **Berry Bros.**, **S.H. Jones**, **Lay & Wheeler**, **James Nicholson**, **Selfridges** and **Wine Society**). Made from two thirds Pinot Noir and one third Chardonnay, this is a heavenly vintage wine for Roederer. There is still some of the incredible 1996 around but squirrel this away in your cellar as the 1997 is forward, expressive and incredibly moreish.

£55.00 **Bollinger**, **Grande Année**, 1997, Champagne, France (**Berry Bros.**, **Fortnum & Mason**, **Harrods**, **Harvey Nichols**, **Lay & Wheeler**, **Lea & Sandeman**, **Maj**, **Odd**, **Sai**, **Selfridges**, **Tanners**, **Vintage House**, **Wai** and **Wine Society**). Boy what a pleasure it was to unwrap a package with this sneak preview bottle in it two days before the book deadline. I felt like celebrating early, but I knew I had to sniff, swirl and spit, and write another 10,000 words. So, I kept my cool and just got on with it. As you know I am a massive Bolly fan and Grande Année is always a hedonistic pleasure. This is one of the most forward vintage releases in years, which means you can crack on virtually immediately

– thank God, I hear you cry! Usually GA needs time to evolve – the 1996 is still a baby – but this is a blindingly serious creation with dramatic high notes of vanilla and wild berries, and a texture that is uniquely Bollinger's. 1997 Grande Année is like no other wine on the face of the earth.

£65.00 **Gosset**, **Celébris**, **1995**, Champagne, France (**Averys**, **Berry Bros.**, **Croque-en-Bouche**, **Handford**, **Harrods**, **Oxford Wine**, **Peake**, **La Réserve**, **Roberson**, **Whitebridge**, **Wine Library**, **Wright Wine** and **Noel Young**). With a little more age than most prestige cuvées out there, this is a truly spectacular wine with heavenly complexity and a never-ending finish.

£75.00 **Veuve Clicquot**, **La Grande Dame**, **1996**, Champagne, France (**Berry Bros.**, **Boo**, **Harrods**, **Maj**, **Odd**, **La Réserve**, **Selfridges**, **Tes**, **Thr**, **Unw**, **Valvona & Crolla** and **Wai**). The mesmerising 1995 runs out in October time and if you see it, buy it – it is heroic. I was lucky enough to be afforded a very early sneak preview of this Olympic 1996. It is an amazing wine with oceans of class and breeding. This is one of the most sleek and impressive vintages of La Grande Dame in years – it is elegant, assertive and flamboyant – all in the same mouthful. It also sits in the best Champagne packaging I have ever seen. So, with that in mind, this is probably the ultimate present because it looks like a million dollars and tastes it, too.

£115.00 **Krug**, **1990**, Champagne, France (**Amps**, **Bacchus**, **Bentalls**, **Berry Bros.**, **Bibendum**, **Connolly's**, **Corney & Barrow**, **Eton Vintners**, **Farr**, **Fortnum & Mason**, **Great**

Western Wine, Harrods, Harvey Nichols, Hayman, Barwell Jones, Haynes, Hanson & Clark, Hoults, Lay & Wheeler, Lea & Sandeman, Philglas & Swiggot, Raeburn, Roberson, Selfridges, Tanners, J. Townend, Uncorked, Valvona & Crolla, The Vineyard, Vintage House and Winchcombe). No complex, florid tasting note here, just a medieval expletive – f**k! This is phenomenal. I opened a bottle for ten friends to taste and every one just sat there grinning like goons. Nobody spoke for about ten minutes (it was bliss!), mesmerised by this unique and otherworldly wine. Is it worth the money? Bloody right it is.

●●●●●●●●●●●●●●●●●●●●●●●●

£3.29 **Bianco Beneventano, 2003**, Campania, Italy (**M&S**). This chirpy little fellow is made from two wonderful and underrated southern Italian grapes, Falanghina and Fiano. It offers more fruit and charm than any other three quider I have tasted this year and, dare I say it, could happily perform many more tasks than just party duty.

£3.99 **Obikwa Chenin Blanc, 2004**, Western Cape, South Africa (**Odd**). I was amazed when I first sniffed and slurped this wine – it is fantastic. There is so much lively, fresh, clean, tropical fruit, and the finish is lovely, luscious and dry. I am a big fan of the Obikwa range at Oddbods and, for me, this perky Chenin is the jewel in the crown.

£3.99 **Santa Julia Fuzion Chenin Blanc/ Chardonnay, 2004**, Argentina (**Unw** and **Wai**). I first tasted this wine way back in May and thought it was a stunner. The stock was due in the summer and it would have sold fast because it's a crisp, cheery, dry white. But there was some problem with transport and it is now coming over just in time for the publication of this book. You see, ESP does work!

£4.99 **Flagstone Noon Gun**, 2004, Coastal Region, South Africa (**Odd**). Now that Noon Gun has a screwcap, it is in a different dimension. This is a buffet lunch dreamboat, as its complex blend of different varieties (Riesling/Chenin Blanc/Chardonnay/Pinot Blanc/Sauvignon Blanc/Semillon) makes it perfect for matching to a wide range of dishes. It is also a perfect picnic wine, for the very same reason.

£4.99 **Racina Ianca Grillo**, 2003, Sicily, Italy (**M&S**). This is a funky one – Grillo is usually a sweaty, fat, lumpy variety with little charm or poise. This version couldn't be more different. It is lean, tangy and shiveringly refreshing. The quince, greengage and lime fruit soothes the palate and primps it up in one go. I would drink it alongside grilled fish with lemon and fresh herbs.

£4.99 **Stellenzicht**, **Hill and Dale Sauvignon Blanc**, 2004, Stellenbosch, South Africa (**Mor** and **Saf**). Inexpensive South African whites are in vogue this year, as they offer so much life, vitality and thirst-quenching acidity. This cheeky, budget, lime, asparagus, freshly cut grass and elderflower Sauvignon is a winner. It is everything you'd expect it to be only cheaper. These guys also make a stonking 2003 H&D Pinotage (£4.99, **Mor** and **Saf**).

£4.99 **Tesco Finest South African Chenin Blanc,
2004**, Stellenbosch, South Africa (**Tes**). Ken Forrester
does it again with this incredible white wine. He and
winemaking partner Martin Meinert know how to turn on
the charm with this grape. Tesco is so pleased with the
quality of this gorgeous, zesty, lemon- and lime-imbued
wine that they have, once again, awarded it their 'Finest'
label. A cracker!

£5.95 **Waterford Pecan Stream Chenin Blanc**,
2003, Stellenbosch, South Africa (**Berry Bros.**, **Hoults**,
Revelstoke and **The Vineyard**). Chenin is such an important
grape for our diet and South Africa gives us the world's
best, inexpensive, dry versions. Next to Obikwa, this is a
suave, genial fellow. It is smoother, less jumpy; calmer, less
nervy; and, in truth, classier, but I'd still prefer to glug
Obikwa at a garden party. Waterford is a very important
estate in the Cape (see the awesome Kevin Arnold Shiraz
later) and this is its interpretation of a cheeky, entry-level
wine. What you end up with is a relaxed brew with finesse
and complexity – perfect for aperitif drinking, but fine
enough for a dinner party. Not really reflective of its price,
is it? And the 2004, which arrives in the late autumn, is
wonderfully balanced, too.

£5.99 **Cheverny Le Vieux Clos**, **2003**, Delaille, Loire,
France (**Wai**). Made from a cunning blend of Sauvignon
Blanc and Chardonnay, this fantastic wine tastes like a
cross between Sancerre and Chablis. It is green, crisp
and lively on the nose, with citrus and fresh herb nuances.
The palate is zesty, too, with a luscious lemony finish.

Le Vieux Clos is also a very versatile food companion, covering all bases from canapés, crustacea and all varieties of salad, to spicy food and goat's cheese – a clever wine.

£5.99 **Co-op Côtes-du-Rhône Reserve White**, **2003**, Rhône, France (**Coo**). Grenache Blanc, Viognier and Marsanne combine skilfully to produce a seamless, honeyed, floral wine. There is a minuscule amount of oak here (12%), but I can't spot it and it probably just boosts the embonpoint a tad and leaves this model white looking its very best. This is extremely good value and a stunning wine for fresh fish dishes.

£5.99 **Lugana Villa Flora**, **2003**, Zenato, Veneto, Italy (**Wai**). With more richness and honey going on than most six-pound Italian whites, this is already an impressive bottle. Last year I listed Ca' dei Frati's Lugana, which is three quid more expensive but, I must admit, this is a better wine. It is ripe, smooth, pear- and apple-scented, with good length, a smart label and an air of sophistication. Invite Villa Flora around for dinner, you'll not regret it.

£5.99 **Peter Lehmann Semillon**, **2002**, Barossa Valley, South Australia (**Asd**, **Boo**, **Odd**, **Saf**, **Sai**, **Tes**, **Unw** and **Vin du Van**). I have never tasted a dull bottle of this wine, in any vintage, since it is a perennial over-achiever. The lemon and lime fruit, waxy and honey body, and crisp finish are in line once again. This is every bit a legendary wine, despite the lowly price tag. I recommend that, if you have the chance, you buy the screwcap-sealed version, stocked by Oddbins and Tesco, as it is guaranteed to be in perfect nick.

LIGHT, DRY AND UNOAKED

£5.99 **Stormhoek Pinot Grigio, 2004**, Western Cape, South Africa (**Asd** and **Thr**). Stormhoek is no longer a one wine operation. It is now a veritable team with a stunning, juicy Cabernet, an earthy, plummy Shiraz, a very fine rosé (see page 51), this amazing PG and last year's Top 250 star wine, the Sauvignon Blanc. This seismic growth doesn't surprise me, as these wines are the brainchild of Nick Dymoke-Marr, an ex-supermarket wine buyer and now agent behind some of the most over-delivering wines on the shelves today. The Wine List had the scoop on the Sauvignon last year and has, again, the jump on everyone else this year with this terrific squad of stunners. My chosen Pinot Grigio is positively energetic in the way it pogos on your taste buds. You could spend a week on a Vespa in Friuli and not find a wine as joyous as this. You'll not be surprised to hear that 2004 Stormhoek Sauvignon Blanc (£5.99, **Asd, Odd, Sai** and **Wai**) is, once again, the king of cool. Chase the Storm!

£5.99 **Tesco Finest Gavi, 2003**, Piemonte, Italy (**Tes**). Gavi is what Italian Sloane Rangers (or whatever they're called) drink in trendy bars in Milan. You'd be hard pushed to leave a restaurant without spending more than £25 on an average bottle, so when this accurate, refreshing, classy and inexpensive version appeared I couldn't believe it. The stock control bloke at Tesco reckons there is enough to last until the New Year … we'll see about that!

£6.50 **Davenport Horsmonden Dry White, 2002**, East Sussex, England (**Davenport Vineyards tel. 01892 852 380**, **Vinceremos** and **Vintage Roots**).

Will Davenport quietly gets on with making some of England's most complex and rewarding white wines. His 2002s are world-class creations and Horsmonden Dry, at a mere £6, is a true bargain. 2002 is one of the best vintages England has ever seen and the top wines are a revelation. In terms of value for money, Horsmonden Dry is one of the finest in this book. The counterpoint between the quince, gooseberry, melon fruit and the lime-juice acidity is breathtaking.

£6.99 **Fleur du Cap Unfiltered Sauvignon Blanc**, **2003**, Coastal Region, South Africa (**Odd**). Sipping this wine is like standing under a shower of ice-cold water. The green, racy, grassy Sauvignon fruit is shockingly pure and it jolts the palate, waking up every nerve ending in your body. It also has a fair amount of depth, making this superb wine not only a brilliant apéritif but a mean seafood partner, too.

£6.99 **Pinot Grigio La Prendina**, 2003, Cavalchina, Italy (**M&S**). Balanced, fresh as daisies, spritzy and uplifting. If only all PGs were as delightful as this one.

£6.99 **Raats Original Chenin Blanc, 2004**, Coastal Region, South Africa (**Odd**). Bruwer Raats is a Chenin Blanc expert and his enthusiasm for fine wines is infectious. He does everything in his power to harness every last flavour nuance from his terrific old vines and the result is a smooth, lemony, pineappley wine with fleeting moments of honey and nougat on the palate. Then, suddenly, these genial flavours change to zesty, racy, edgy acidity on the finish. This is a sumptuous yet refreshing wine – a gripping game of two halves – and I love it. Trade up to the noble 2003 Raats Chenin Blanc (£9.99, **Handford**, **Harrogate**, **Odd**) if you so desire and don't forget 2002 Raats Cabernet Franc (£13.99, **Adnams**, **Handford**, **Harrogate Fine Wine** and **Odd**), as it is already one of my favourite 100% Cab Francs in the world. P.S. Keep this under your hat – the 2003 (which I tasted out of the barrel) is nothing short of legendary. Watch out!

£6.99 **Tyrrells Old Winery Semillon**, 2003, Hunter Valley, New South Wales, Australia (**Great Grog**, **Maj**, **Laurence Philippe** and **Selfridges**). Bruce Tyrrell proves in this compact, well-balanced wine, that Hunter Semillon does not have to be ten years old to be enthralling. The lemon butter nuances are really lovely in this excitable wine and it is equally talented with or without grub.

£7.35 **Mâcon-Montbellet**, **2002**, Domaine Talmard, Burgundy, France (**Goedhuis & Co.**). Talmard makes gorgeous, smooth, creamy Chardonnays and this melon, honey and pear juice 2002 is no exception. If you love white Burgundy but find it an awfully difficult region to navigate around, start here.

£7.99 **Burgans Albariño**, **2003**, Rías Baixas, Galicia, Spain (**Odd**). Albariño is a joy when it's good (white pepper, pineapple, gooseberry and peach) and this 2003 is not only totally precise and downright delicious, it is also one of the cheapest versions out there.

£7.99 **Twin Wells Semillon**, **1999**, Hunter Valley, New South Wales Australia (**M&S**). Made by the legendary Bruce

Tyrrell, this is a phenomenally attractive wine and it is a complete steal at eight pounds. With five years under its belt already, this incredible wine boasts lime, hazelnut, orange zest, fresh herbs and a minutes-long finish. Any fish dish would beg to be eaten alongside a wine of this class and breeding.

£7.99 **Wither Hills Sauvignon Blanc, 2004**, Marlborough, South Island, New Zealand (**Ballantyne**s, **Boo**, **Simon Charles**, **Great Northern Wine**, **Great Western Wine**, **Charles Hennings**, **Jeroboams & Laytons**, **Odd**, **Edward Sheldon**, **T&W**, **Villeneuve**, **Wai** and **Wine Society**). With seven wines appearing in the Top 250 in the past three years (and another two this year), you'd be right to think that Brent Marris, winemaker at Wither Hills, is doing some good work. This is a benchmark Wither Hills Sauvignon, bursting with vitality and life. The epic lemon and lime fruit invades your senses and the finish is as exciting as walking a tightrope. Seven pounds ninety-nine. I repeat, seven pounds ninety-nine – and just a flick of the wrist and the screwcap is off. This is a very small price to pay for letting your senses experience nirvana.

£8.49 **Springfield Special Cuvée Sauvignon Blanc**, **2004**, Robertson, South Africa (**Bibendum**, **Sai**, **SWIG**, **Thr** and **Wai**). I plunged my tasting glass into the top of the tank that held this fledgling wine back in April '04. It had just finished its fermentation and Abrie Bruwer, owner and winemaker at Springfield, agreed with me that it was one of the finest ever Special Cuvées from this stellar estate. It is frighteningly precise and bracingly racy, and yet the core

LIGHT, DRY AND UNOAKED

fruit is knowing, settled and calm. The nettle and asparagus fruit on the nose is the prelude to a wonderful lemon tart and fresh pineapple palate. The classic rapier sharp finish is there, but with even more length than usual. This is a top-flight Sauvignon that puts almost every 2003 Sancerre I have tasted in the shade.

£8.75 **Menetou-Salon, Domaine Henry Pellé, 2002**, Loire, France (**Goedhuis & Co.**). 2002 was a perfect vintage in the Loire. (2003 wasn't because it was too hot for the acidity-loving Sauvignon variety. Consequently a lot of 2003 Sancerres and the like are flabby, forward and overripe.) This Menetou (the village next to Sancerre) is a tight, zippy, aromatic, grassy, lemon and lime juice beauty. It has so much electricity buzzing around the bottle it is a total and utter delight to drink.

£8.99 **Curious Grape Bacchus Reserve, 2003**, Tenterden, Kent, England (**English Wine Group at Tenterden Vineyard tel. 01580 763033, Handford** and **Philglas & Swiggot**). If 2002 was a great vintage in England, then 2003 could turn out to be even better – remember the heat wave? With weather like that anything is possible, as this wine clearly shows. It is bursting with juicy, fresh fruit cocktail aromas, and there is more texture and length on this wine than ever before. In my tasting notes I awarded '03 Bacchus Reserve the highest-ever score for an English wine.

£9.99 **The Berrio Sauvignon Blanc, 2003**, Flagstone Winery, Elim, South Africa (**Odd**). Sealed with a screwcap and hailing from surely the most exciting new region in SA,

Elim, this is a blindingly serious Sauvignon. The flavour is piercingly fresh and dominated by limes and fresh herbs. The finish is magical, minutes long and it enlivens your senses as every second passes. Made by wine alchemist Bruce Jack this is one of the most important and quietly influential Sauvignons in the world – everyone is watching, whether they admit it or not. The 2004 turns up in the New Year and it will continue an unbroken series of excellent vintages for The Berrio.

£9.99 **The Gum Sauvignon Blanc, 2004**, Adelaide Hills, South Australia (**M&S**). I tasted a tank sample of this and it practically floored me. It was like a surprise uppercut that nearly took my head off. The nose is rapier sharp, pure and wickedly exciting, and the palate buzzes with limitless citrus energy. If you want to put this menacing flyweight together with a venomous welterweight, look no further than 2002 The Gum Shiraz (£12.99, **M&S**) – it's a belter. What a combo – you will be dizzy with excitement when these two get to work.

£9.99 **Hunter's Sauvignon Blanc, 2003**, Marlborough, South Island, New Zealand (**Castang, Pierre Henck, Jeroboams & Laytons, Christopher Piper, Tanners** and **Wine Society**). This crystal clear, totally focused wine is amazingly lively on the nose and palate. The taut lemon and lime fruit is terrific, and the finish is exceptionally long and cleansing. This is a remarkable creation and it's an awful lot of wine for a tenner. The only problem is that once you've cracked off the screwcap, it won't last very long – you'll tuck this away in a matter of seconds.

LIGHT, DRY AND UNOAKED

white 29

£9.99 **Starvedog Lane No Oak Chardonnay**, 2003, Adelaide Hills, South Australia (**Amps**, **Best Cellars**, **D. Byrne**, **Andrew Chapman**, **Cheers**, **Constantine**, **Corkscrew**, **Great Grog**, **Inspired Wines**, **Noble Rot**, www.tesco.com and **Noel Young**). Class, finesse, breeding and a little dash of the X factor – this wine tastes like an ethereal, top vintage, super cuvée Chablis, but it hails from thousands of miles away in the idyllic Adelaide Hills. 'No Oak' proudly exhibits a harmonious, ripe, creamy palate and, as the label says, no oak barrel nuances whatsoever. On the nose you can detect ripe pears, red apples and a whisper of lime and honey, and all that before you've even tasted this tremendous, harmonious and engaging wine. This is what unadulterated, fresh, pure Chardonnay tastes like, and I love it.

£11.49 **Iona Sauvignon Blanc**, 2004, Elgin, South Africa (**Boo**, **Peter Green**, **Henderson**, **J & H Logan**, **Luvian's**, **Peckham & Rye**, **R&R**, **Sommelier**, **SWIG**, **Valvona & Crolla**, **Villeneuve**, **Wimbledon Wine** and **Winecellars**). The 2003 vintage of Iona is one of the most unnerving wines I have ever tasted. It still sends a citrus shiver down my spine every time I think of it. First-class, world-beating Sauvignon Blanc should do this, but very few actually do. The phenomenally exciting nose of high tensile lemon and lime fruit, and gripping, mineral palate with its keen, rapier-sharp acidity, combine to mug your senses and re-align your taste buds. I tasted several component parts of the 2004 wine, back in April while it was fermenting, and I am in no doubt that it will be even more impressive than the staggering 2003. Owner Andrew Gunn only started Iona a few years ago but his speed in establishing this as one of the most important estates in South Africa is nothing short of astounding.

£11.99 **Villa Maria Reserve Clifford Bay Sauvignon Blanc, 2003**, Marlborough, South Island, New Zealand (**Odd**). If you like a rich, full Sauvignon, as opposed to the rapier-like style of Hunters above, then Villa Maria's Clifford Bay is the wine for you. This is a flamboyant and intense glass of citrus-imbued wine with a heroically long finish. Villa Maria has launched a new single vineyard series this year as well – 2003 Taylor's Pass Single Vineyard Sauvignon Blanc (£12.99, **Wai**) is the pick of the wines. It is finer and less explosive than Clifford Bay and would be more suited to milder fish dishes than its stable mate's repertoire of full-on Asian cuisine.

£12.95 **Keith Tulloch Semillon, 2003**, Hunter Valley, New South Wales, Australia (**Haslemere** and **Vin du Van**). This is a phenomenal wine, brimming with taut limejuice fruit and sporting a never-ending finish. Keith Tulloch is a fastidious winemaker with an eye for detail and an endless desire for perfection. On this showing, he is very close. The screwcap keeps this wine in tiptop condition, so unscrew and dive in.

£12.99 **Chablis, Saint Martin, Domaine Laroche, 2002**, Burgundy, France (**Amps**, **Bibendum**, **Evertons**, **ND John** and **Jolly Vintner**). Goodness me, this is a fantastic wine. The fruit for the Domaine Laroche wines comes, as the name suggests, from the Michel Laroche's own vineyards. The main difference between this and his basic

Chablis 'village' is the sheer intensity of fruit and length of flavour on the palate. If the straight Chablis is a ham and cheese baguette, Saint Martin is a gastronomic dinner at La Tour d'Argent. It may be pretty full-on for a novice, but for a seasoned Chablis lover this is a dreamy bottle. And remember, the 2002 vintage was lithe, leggy and simply superb, so take advantage because the 2003 was a bit of a fatty! If you want to push the envelope even further, grab a bottle of 2002 Chablis, 1er Cru Les Fourchaumes Vieilles Vignes, Domaine Laroche (£20.59, **Bibendum**) – it is totally awesome.

£13.99 **Frog's Leap Sauvignon Blanc**, **2003**, Napa Valley, California (**Flying Corkscrew**, **Harvey Nichols** and **Theatre of Wine**). Winemaker John Williams is one of the coolest guys on the planet. His famous Frog's Leap label is seen in some of the greatest restaurants in the world but rarely gets an airing in UK households. It is time to change all that. This is California's leading Sauv house and it is a doddle to see why. The pure, green, tight, lifted, crisp fruit is astounding. Make sure you find this wine, as it is a work of art to look at and an inspiration to taste. John's 2002 Carneros Chardonnay (£18.50, **Butlers**) is another jaw-droppingly precise wine.

£15.99 **Sauvignon Bianco**, **Ruttars**, **2003**, Giovanni Puiatti, Collio, Friuli-Venezia Giulia, Italy (**SWIG**, **Wimbledon Wine** and **Winecellars**). Giovanni Puiatti is a living legend. He is one of the most elegant gents in the world and is always impeccably turned out, generous to a fault, gracious, affable and he makes sure that every

LIGHT, DRY AND UNOAKED

moment that passes is celebrated in style. You can see all of these attributes in his wines. Ruttars Sauvignon is totally pure, intense, focused and minutes-long on the palate. It is crystal clear – the nose alone is a masterclass in restraint and aromatic finesse. Sauvignon fans must spend an evening with Puiatti.

● ●

£4.99 **Casillero del Diablo Viognier**, 2004, Central Valley, Chile (**Asd**, **Boo**, **Odd** and **Saf**). After two stellar vintages of Casillero Viognier (Top 250, of course) where could winemaker Marcelo Papa go? Well, he was already responsible for the most impressive, inexpensive Viognier I had ever tasted, so it had to be more of the same. In fact, he has further improved the magical recipe by keeping all of the heady, peachy, almond aroma and luscious, sexy palate, but has refined the finish and moderated the alcohol, and, therefore, the power of this wine. It is beautiful. There is no other word for it.

£4.99 **Dry Muscat**, 2003, Vin de Pays des Côtes Catalanes, France (**M&S**). OK, it's a boring name and there aren't many clues on the bottle as to what this wine tastes like, so it is up to me to tell you that this is a sensational glass of wine. Forget dry Alsatian Muscat at £15 a bottle – slot this instead. Made in the Pyrenees, near the Spanish border, the grapey nose leaps from the glass and pulverises your olfactory system like a nubile masseuse, administering an aromatherapeutic body rub. It's a fab apero or the perfect wine for spicy takeaways – and it's only a fiver!

LIGHT, DRY AND UNOAKED/AROMATIC

£5.99 **Neethlingshof Gewürztraminer, 2004,** Stellenbosch, South Africa (**Sai**). These guys won a place in TWL'02 with this very wine, but then they lost their way for two vintages, making pulpy, flabby, boring wines. 2004 is a return to fitness and this is spectacular. Rose petal and pretty perfume on the nose, and a lithe, juicy body make the initial flavour raid a joy. Then the finish looms with buckets of racy acidity and it mops up the more aromatic elements and leaves you with a dry, tangy palate, wanting more. This is the definitive Thai food wine, as it loves chilli, lemongrass and all things spicy. It's amazing how much wine there is here for only six pounds.

£5.99 **Torres Viña Esmeralda, 2003,** Penedès, Spain (**Bentalls, Boo, The Grape Shop, Harvey Nichols, S.H. Jones, Laymont & Shaw, Odd, Oxford Wine, Portland, Sai, Tes, Thr, Unw, Wai, Weavers** and **Noel Young**). Four years in a row! Esmeralda is one of the most consistently brilliant labels on the wine shop shelves. Every vintage improves seemingly on the last. It is the screwcap and its associated freshness and vitality that lift this wine above its competitors. The blend is still the same – a large chunk of Muscatel (Muscat) and a smaller but very important sploosh of Gewürztraminer. The nose and initial attack of Esmeralda is so exciting – papaya, guava and juicy pineapple pulp welcome you into the glass, and then the palate gets keener and edgier, finishing in a crescendo of thirst-quenching acidity. You'll not find a cheaper or more impressive Asian food wine anywhere in the world. Miguel Torres is a legend and this wine, despite its lowly price and ephemeral appeal, is a vital part of his armoury.

simply *breathtaking*

£6.25 **Les Grès Viognier**, **2003**, Vin de Pays d'Oc, France (**Jeroboams & Laytons**). Peaches, apricots and a sprinkling of nutmeg on the nose, honey and tropical fruit on the palate, and a bone-dry finish – just what you want but rarely actually find in a Viognier, particularly at this price. Les Grès is a terrific set up and winemaker Xavier Luc manages not only to crack this grape variety but he also makes a brilliant, inexpensive Grenache rosé (£5.45, J&L).

£6.99 **Cazal Viel**, **Viognier Reserve**, **2003**, Languedoc-Roussillon, France (**Thr**). This busty Viognier with its enticing peachy perfume and open, friendly nature is a beauty. It you fancy a blind date wine then rush this way.

£6.99 **Leasingham Magnus Riesling**, **2003**, Clare Valley, South Australia (**Sai**). This is a beautiful, exotic, hypnotic Riesling from the idyllic Clare Valley. I tasted all of the 2003 Rieslings in one sitting in Clare back in March and this was my joint highest scoring wine. It was also the cheapest. Unlike a lot of Clare Rieslings, it doesn't need age to show its beauty, as it is simply jaw dropping right now. For a zestier style with more mystery and age-ability, 2003 Leasingham Bin 7 Riesling (£7.99, **Wai**) is another wondrous creation. I have been lucky enough to taste the component parts for the 2004 vintage releases as well and they are simply breathtaking – no change there then.

£6.99 **Mineralstein Riesling**, **2003**, Mosel/Pfalz, Germany (**M&S**). A delicious cool, blue-slate feel permeates your senses when you sip this floral Riesling. It is a delightful wine with wonderful, pure fruit.

AROMATIC

white   35

£6.99 **Yalumba Y Series Viognier**, 2003, South Australia (**Maj**, **Sai**, **Selfridges**, **Unw** and **Wai**). This wine gets better every year. The 2002 made the Top 250 last year and when the 2004 turns up in the New Year it will sport a flash new screwcap (at last!). But, for now, set your sights on this gloriously luscious peach, mango and honey cocktail. The nose is alluring and the smooth, floral palate oleaginous and sexy. This wine has the knack of smelling lusciously tropical yet tasting bone dry – great stuff.

£6.99 **Zontes Footsteps Verdelho**, 2004, Langhorne Creek, South Australia (**Sai**). The brand-new, screwcapped Zontes Verdelho, due on the shelves in September (perfect timing!), is a big step up, both aromatically and texturally, on last year's wine. This is a Thai food dream date with its crisp, pineapple-chunk fruit and grapefruit tang, and I feel it is going to age beautifully (not that you'll give it the chance!). Also, watch out for a fresh, new 2004 Zontes Viognier (£6.99, **Unw**).

£7.99 **Basilisk, Marsanne/Viognier**, 2003, McPherson, Goulburn Valley, Victoria, Australia (**La Forge**, **Hendersons** and **Oz Wines**). This debut white blend from the highly motivated McPherson team is perfectly balanced, cleverly blended and incredibly yummy. If you want a cool, mildly aromatic, tropical white wine with no overt oak and a hint of mystery, this is it.

£7.99 **Brampton Viognier**, 2003, Stellenbosch, South Africa (**Wai**). This Viognier, from Rustenberg Estates, is sublime, bursting with peach, nectarine and lime on the

nose, and boasting an exquisite, dry, moreish finish. Eight
pounds is a pittance to pay for the quality of flavour in this
heavenly wine. Sealed with a screwcap, simply spin the top
off and relax. It is such a frisky little number, it should really
be renamed Brampton viagra.

£7.99 **Chapel Hill Verdelho, 2004**, McLaren Vale, South
Australia (**Australian Wine Club** and **Oz Wines**). If you want
to experience some eye-popping palate gymnastics and
spring clean your olfactory kit, then pour yourself a pint of
this white-knuckle ride Verdelho. This wine is glass-
shatteringly fresh, ear-splittingly zesty and toe-tinglingly
nervy. If you are cooling down your palate from a chilli and
lime dip, or dousing your uvula cryogenics mid-Thai green
curry, then this wine is the epitome of cool. The ice cold,
green herb and white peach fruit is sublime. If you like the
sound of this wine, sink your teeth into 2004 Chapel Hill,
Unwooded Chardonnay (£6.99, **Tes**) and drop your body
temperature a degree in the process.

£7.99 **Esk Valley Black Label Riesling, 2003**, Hawke's
Bay, New Zealand (**Amps**, **Cairns & Hickey**, **Peckham & Rye**,
Vicki's and **Wimbledon Wine**). I have always enjoyed the
wines from Esk Valley – they are subtle, not showy. This
Black Label Riesling is a delicious lime- and rhubarb-themed
wine, and it has more integrity and depth than many NZ
versions twice its price.

£7.99 **Jacob's Creek Reserve Riesling, 2003**, Barossa
Valley, South Australia (**Sai**). The JC reserve range is
fantastic value for money and the quality of fruit in this

AROMATIC

Riesling is top class. I have tasted this wine many times this year and it is always refreshing, lithe, lime juicy and long. JCRR is a jewel in the crown of this tremendously successful company.

£7.99 **Tim Adams, Riesling, 2004**, Clare Valley, South Australia (**Tes**). Spectacular, titillating, refreshing, light and airy initially … then, when you least expect it, the flavour changes and builds until the sunny lemon-grove theme hurtles into an explosive, zesty finish. This wine is wonderfully long and beautifully balanced, and it is anchored to your palate, willing you to sniff, sip and sigh, and ultimately unwind.

£8.99 **Pewsey Vale Riesling, 2003**, Eden Valley, South Australia (**Odd** and **Wai**). This fabulous, dry Riesling is in its first flush of youth and is wonderfully aromatic and effervescent. There is spritzy lime zest, rhubarb compote and icy pineapple chunk notes on the nose and palate, and the finish is very grand for a wine of this price. This is not overly tropical, that will come with time, but right now this is one of the yummiest aperitif or Asian-food-matching whites on the shelves.

£8.99 **Redbank Sunday Morning Pinot Gris, 2003** King Valley, Victoria, Australia (**Selfridges**, **Roberson**, **Vin du Van** and **Wimbledon**). Year in, year out, I fall for this cheeky, chirpy, screwcapped PG. It is spicy, near-tropical, bracingly dry and bloody good looking. This is an Asian-food-matching banker. The 2004 turns up in the New Year and early reports are that it is a stunner, too.

AROMATIC

£9.00 **Vis a Vis Viognier/Chardonnay by Linda Domas**, 2004, Fleurieu Peninsula, South Australia (**Novum**). Scoop – this is the very first write up in the UK for this sensational white blend. Linda is a gifted winemaker and her partner Steve Brunato is a viticultural wizard – they have a work ethic unlike anyone else I have ever seen. They slave away in the winery and then play very hard after dark. Vis a Vis is floral and peachy yet bracingly dry on the finish. It is a Jekyll and Hyde wine – pretty then stern – a bit like Linda, come to think of it!

£9.49 **Nepenthe Pinot Gris**, 2003, Adelaide Hills, South Australia (**Odd**). The screwcap helps lift and augment the startling nose on this PG to hitherto unknown levels of sweet-spice and stone-fruit aromas. This is an intellectual food wine so only competent chefs need apply!

£9.99 **Petaluma Riesling**, 2003, Clare Valley, South Australia (**Bibendum**, **Odd**, **Sai** and **Tes**). This is a serious, furrowed-brow Riesling that will age incrementally over the next ten years. Petaluma makes almost masochistically beautiful wine. Every time I open a bottle I know in my heart it would have been even better in a year's time! This is only because I have had the pleasure of tasting some old bottles and I know they are sublime. Having said that, this is already a wickedly fine wine at a very reasonable price, so twist the top off now and revel in this hedonistic fruit.

£9.99 **Zeltinger Himmelreich Riesling**, **Ernst Loosen**, 2003, Mosel Valley, Germany (**M&S**). This stunning Riesling is a masterclass in the crucial balance between phenomenally attractive fruit flavours and bracing acidity. The nose on this heart-achingly beautiful wine is so enticing and all-encompassing it is a shock. The tropical, fruit cocktail aromas are bright, exciting and multi-layered. The palate follows this theme but, just when you think this wine will slip into being medium-sweet and old-fashioned, it tightens, loses its richness and finishes icicle sharp and shiveringly refreshing. This is one of the most captivating white wines of the year so far and if you were planning a posh dinner party, it would be a staggeringly successful apéritif.

£10.49 **J. Leitz, Rudesheimer Magdalenenkreuz Riesling Spätlese, 2003**, Mosel-Saar-Ruwer, Germany (**D. Byrne, Hedley Wright, Richard Kihl, Philglas & Swiggot, Howard Ripley** and **Seckford**). Leitz was a new name to me this year but is one I'll never forget. I first tasted the 2002 of this wine (£9.99, **Odd**) and fell for it in a moment. This 2003 is every bit as gripping. There is fantastic concentration here and it is unmistakably fine German Riesling, but it has more than enough weight to please a lover of Alsace wines or those from the Clare Valley in South Australia. Add to that the elegance of the acidity on the finish and the layers of fruit, and this is a truly celestial bottle.

AROMATIC

£11.99 **Bonterra Roussanne, 2003**, Mendocino, California (**Odd**). There are only a handful of mind-blowing 100% Roussannes in the world and this is the only organic one that I know of. It is Bonterra's finest wine in their cellar and 2003 is the best vintage to date. If you want to move away from lusty, full-on Chardonnays, but still want to have depth and complexity in your glass, try this wine. The nose is floral with green apple, honeysuckle, mango and lime, and the palate is linear and expressive. It is very long and taut and is imposing enough to cope with roast chicken and main course fish dishes. If you want to turn the aroma up to eleven, then try 2003 Bonterra Viognier (£11.99, **Odd** and **Thr**), which arrives in the UK before Christmas. It has more luxurious peach and apricot on the nose, and a little more weight on the palate than my brilliant, high-tensile Roussanne.

£11.99 **Matakana Pinot Gris, 2003**, Matakana, North Island, New Zealand (**Berkmann**, **Luvian's**, **Veritas Wines** and **Wine Barrels**). I was totally amazed with the 2002 vintage of this wine last year (Top 250) and I jumped at the chance to taste the new 2003. It is a sensational achievement for such a teeny, tiny winery and, while the distribution is limited, you simply must pick up the phone and order a bottle if you have ever been intrigued by this alluring white grape variety. The spicy, near-tropical fruit in this Pinot Gris is honeyed, refreshing, mouth-filling and phenomenally long. The texture is creamy and smooth, and the overall experience is simply brilliant. You will, I guarantee, fall completely in love on the very first sniff. I know, as everyone I have opened it for has been speechless for minutes!

£12.75 **Yering Station MVR, 2003**, Yarra Valley, Victoria, Australia (**Winecellars**). Yering's Marsanne/Viognier/ Roussanne blend is a high-tensile concept with bracing acidity and a white-knuckle finish. The fruit is, for a fleeting second, very exotic, before the crisp nature of this wine shuts everything down and keeps it balanced. This is a wonderful wine with a broad range of dishes simply begging to have the chance to dance with it.

£12.95 **Quinta dos Carvalhais Encruzado**, 2002, Dão, Portugal (**Amps**, **Stevens Garnier**, **Peter Green** and **Whitebridge**). This is the most senior Portuguese white wine I have ever tasted. It is absolutely heavenly with amazing complexity on the nose and palate. The peach, pear, lime-leaf and white-flower aromas are even more intriguing on the palate, and the finish is minutes long. I found myself slowing down (from my normal, hectic tasting speed) and wallowing in the stunning aromas and flavours of this wine. It is hard to compare it to any others that you might be used to, so I won't. Suffice to say, I would be amazed if you didn't fall head over heels for this creation.

£12.99 **Riesling**, **Le Kottabe**, **Josmeyer**, 2003, Alsace, France (**D. Byrne**, **Harvey Nichols** and La Réserve). This Riesling has a stunning aromatic nose, brilliant attack on the palate and a surreally long, savoury finish. Alsace wines, when on top form, really excite and Josmeyer is at the top of the League.

● ●

£4.99 **Casillero del Diablo Chardonnay**, 2003, Concha y Toro, Casablanca Valley, Chile (**Asd**, **Maj**, **Odd**, **Sai**, **Thr** and **Wai**). The Casillero range continues to amaze me, both in terms of value for money and also, forgetting for a second that they are only a fiver, in pure quality. The skill with which the fruit and oak is balanced in every one of the different grape varieties is the key to the success of this brand. Only 30% of the wine ferments in oak barrels and the rest is done in stainless steel tanks. This means any oak flavours are cleverly woven into the core of the wine, providing weight and texture rather than overt characters on the nose or palate – stunning and very, very clever.

£7.49 **Donatus**, **2003**, Dornier Wine, Stellenbosch, South Africa (**Wine Society**). This is one of the cleverest white blends I have ever tasted. Donatus is a Chenin Blanc/Semillon/Sauvignon Blanc mix and it is delicately but cleverly oaked. It cunningly steals the highlights from each of the three varieties and then splices them together with consummate accuracy. You will fall for this in a heartbeat.

£7.99 **La Bégude Chardonnay**, **2002**, Limoux, South of France (**Wai**). La Bégude Chardonnay is impeccably balanced and it is pinned together with sublime and invigorating lime-juice acidity. It hails from biodynamically managed (organic to the extreme!), low-yielding, high-altitude vineyards in Limoux. This wine spends a brief spell in oak barrels, and the result is both brilliant and awesome value. Tasted blind, you are certain to think it white Burgundy (around the fifteen-pound mark) but, in truth, very few white Burgundies have remarkable, cleansing minerality and intense citrus fruit. This is a stunning wine with a brilliant, heavy glass bottle and classy label. You and I know it only costs eight quid – let's keep it that way.

OAKED

£7.99 **Kaituna Hills Reserve Chardonnay**, 2002, New Zealand (**M&S**). Kaituna is made by wine giant Montana and it is a real find. Montana's own reserve level Chardonnay is a big, clumsy, tropical wine with lashings of full-on, lolly-stick fruit, but this M&S beauty is leaner, more elegant and focused. It is very much along the lines of the modern UK palate, and for eight pounds this is a very successful wine indeed. The M&S team selected the Chardonnay lots with the most overt lime juice flavours and left the more exotic fruit or oaky flavoured cuvées out of the mix. This was a very smart move and I don't think you'll find a more racy NZ Chardonnay, at this price, in the UK.

£8.99 **Bonterra Chardonnay**, 2002, Mendocino, California (**Boo**, **Maj**, **Odd**, **Sai**, **Thr** and **Wai**). Bonterra is the organic arm of the Fetzer dynasty and this sumptuous wine has oodles of orange blossom and acacia honey nuances. This is very much a fruit-driven style as the wine only spends about four and a half months in oak. They use French oak to give subtle flavours of hazelnut and fresh baked bread, and American oak to lend butterscotchy, vanilla notes. Both styles work well with Bonterra's perfumed fruit, making the finished wine very delicious indeed.

£8.99 **Penfolds Thomas Hyland Chardonnay**, **2003**, South Australia (**Asd**, **Maj**, **Tes** and **Thr**). This is my favourite ever Penfolds Chardonnay. It totally over-delivers and it is ridiculously under-priced. Hyland is a lesson in fine, balanced, classy Aussie Chardonnay – don't miss it, this is a landmark wine.

OAKED

£9.99 **De Loach Russian River Estate Chardonnay**, **2002**, Sonoma County, California (**Bibendum**). I remember visiting this estate ten years ago and being very impressed with the wines. These days De Loach is owned by the dynamic French family Boisset and they intend to bring these wines back to the marketplace with a bang. Both this wine, with its dreamy, honeyed, floral fruit, and the bright, plum and blueberry 2001 De Loach Russian River Estate Pinot Noir (£9.99, **Bibendum**) are extremely good value and classic examples of just how delicious Californian wines can be. Jump in quick because, with this quality of fruit and definition of flavour, the prices will surely rise.

£9.99 **Gallo Coastal Vineyards Chardonnay**, **2002**, California (**Asd**, **Saf**, **Sai** and **Tes**). This is a cracking piece of winemaking from Gina Gallo and her skilled team. It is balanced, fresh, cool and classy. The fruit is ripe, there is no doubt (it's California after all), but the oak is sensitively administered and the synergy on the palate is a joy. If you want to step up a gear then find a bottle of 2001 Gallo Laguna Ranch Single Vineyard Chardonnay (£13.99, **Harrods**, **Hayman**, **Barwell Jones**, **Selfridges** and **Sai**) – it is even more of a showstopper.

£9.99 **Springfield Estate**, **Wild Yeast Chardonnay**, **2002**, Robertson, South Africa (**Bibendum**, **N.D. John**, **Magnum Wines**, **Charles Steevenson** and **SWIG**). This pagan sounding 'wild yeast' Chardonnay is made without the use of manmade yeasts. Nothing unique about that, many wineries choose not to inoculate, it's just that the name conjures up debauched images (for me anyway). Thank

OAKED

goodness the wine is a winner – the sheer intensity and quality of fruit is amazing, and you will feel you are drinking a wine that is at least double the price.

£9.99 **The Willows**, **Barossa Valley Semillon**, 2001, South Australia (**Oz Wines** and **Thr**). Willows is a delectable, intense, aromatic Semillon from the heart of the Barossa Valley. It has honeyed lime-juice notes on the nose, a lovely, creamy lanolin palate, and a sprightly citrus finish. There is more than enough richness here to cope with main course chicken or veal dishes, so it makes a welcome change of direction if you have the Chardonnay blues.

£10.50 **Rijk's Private Cellar Chardonnay**, 2002, Tulbagh, South Africa (**Ballantynes** and **Simon Charles Vintners**). Pronounced Rakes not Rikes (I can never get it right), this is a stunning debut wine for the UK market. I love the ripe, smooth, intense, all-pervading, flashy Chardonnay fruit. It is extremely attractive and, just when you think there is possibly too much of a good thing, the trademark South African acidity thankfully zooms in and bodychecks the palate. The result is really electrifying.

£11.75 **Bourgogne Blanc**, **Vieilles Vignes**, 2002, Domaine Jean-Philippe Fichet, Burgundy, France (**Goedhuis & Co.**). This old vine Chardonnay is made from three small parcels of vines, two thirds of which are over the fence from Les Gruyaches (a stunning and expensive Meursault vineyard). I have long been a fan of this wine and the 2002 is by far the most serious VV to date. It has a

OAKED

true old vines feel of focused, honeyed fruit and, in every respect, this is a mini-Meursault. It just happens to be half the price!

£11.99 **The Gum Chardonnay**, **2002**, Adelaide Hills, South Australia (**M&S**). Made for M&S by the first-class team at Starvedog Lane (Top 250 honours graduates!), this is one of the best Aussie Chardonnays I have tasted this year. The nose is like walking into a breezy, sunny breakfast room and catching the intimate scents of crisp white linen, just buttered honey croissants and fresh picked white flowers. The palate is deeper, like a mellow, lazy late lunch, with orange and gold décor and dazzling reflected light. The finish is sultry, sexy and thoughtful, daring you to take another sip and promising even more intrigue and exhilaration when you return to the glass – a temptress.

£12.99 **Villa Maria Fletcher Single Vineyard Chardonnay**, **2002**, Marlborough, New Zealand (**Eagle's**, **www.everywine.co.uk**, **Valvona & Crolla**, **Veritas** and **Wimbledon Wine**). Villa Maria is firing on all cylinders with its new single vineyard releases. The hazelnut, papaya, honey and nougat notes on Fletcher Chard are mellow and ever so dreamy. Villa Maria's vast portfolio is one of the safest around, and this is one of the true gems.

£14.99 **Forrester Meinert Chenin Blanc**, **2002**, Stellenbosch, South Africa (**Les Caves de Pyrene** and **Wai**). This is my absolute favourite, full-steam-ahead, world-model, dry Chenin Blanc. Ken F and Martin M make cosmic wines, and this is the very, very best bottle they have ever

OAKED

given us. I have tasted it many times and drunk it a few, too, and every time I get within an arm's length of this wine I am completely helpless and caught in its tractor beam. If you have not yet had the palate-altering, life-enhancing, out-of-body experience of tasting this wine, then make sure you do – and soon.

£15.95 **Sonoma Cutrer Russian River Chardonnay, 2002**, California (**Lea & Sandeman**). This fabulous oaked Chardonnay, from the famous Sonoma Cutrer Estate, is a bargain. 'A bargain? At north of fifteen quid?' I hear you cry. Well, this is top flight Californian Chardonnay from a cult estate and it tastes as good as this grape gets anywhere in the world – hence I believe this is a very competitive price. Don't worry, you'll fall head over heels for the sexy, praline, orange blossom and wild honey nose, and cartwheel around the room (whoa!) when you taste the voluptuous palate.

£16.50 **Seresin Estate Reserve Chardonnay**, 2002, Marlborough, South Island, New Zealand (**John Armit**, **Philglas & Swiggot** and **Selfridges**). This is a slightly riper and more pliable style of Chardonnay than I normally go for, but the fruit is so genuinely tasty I am really drawn to it. Also, the sensitive use of oak, which brings a nutty creaminess to the party, only serves to make this wine even more endearing. This 2002 is drinking perfectly now, despite its apparent youth. Seresin wines are always precocious, polished and pretty, and I look forward to tracking this wine to see how well it develops. Drink it with lobster and chips and aïoli on the side.

OAKED

£16.95 **Robert Mondavi Fumé Blanc**, **2001**, Napa
Valley, California (**Wine Direct tel. 08450 661 122**). There
are other merchants that sell this brilliant wine in the UK,
but these guys ship it direct and consequently it's a fiver
cheaper than anywhere else. The only downside is that you
have to buy a case, but get some friends involved and you'll
save sixty quid just by picking up the phone. Mondavi Fumé
Blanc is an iconic wine. Sensitively oaked Sauvignon was
invented by the great man and, when I saw him this year (he
is in his 92nd year), he was eager to explain that innovation
in his winery still continues apace today. With almost the
weight of a Chardonnay but a completely different flavour
profile and acid structure, this is a rich but refreshing wine
and I heartily recommend it to you.

£16.95 **Shaw & Smith M3 Chardonnay**, **2002**, Adelaide
Hills, South Australia (**Bennett's**, **Andrew Chapman**,
Execellars, **Flying Corkscrew**, **Harrods**, **Harvey Nichols**,
Liberty, **Luvian's**, **Nidderdale**, **Philglas & Swiggot**, **Tes**,
Villeneuve and **Noel Young**). This is the very best
Chardonnay that Martin and Michael (S&S) have ever made.
The oak and fruit balance is the cornerstone to the success
of M3. Fermented and matured in French oak barrels, this
wine gets the full five-star treatment but its core fruit can
handle this pampering, so you are left with a wine that is
the equal of many white Burgundies but a tenner less.

£27.50 **Puligny-Montrachet**, **Domaine Louis
Carillon**, **2001**, Burgundy, France (**Fortnum & Mason**).
I was lucky enough to taste all of Carillon's 2001s and 2002s
in his cellar last November. It was a spectacular tasting from

OAKED

start to finish. This wine is made from 11 lieu dits (different mini-sites) with an average vine age of 35 years old. It only saw 15% new oak (15% one-year-old, 15% two-year-old and so on to six-year-old barrels) and was one of the finest white wines I tasted in ten days of frantic work. I wrote 'textbook' in my notes, indicating that this was everything I could possibly want from a glass of Puligny. The lively nose and rich, complex palate really impressed me, and the length was phenomenal. The excellent 2001 is under Fortnum's own label and the sublime 2002 will follow next year.

●●●●●●●●●●●●●●●●●●●●●●●●●●●

£5.49 **Torres San Medin Cabernet Sauvignon Rosé, 2003**, Curicó Valley, Chile (**Sai** and **Wai**). This is the new retail name for Torres Santa Digna, last year's star rosé. This 2003 is every bit as good as the 2002 (and it's 50p cheaper). Cab Sauv is not usually used for rosés, but I can't fault the expressive cassis, cherry and berry aromas. You could drink this wine with main course pork or lamb dishes, or simply chill it down really cold and have it as a funky apéritif with zany canapés.

£5.79 **Jacob's Creek Shiraz, Rosé, 2004**, South Eastern Australia (**Asd**). Scoop – with a drop-dead colour of vibrant pink and an ethereal, floral, candyfloss and raspberry nose, on first impressions this is a very girly wine. But JC cunningly keeps the boys on side by making sure the palate is ripe and the finish is vital, dry and crisp. They could so easily have dropped the ball and made this wine too soft, commercially 'safe' and sloppy, but they didn't –

OAKED

punk rock rosé

JC Shiraz rosé sprints down the pitch and scores under the posts, as the Aussies are so often prone to do.

£5.99 **Stormhoek Rosé, 2004**, Western Cape, South Africa (**Odd**). Shiraz, Pinotage, Cinsault and Muscat, who'd 'a thought it? Stormhoek, that's who! This is a crazy rosé with an irreverent air, that holds two large fingers up to traditionalists and gets away with it. Punk rock rosé never tasted so good.

£6.60 **Château de Fontenille, Clairet Rosé, 2003**, Bordeaux, France (**Haynes, Hanson & Clark**). Fontenille, an unashamedly old style Bordeaux rosé, is made entirely of cabernet franc. The colour is fairly deep, almost red, and the nose is really stunning – violets, herbs, blackberries and mulberries. The palate is moderately intense, but not as forceful as the colour might suggest, and the finish is crisp and mouth-watering. In short, this is a tremendous find with integrity and charm.

£7.50 **Shotbull Shiraz Rosé by Linda Domas**, 2004, Fleurieu Peninsula, South Australia (**Novum**). Scoop (again) – this roller coaster rosé transports your palate up a long, slow build up, teeters at the top, and then hurtles down your palate, knocking over at eye watering speed every black and red berry and sweet spice flavour on the way – a simply exhilarating flavour ride!

£7.99 **Wirra Wirra Mrs Wigley Rosé, 2003**, McLaren Vale, South Australia (**Odd** and **Sai**). Awesome value, bursting with bitter cherry, cranberry and raspberry fruit with a vivid garnet hue, this is my favourite Grenache rosé on the planet (and that includes even the most expensive Tavel rosés from the southern Rhône)! It is screwcap sealed, fresh as a PYO punnet and wickedly invigorating on the palate.

£8.99 **Château de Sours Rosé, 2003**, Bordeaux, France (**Corney & Barrow, Goedhuis & Co., Maj, Playford Ros** and **Tanners**). Three years in a row for this terrific rosé and, with a stunning, hot vintage like 2003, it was always going to be a blockbuster. This wine has a cult following in the UK and there is always a stampede when it is released. But don't worry, as there is still plenty of stock to go around. The fabulously ripe Merlot grapes that form the turbo thrust in the core of this stunning wine are in absolute peak condition. The colour is deep and rich, and the flavour luxurious and stuffed with red cherry fruit. Stunning.

£8.99 **Redoma Rosé, 2001**, Douro, Portugal (**Butlers, Fortnum & Mason, Philglas & Swiggot** and **Haslemere Cellar**). Redoma rosé is a fascinating wine. It is delicious now but, in comparison to the others in this chapter, it is a veritable Grandpa. What is even more intriguing is that I suspect it will continue to evolve further over the next few years. This wine is clearly made of stern stuff. Unlike the others, this is strictly a foodie rosé, made to be enjoyed with main course fish and chicken dishes and spicy, veggie recipes. The fruit is strawberry and raspberry imbued, but there is also a touch of liquorice and herb to keep your mind from wandering.

£3.05 **Cuvée de Richard Rouge, 2003**, Vin de Pays de l'Aude, France (**Maj**). Majestic always do well with budget reds and this wine is no exception. It is a smooth, light and juicy Grenache, with vibrant red fruit and a clean, tidy finish.

£3.99 **Palacio del Marqués Tempranillo/Syrah**, 2003, La Mancha, Spain (**M&S**). There is only 5% Syrah in here, so the main flavour is that of vibrant cherry- and raspberry-imbued Tempranillo. All the Syrah does is act as a condiment – lifting and pepper-spicing the nose. This is a benchmark pizza and pasta wine that will give you immense pleasure at a teeny price.

£3.99 **Santa Julia Fuzion Tempranillo/Malbec, 2003**, Argentina (**Unw**). Cheap, fresh, ripe, juicy, funky, cheeky and forward – what more could you wish for in an everyday 'house' wine?

£4.99 **Marks & Spencer Casablanca Pinot Noir, 2003**, Chile (**M&S**). This cheeky new label at M&S is a winner. It's full to the brim with creamy raspberry and strawberry fruit, and the texture is velvety smooth. There is even a gorgeous, extra little touch of savoury spice, which comes from six months spent in oak barrels. Add to that a bonus twist of earthiness in the finish and this bottle totally over-delivers for a fiver. Bearing in mind it's made from the notoriously difficult Pinot Noir grape, it is simply astonishing.

£5.03 **Leopards Leap The Lookout Red, 2002**, Western Cape, South Africa (**Tes**). The Lookout Red is a blend of no less than seven different red grape varieties.

LIGHT AND FRUITY

red 53

It has superb flavour complexity – terrific, ripe, summer pudding notes and a liberal dusting of sweet and sour spices. The texture is velvety smooth and there is virtually no tannin whatsoever, so it is ready right now. A fiver is a very small price to pay for this calibre of wine and, guess what, the 2003 is even better.

£6.49 **McPherson Merlot**, 2003, Murray Darling, Victoria, Australia (**Cairns & Hickey**, **Eagle's**, **East Coast Wines**, **La Forge**, **Henderson**, **Kelly of Cults**, **Kendalls**, **J & H Logan**, **Peckham & Rye**, **Richardson**, **Vintage House** and **T.B. Watson**). The purity and focus in this inexpensive Merlot defies belief. This is a mighty effort from McPherson and is precisely the wine we should all have at home for emergency, off the cuff drinking. It is about as flexible as any red wine can be in terms of food matching and, as you know, Merlot is a tried and tested crowd-pleaser, so all of your friends are guaranteed to love it.

£6.99 **Beaujolais-Villages, Louis Jadot**, 2003, Burgundy, France (**Asd**, **D. Byrne**, **Luvian's**, **Peckham & Rye**, **Saf**, **Tes**, **Vicki's**, **Wai** and **Wimbledon Wine**). 2003 was a boiling hot vintage in Beaujolais and the wines are more pumped up and red fruit stuffed than ever. Chill this down a few degrees (fifteen minutes in the fridge) and you'll see the nose hurdle out of the glass and the cool, raspberry, cherry and strawberry flavours will glide over your palate. Jadot is a Premier League set up and you won't find better B-V than this bottle. Always have some on board because this wine is the consummate food-matching king.

£7.95 **Chinon, Cuvée Terroir, Charles Joguet, 2002,** Loire, France (**Jeroboams & Laytons**). Pristine, first-class, boutique production wine does not need to be fifty quid a bottle. Joguet's Cabernet Franc is as good as it gets and, as you can see, it is a snip. The Loire is a treasure chest of underrated, underpriced wines and this is one of them.

£7.99 **Swan Bay Pinot Noir, 2003,** Scotchman's Hill, Geelong, Victoria, Australia (**Odd**). Scotchman's Hills' second label, in 2003, with its screwcap and awesome flavour, is this year's finest, inexpensive Pinot in the world (and that's the result of twelve months of non-stop tasting!).

£10.95 **Hunter's Pinot Noir, 2002,** Marlborough, South Island, New Zealand (**Jeroboams & Laytons**). Not really a 'light' wine, but it is seamlessly smooth and very fruit driven, so I have shoved it in this section. Hunter's Pinot is plummy and velvety and a delight to drink. The only problem I can foresee is that it might disappear too fast from the glass (evaporation?).

£11.95 **Brouilly, Château de Pierreux, 2003,** Beaujolais, France (**Liberty Wines, Luvian's** and **Moriarty**). This incredible wine is made by Pascal Marchand from the famed Domaine de la Vougeraie in Burgundy. It is 100% Gamay, like every other bottle of Beaujolais, but somehow it tastes totally different. Pascal has transformed the happy-go-lucky Gamay grape into a sublime, totally focused, red fruit jamboree with an undercurrent of darker, spicier fruit and a whisper of oak (I think?). Anyway, this is a gob-smackingly serious Beaujolais from one of the ten famous

LIGHT AND FRUITY

'Cru' villages, Brouilly, and I guarantee you've not had anything like it before. It's possibly even the most impressive wine I have ever tasted from this region.

● ●

£3.49 **Cuvée des Amandiers Rouge**, 2003, Vin de Pays d'Oc, France (**Maj**). This innocent Syrah/Grenache blend is surprisingly chunky and rewarding. It is a good party wine as there is little or no tannin but it will keep the wine bores happy, too, as there is enough interest on the nose and palate.

£3.99 **Cortello**, 2003, Estremadura, Portugal (**Flying Corkscrew**, **FWW**, **Saf** and **Sommelier**). Safeway may or may not take this phenomenal wine. When Morrisons took over earlier this year, they unfortunately chucked out a load of Safeway's star wines and, at the time of writing, they had not decided whether this wine was getting the guillotine or not. Anyway, there are a few other very good merchants who can supply you with what is the best value Portuguese wine on the shelves today. Cortello is stuffed with blackberry and red cherry fruit, and there is a staggering level of complexity for the price.

£3.99 **Snake Creek Shiraz**, 2003, South Eastern Australia (**Odd**). If you are feeling skint and need to be perked up, this is the chunky blackcurrant and funky plum wine for the job. It may be cheap, but there is enough fruit and backbone here to please even the sternest critic – it works for me.

sausage-and-*mash* evenings

£4.99 **Beau-Mayne Merlot**, **2003**, Bordeaux (**Saf** and **Tes**). This is a screwcap-sealed inexpensive red Bordeaux that totally performs. It is from the super-ripe 2003 vintage and is stuffed with cassis and blackberry fruit. Beau-Mayne is a lovely everyday wine, perfect for uncorking on a whim.

£4.99 **Jacob's Creek Cabernet/Merlot**, **2002**, South Eastern Australia (**Sai**). For a quick and easy fiver, you can sit back and sink into this juicy Ribena-scented red. Cleverly blended and frighteningly well made, this is a sign to the wine world that you can, despite hideously high duty, excise and VAT charges, release superb wine at a low price.

£4.99 **Norton Barbera**, **2003**, Mendoza, Argentina (**Berkmann**, **Henderson** and **Wai**). Unoaked, bright, juicy and plummy, this is a gorgeous, easy, switch-your-brain-off wine, which is lusciously smooth and the perfect partner for pizza, pasta or sausage-and-mash evenings. It has the quality of fruit of a ten-pound wine but, luckily, has saved loads of cash by not using oak, so you can enjoy this stonking wine for a fiver.

£5.49 **Oracle Pinotage**, **2003**, Coastal Region, South Africa (**Odd**). This is a pristine, entry level Pinotage and it is the perfect wine for char-grilled burgers or spare ribs. The punchy plum fruit is all there and in addition there is a tang of acidity and aniseed bringing up the rear – a pocket rocket.

£5.99 **Château Ducla**, **2002**, Bordeaux, France (**Boo** and **Unw**). Ducla is a competent Bordeaux Supérieur but not one that has troubled the Top 250, until now. The 2002 is a

MEDIUM WEIGHT

mile ahead of previous vintages on account of its bright
berry fruit and ripe, savoury finish. *Incroyable*!

£5.99 **Quinta das Sentencostas**, 2003, Alenquer,
Portugal (**Sai**). Portugal has its fair share of unusual grape
names – this is made from Periquita, Camarate, Tinta Miuda
and Preto Martinho. It's a stunning, smoky, barbecue-style
red and it's crammed with cherry and plum fruit. Like many
Portuguese reds, it also has delicious mouth-watering
acidity and tanginess on the finish, refreshing the palate.
Great wine, great price, quirky taste and perfect with Indian
lamb shank or Moroccan stews.

£5.99 **Tupungato Cabernet/Malbec**, 2003, Mendoza,
Argentina (**M&S**). Made by the top-class outfit Catena
Zapata, this is a gorgeous, medium-bodied red with
oodles of dark berry fruit and a delightful twist of spice
and herbs on the finish. Treat this glossy dark beauty to
a serious steak.

£6.49 **McWilliams, Hanwood Estate Cabernet
Sauvignon**, 2003, South Eastern Australia (**Tes** and
Thr). It is so difficult to get inexpensive Cabernet right. You
need charm and complexity but not too much oak or tannin.
Hanwood is a very clever wine with calm, multi-layered,
accurate fruit. This is a worthy rival to Cabernets across the
planet and, don't worry, there is enough to go around.

£6.99 **MM Reserva Privada**, 2000, Marqués de Monistrol,
Penedès, Spain (**www.tesco.com** and **Unw**). Stunning,
charred plum and blackberry fruit is augmented with dark

MEDIUM WEIGHT

chocolate, bonfire, damp potting compost and Cuban cigar moments. This, as you can probably tell already, is a very complex bottle with masses of charm and an ever-evolving flavour. For seven pounds you'll not find a more captivating, involving or intriguing red wine for late night sipping.

£6.99 **Peter Lehmann Clancy's**, **2002**, Barossa Valley, South Australia (**Coo**, **Odd**, **Unw**, **Vin du Van** and **Wai**). Clancy's is a mesmerising red blend, masterminded by the great man himself and made by the self-deprecating, yet awesomely talented Andrew Wigan, and drunk in huge quantities by myself. This is a gob-smackingly great wine with more layers of fruit and subtle flavour nuances than ever before. I adore this wine, and if you've never tasted it, you're in for a shock.

£6.99 **Sainsbury's Classic Selection Western Australian Cabernet Merlot**, **2003** (Sai). Made at Forest Hill by laid-back (near horizontal, in fact) wine alchemist Larry Cherubino, this is a youthful, vibrant, ballistic wine, bursting with sensational, high-quality fruit – it is, not surprisingly, one of my wines of the year. Claret simply can't compete on the same playing field as this unbelievably inexpensive wine. The nose alone suggests this is a fifteen-pound bottle!

£7.49 **Vega de Castilla**, **2002**, Ribera del Duero, Spain (**Wai**). Ribera del Duero is the Mayfair of vineyard real estate in Spain, but somehow this delicious red wine has missed out on a typically exorbitant Ribera price tag. No stranger to the Top 250, Vega is made from the fabulous Spanish red grape Tempranillo and it is harvested from 50-year-old 'bush' vines. Where the winemaker really gets this wine right, though, is that he only gives it six months in French and American oak barrels. Any longer would have made it too oaky and coarse. You are left with vibrant mulberry fruit, beguiling depth and true Ribera class in spades.

£7.99 **Bon Cap Organic Syrah, Robertson, 2003**, South Africa (**Wai**). I didn't know the price of this wine when I first tasted it in Cape Town back in April. I certainly didn't pick it for a sub-ten-pound bottle. Bon Cap is a lovely, inexpensive, organic Syrah, with loads of charm intensity and a true 'sense of place'. By that I mean it is unmistakeably South African with its distinctive spice, earth and warm leather nuances, and that makes it all the more enjoyable.

£7.99 **Bush View Shiraz, 2002**, Margaret River, Western Australia (**M&S**). Lighter and more aromatic than most Aussie Shiraz, this is a delicious, relaxing plummy red, with a salt-and-pepper nose and a smooth, berry and briar palate. Allow this soothing wine to bring you down slowly after a hectic day at work.

£7.99 **Château Ségonzac, 2002**, Premières Côtes de Blaye, Bordeaux, France (**Wai**). Great impact on the palate with tight cherry fruit, lovely freshness and style, this Cabernet/Merlot blend is a real success for Ségonzac. I remember the Château from days gone by and it has a fairly useful pedigree. On this showing it has zoomed into my hard-fought hit list of overperforming, underpriced wines.

MEDIUM WEIGHT

£7.99   **Leasingham Magnus Shiraz/Cabernet**, 2001,
Clare Valley, South Australia (**Sai**). This and the 2002 that
follow it are two of the finest, most impressive budget reds
from the Clare Valley. Shiraz and Cabernet are made for each
other and this natural synergy is in total harmony here. The
balance is spot on and the warmth and touch amazing. You
won't believe it but the 2003s that I tasted out of barrel this
year continue the unbroken run of excellence – delectable.

£7.99   **Marqués de la Concordia Crianza**, 2000,
Rioja, Spain (**Unw**). This is spectacular Rioja. In fact, it is
one of the finest versions I have tasted – at any price! The
quality of fruit and the texture alone are simply amazing.
Black cherry, plum, spice and vanilla nuances cavort on the
palate, and the finish is dreamily long. You will not believe
Concordia – it is a phenomenal bottle.

£7.99   **Yarra Burn Shiraz/Viognier**, 2002, Yarra Valley,
Victoria, Australia (**Philglas & Swiggot**). Brand new on the
market and currently only sold in Aussie specialists Philglas
(no surprise they were on to it quickly), this wine is the
vanguard of a new and not wholly welcome Australian
fashion – the Shiraz (red)/Viognier (white) blend. Now,
Côte-Rôtie (the greatest of all French Syrahs) uses this trick
with skill, experience and great results. The majority of
Aussies who are putting a dribble of Viognier into the mix
for added aroma and complexity seem to be a bit shaky-
handed and tip in far too much. They also hoik the price up
to a high-trousered level and the wines are simply not worth
it. Yarra Burn's version is clever, accurate and inexpensive,
and it has got it right in one. My advice – buy it now!

MEDIUM WEIGHT

£8.00 **Saumur-Champigny, Château du Hureau, 2002**, Loire, France (**Haynes, Hanson & Clark**). This is 100% Cabernet Franc and it is from one of the top estates in the Loire Valley. The herbal, blackberry fruit is so attractive and juicy it is amazing. Drinking beautifully already, Hureau's S-C is a perfect introduction to this fantastic variety.

£8.60 **Moss Wood, Ribbon Vale Cabernet Sauvignon, 2001**, Margaret River, Western Australia (**Jeroboams & Laytons**). Ribbon Vale is Keith Mugford's second label and it is finally hitting a rich seam of quality. 2001 is a first-class vintage and these vineyards are smack in the heart of Margaret River's prime turf. Why this is a mere £8.60 Lord only knows, but I can tell you that when I opened this wine for a room of connoisseurs they simply couldn't believe it. When Ribbon Vale's fame spreads the price will go north towards Moss Wood's own of around £40 per bottle. My advice is to get in there early because this wine is likely to fly.

£8.99 **Barbera Parpan, 2001**, Fontanafredda, Piemonte, Italy (**Henderson, Peckham & Rye**, **Valvona & Crolla** and **Winecellars**). This top-flight estate has pulled itself out of a nose dive over the last few years and is now making some of the most dramatic wines in northern Italy. I cannot believe the quality of this relatively inexpensive Barbera – it is spectacular. The red and black fruit is bright, chunky, smooth and satisfying. Well done guys – keep it up and this historic name will once again be seen on wine lists and in cellars across the country.

MEDIUM WEIGHT

£9.50 **Coyam, Viñedos Organicos Emiliana**, **2001**, Central Valley, Chile (**Asd**, **Vintage Roots** and **www.virginwines.com**). This multi-layered, organically grown Merlot/Carmenère/Cabernet Sauvignon/Syrah/Mourvèdre blend (phew) from Chile is made by one of the greatest winemakers in South America, Alvaro Espinoza. Coyam is an incredible bottle – it is phenomenally classy and, although it is under ten pounds, it has the depth, intensity and aura of a much more expensive wine. A darker, fiercer 2002 turns up in the New Year.

£9.50 **Domaine Gardiés**, **Les Millères**, **2001**, Côtes-du-Roussillon Villages, France (**Jeroboams & Laytons**). Gardiés is one of my favourite recent finds from the South of France. The intense, inky fruit is stuffed with blackcurrant, loganberry and plum, and there is a hefty dose of pepper and fresh herbs to lift the nose. 2001 was a superb vintage and this shows in the intensity of flavour and sheer size and length of the aftertaste. Sneaking in under a tenner, this is a fabulous wine with a massive amount of class and concentration. Also, look out for the devastating 2002 Gardiés Vieilles Vignes Blanc (£11.95, **J&L**), as it is rare to find a white with this degree of sophistication and intrigue.

£9.50 **Jordan Merlot**, **2002**, Stellenbosch, South Africa (**Connolly's**, **Rodney Densem**, **Garland**, **Peter Graham**, **Jeroboams & Laytons**, **Christopher Piper Wines**, **Frank Stainton** and **Noel Young**). Every wine that Gary and Cathy Jordan make is spot on. This is a five-star estate and a safe haven on an unfamiliar wine list. 2002 Jordan Merlot is not overly complex, it's not wondrously age-worthy, nor is it

MEDIUM WEIGHT

red 63

the highest-scoring wine in their portfolio, but it is the one that made me smile the widest when I tasted the range this year. It is, quite simply, a downright delicious wine – you'll need two bottles, it is just too easy to drink.

£9.50 **Neagles Rock Grenache/Shiraz, 2003**, Clare Valley, South Australia (**Yapp Bros.**). With raspberry, fresh herbs and red cherries leading the way, this fragrant, garnet-hued, Grenache-dominant red is a perfect bottle for autumnal dishes and well-stocked cheese boards. It should zoom into the country by Christmas, so keep yourself amused with the delightfully plummy 2002 in the meantime.

£9.99 **Flagstone 'BK5' Pinot Noir, 2003**, South Africa (**Odd**). 2003 BK5 is the juiciest incarnation of this wine to date. The balance is exact and the fruit and oak are in perfect synergy. Despite its youth, this is a cracker, and with a screwcap it will inevitably live a long and healthy life. The velvety berry fruit rolls over the palate, occasionally enlivened with herbal twists, earthy turns and plummy switchbacks that enliven the journey along the way. If you like this then try Bruce Jack's other smart Pinot, 2003 Poetry (£14.99, **Odd**). It's like BK5 reclining naked on a Louis XIV chaise longue.

£9.99 **Glen Carlou Pinot Noir, 2003**, Paarl, South Africa (**Eagle's**, **Odd**, **Christopher Piper**, **Frank Stainton** and **SWIG**). David Finlayson, son of Walter, now runs Glen Carlou and he is a very smart winemaker. Having worked at Peter Lehmann in the Barossa Valley and Château Margaux in Bordeaux, among others, his experience abroad has been

MEDIUM WEIGHT

invaluable. This bright, vibrant Pinot is classically dimensioned with explosive cherry and plum fruit on the nose, and a fine, luxurious texture on the palate. There is also a welcome South African 'gout de terroir' (funky, earthy nuances coming from the soil in the vineyards) that gives it an authenticity that undoubtedly broadens its appeal.

£9.99 **Lacrima di Morro d'Alba, Fonte del Re, 2003**, Umani Ronchi, Marche, Italy (**SWIG, Wimbledon Wine** and **Winecellars**). Of all of the bizarre grape varieties in the world, this must surely be the King. But which of the words in this wine's name is the grape? Well, 'Lacrima di Morro d'Alba' is the answer, and it smells like a bunch of red roses, a slice of Ma Jukesy's summer pudding and a liquorice-stick forest all rolled into one. The taste is not unlike a purple-hued, extraterrestrial, fruit-frenzy cocktail. It is tangy and refreshing, too, and I can guarantee you'll never have experienced such a strange and yet wonderful wine in your life. Drink it slightly chilled with Indian food.

£9.99 **Vacqueyras, Les Christins, 2002**, Perrin, Southern Rhône, France (**Tes** and **Thr**). Thresher is still on the 2001 (which is a cracker) but they will move on to this phoenix-like 2002 in due course. It was an awful year in the southern Rhône but the Perrin team is immensely skilled and this meaty Vacqueyras rose from the mire. It is spicy, briary and desperate for a wintry stew to be served alongside it.

£10.99 **Chianti Classico Brolio, 2002**, Tuscany, Italy (**Sai** and **Winecellars**). After the awesome 2001 vintage, you might expect the 2002 (a more difficult vintage) to be a less impressive wine. But no, Francesco, or the Barone Ricasoli to be more precise, decided to tighten the quality control to strangulation point and disregard any grapes that were not 100 per cent perfect. He also decided not to make his top cuvée, Castello di Brolio, so those grapes flowed down the ladder into this wine. Consequently, this is probably the most delicious, early-drinking Chianti Brolio he has made to date. This wine is a stunning expression of Tuscany and it will romance your palate and warm your heart.

£11.99 **Château Cambon la Pelouse**, **2001**, Haut-Médoc, Bordeaux, France (**Wai**). Cambon is elegant, balanced, effortlessly classy claret, and it is a dream date for a proper English Sunday lunch. The bright cassis and black cherry fruit is simply heavenly and the oak nuances are beautifully integrated – class in a glass and perfect with roast lamb.

£11.99 **Mount Langi Ghiran**, **Cliff Edge Shiraz**, **2001**, Ararat, Victoria, Australia (**Andrew Chapman**, **Dunells**, **Moriarty**, **Philglas & Swiggot**, **La Réserve**, **Villeneuve** and **Noel Young**). Winemaker Trevor Mast scored a huge hit in 2001 with his second label Cliff Edge. It is highly scented, aromatic Shiraz, with a lovely plump cassis texture, a touch of tar and spice, and a heroic finish.

£11.99 **Scotchman's Hill Pinot Noir**, **2003**, Geelong, Victoria, Australia (**Odd**). Scotchmans' 2003 Pinots are the best they have ever made (see Swan Bay, too). Thankfully they are also sealed with a screwcap, guaranteeing the perfect condition of the contents. The dense strawberry, black cherry and sweet plum aromas are complemented by fertile earth nuances, and the texture is pure liquid velvet. These various elements meld harmoniously together in this wine and, as this wine has such an ethereal aroma, you may even find yourself sniffing more than sipping.

£12.50 **Crozes-Hermitage, Domaine Alain Graillot, 2002**, Northern Rhône, France (**Yapp Bros.**). Graillot is nothing short of a legend in Crozes, despite a pretty short time as a winemaker in this hallowed land of Syrah. I remember tasting his first vintage (1985) and marvelling at the fresh, ground pepper nose and plump blackberry fruit. Nothing has changed and even this fairly ordinary 2002 vintage cannot deflect this wine from its purpose – that is, to entertain the palate. This is a Graillot Crozes that is ready to drink (hurrah) and, first and foremost, it is world class and only twelve quid.

£12.95 **Clonakilla, Hilltops Shiraz, 2003**, Canberra, New South Wales, Australia (**Bennett's Hedley Wright** and **Liberty**). The brand new release of Hilltops '03 hadn't had more than a second to get over its jetlag before I whipped off its screwcap and dived right in. Considering it was a little bashed up, it still looked absolutely phenomenal. The pepper and iodine nose was pungent, the core of sleek and unruffled black fruit heightened my anticipation, and then the finish was majestic. I had to pinch myself to remember this was only a shade over a tenner.

£12.99 **De Toren Diversity Gamma, 2002**, Stellenbosch, South Africa (**Bergerac Wine Cellar, Berry Bros., Andrew Chapman, Cooden Cellars, Corkscrew, The Flying Corkscrew,**

MEDIUM WEIGHT

Peter Green, Halifax, Handford, Harrogate Fine Wine, John Kelly, Moriarty, Nobody Inn, Odd, Thos. Peatling, Penistone Court, Philglas & Swiggot, Raeburn, Charles Steevenson, SWIG, Wimbledon Wine, Wine Society and Noel Young). Diversity is the second wine of De Toren's famous Fusion V. The 2001 was called Beta and there is still some stock out there. But hold fire for the 2002 Gamma, due into the country in the autumn – it is fantastic. This is one of South Africa's gems and if you compare it to red Bordeaux, you have to spend a tenner (minimum) more for the same impact, harmony and class.

£14.25 **Réserve de Léoville-Barton, 1999**, Château Léoville-Barton, St-Julien, Bordeaux, France (**Goedhuis & Co.**). Totally famous Château; excellent vintage; drinking beautifully now; bargain price; lots of stock – this never happens. Until now! What are you waiting for?

£14.95 **Spécial Cuvée du Château Lezongars, 2001**, Bordeaux, France (**Jeroboams & Laytons**). At the very top of the Lezongars tree, above the Château wine and even above the delicious L' Enclos, is the Spécial Cuvée. This is claret with a difference – it is modern, without being over extracted, and the oak is in perfect balance. If you want to try a wine with flair but also a true sense of place, this is it.

£14.99 **2002 Nepenthe Zinfandel, 2002**, Adelaide Hills, South Australia (**Odd** and **Sai**). Zinful and unashamed in its blueberry pie nose and broad brush strokes of glossy black fruit flavours, this is a dead impressive bottle of wine and one of the few Aussie Zins to get anywhere near the goal.

MEDIUM WEIGHT

£14.99 **Wither Hills Pinot Noir**, 2003, Marlborough, South Island (**Ballantynes**, **Boo**, **Simon Charles**, **Great Northern Wine**, **Great Western Wine**, **Charles Hennings**, **Odd**, **Jeroboams & Laytons**, **Edward Sheldon**, **T&W**, **Villeneuve**, **Wai** and **Wine Society**). I tasted the very first bottle of this vintage in the country earlier this year and it is a sublime effort from master craftsman Brent Marris. The wondrous nose of sweet spices, polished oak, mulberries and damsons is hypnotic. The palate is silky smooth and long, even by Wither Hills' cosmic standards. Once again, it is proudly topped off with a screwcap, sealing in all of the profound aromas and assuring you a perfect glass.

£17.95 **Chard Farm**, **Finla Mor Pinot Noir**, 2002, Central Otago, South Island New Zealand (**Lea & Sandeman**). Central Otago is fast becoming the trendiest place outside of the Côte d'Or in Burgundy to plant the Holy Grail of grape varieties, Pinot Noir. 2002 is also the best vintage to hit this region in living memory, so you are now up to pace. Otago Pinots are not cheap, but a few of them are worth the steep price tag. Chard Farm is a top-flight producer and the nose, texture and flavours in this wine are nothing short of benchmark. Strawberry- and red-cherry-scented nuances weave their way into your olfactory system and never let go, and the fruit on the mid-palate is relaxed, smooth, ethereal and ever so generous.

£19.50 **Mount Michael Pinot Noir**, 2002, Central Otago, South Island, New Zealand (**Butlers**, **Andrew Chapman**, **Cellar Door**, **Cooden Cellars**, **Eagle's Wines**, **Hailsham Cellars**, **Philglas & Swiggot** and **The Vineyard**).

MEDIUM WEIGHT

From the highly respected Cromwell sub-region of central Otago, this is a deep, rich Pinot with more intensity and gravitas than the Chard Farm above. This is a Vosne-Romanée to Chard Farm's Beaune, if you know what I mean, and it is sumptuous (you can tell I'm a Burgundy bore!). The fruit is sappy, pure, brooding and balanced – keep your eyes peeled for it.

£19.99 **Planeta Merlot, 2002**, Sicily, Italy (**Boo, Bacchanalia, Great Northern Wine, Harvey Nichols, Philglas & Swiggot, Villeneuve, Wimbledon Wine, Winecellars** and **Wine Society**). 2002 was a stunning vintage in Sicily (unlike most of the rest of Italy and a lot of southern France) and this Merlot is bursting with intensity and class. It treads a fine line between red- and black-fruit flavours, sometimes hopping from one camp to the other mid-sip. The oak is first class and, even though it is strictly speaking too young, this is a very moreish wine already. Planeta is a stellar estate, so look out for their wines – every label is worth a try and you can't say that very often.

● ●

£3.99 **Navasqüés Tinto, 2003**, Navarra, Spain (**Mor** and **Saf**). Scoop – Navasqüés makes incredible wines at incredible prices. This is the third time in as many years that one of their wines has made TWL. Made from Tempranillo and Garnacha (exactly the same recipe as top flight Rioja) this is a heroic wine with acres of dark berry, chocolate and mocha fruit. Four quid for massive texture, weight, class and length – how do they do it?

MEDIUM WEIGHT/BLOCKBUSTER

£5.49 **Casillero del Diablo Cabernet Sauvignon**, **2003**, Maipo Valley, Chile (**Asd**, **Boo**, **Odd**, **Saf**, **Sai**, **Tes**, **Thr** and **Wai**). I think we can allow this wine to go up 50p for the 2003 vintage – after all, it is one of the best-value Cabernets on the planet. Casillero Cab is a spectacular creation with brooding plum, blackcurrant and leather notes, and it is thankfully on virtually every supermarket shelf. If you are in a rush and you need a fail-safe wine for dinner, this is it. 2003 CdD Carmenère (£4.99, **Maj**, **Sai**, **Tes** and **Thr**) is another wonderful wine with less brawn and more coffee and red fruit aromas than the Cabernet.

£5.59 **Aglianico Guardiolo**, **La Guardiense**, 2002, Southern Italy (**Bibendum Wine**). Believe it or not, this is the super cuvée from this estate and it is only a fiver! Aglianico is a superb indigenous Italian red grape variety. It doesn't have the portiness of fellow southern Italian stalwart Primitivo and, for this reason, more often than not I prefer it. The flavour is rich and black fruit driven, with oodles of spice and liquorice, and a warm, southern demeanour. Add to this a level of true complexity rarely found in wines three times its price and some very snazzy packaging, and this wine is a demon that, on a good day, could beat the pants off many a bottle of the Super-Tuscan bluff and bluster brigade. If you are having a party with an Italian theme, get a case of this wine – you know you've got nothing to lose!

£5.99 **Anubis Malbec**, **2003**, Mendoza, Argentina (**Wai**). My goodness this is a terrific wine for the money. It is massive and inky, but extremely smooth and velvety on

BLOCKBUSTER

red 71

the palate. The core fruit is dark and dense, and this is a massive mouthful, but it is seamless and luxurious – dive in.

£5.99 **Concha y Toro, Lot 34 Malbec, 2003**, Cachapoal Valley, Peumo, Chile (**Odd**). Marcelo Papa continues to make some stunning small 'lots' for Oddbins. In the 2003 vintage they are, once again, all very good, but my picks are this inexpensive Malbec, with its bravado, brazen fruitiness and mass of dark berry fruit, and the 2003 Lot 453 Carmenère (£8.99) with its sumptuous core of red berries and smoky, sweet oak. The other wines (a Syrah, Cabernet and Merlot) are all brutally tannic, and this is a shame because I bet most people will take them home and drink then immediately, when they'd be better left for five years.

£6.99 **Dourosa, Quinta de la Rosa, 2002**, Douro, Portugal (**Wai**). All of the big port houses are now gunning for each other in not just the port game but also the red wine sector. Dourosa is certainly the cheapest of the wines worthy of note and it sacrifices pure unadulterated power for a degree of balance and control. If the other wines in this 250 are wintry dinner wines, this could even be barbecue food, such is the lift and drive of the plummy, juicy fruit – bravo.

£6.99 **Porcupine Ridge Syrah, 2003**, Coastal Region, South Africa (**Som**, **SWIG**, **Wai** and **Wine Society**). I have always been a fan of this legendary wine. I tasted the 2003 vintage with winemaker Marc Kent at his winery and it is a complete stunner. I can't think of many other seven-pound wines that are as profoundly and memorably satisfying as

triceratops burgers

this unassuming wine. It is quite simply one of the best-value reds in the world. Whack it in a decanter and let it open up, and then marvel at the drama in the glass.

£7.49 **Cazal Viel, Cuvée des Fées, 2003**, Saint-Chinian, Languedoc-Roussillon, France (**Wai**). This is the brand-new vintage of Cuvée des Fées and it's a winner. A feisty Syrah, brimming with black fruit and pepper, it's the perfect all-purpose winter wine for stews, game and carnivorous frenzies. Cheers.

£7.95 **Vega del Castillo, Garnacha 100, 2002**, Navarra, Spain (**Wine Society**). Made from 80/100-year-old vines and completely unoaked, this is a staggeringly impressive creature with a core of the blackest fruit and a fascinating herbal aura. Drink it with massive meaty dishes – triceratops burgers, perhaps?

£7.99 **Heartland Shiraz, 2002**, Limestone Coast, South Australia (**Odd**). I have opened this bottle a number of times at wine tastings and every time that people try to guess the price, they overshoot by a fiver! This is a benchmark wine and it is setting the pace for all others to follow. The intensity of the black cherry and berry fruit, coupled with the smart oak, whisper of mint and whiff of leather gives you plenty to savour as you swirl this wine around the glass. If you want an everyday wine from the same stable, try 2003 Stickleback Red (£5.95, **deFINE**, **Great Western Wines**, **Michael Jobling**, **Wine in Cornwall**). It's a funky little Cabernet/Syrah/Sangiovese blend that offers a welcome change from the usual formulaic Aussie cheapies.

BLOCKBUSTER

red 73

£7.99 **Peter Lehmann Shiraz**, **2002**, Barossa Valley, South Australia (**Asd**, **Boo**, **Mor**, **Odd**, **Saf**, **Vin du Van** and **Wai**). Arriving in the autumn, this is another spellbinding vintage of PL Shiraz. No note because it doesn't need it. You already know all about this multi-award-winning wine. If you want to taste the 'greatest wine we have ever made', then hurry along and grab one of the last few bottle of the monumental 1998 Stonewell Shiraz (£29.99, **Bibendum**, **Odd**, **Vin du Van** and **Wai**). I gave it one of my elusive perfect 20/20 scores.

£7.99 **Robertson Winery, Wolfkloof Shiraz, 2003**, Robertson, South Africa (**www.sainsburyswine.co.uk**). Wolfkloof is a soaring wine with acres of crushed velvet black fruit and a handful of cracked pepper floating atop every glass. The sappy, black cherry fruit merited one clear and rarely written word to finish off my gushing tasting note – unbelievable. The 2003 arrives just before this book is published and is a revelation. Eight pounds is a snip for a wine of this quality. Don't miss it.

£7.99 **Tukulu Pinotage**, **2002**, Groenekloof, South Africa (**Odd**). When it comes to 100% Pinotage wines, I am very fussy and aim for modern, fruit-driven styles over the bad eggs, sour cranberry and undergrowth wines of the past. Tukulu is a perfect example of how to make a wonderfully lush, dark, spicy wine, load it with cinnamon and blackberry, raspberry and strawberry nuances, and then just let it go on to the market without over oaking or mucking it around. For that reason alone it wins a slot in the hallowed 250. It also happens to be a stunner.

£8.99 **Ravenswood Amador County Zinfandel**, **2001**, California (**Thr** and **WRa**). One of my favourite tastings of the year was at Ravenswood, in Sonoma, earlier this year. I strolled through barrel samples of weird and wonderful Zinfandel from ancient parcels of vines dotted across California. This is where I found this stunning cuvée and I gave it a massive score in my notes. Amador is a startlingly serious wine for its reasonable price tag. It is packed tight with blueberries, tar, violets, cinnamon, vanilla, dark chocolate, woodsmoke, blackcurrants and boot polish (not literally, you understand). There is so much going on in the glass it is amazing. If you want a sofa-sippin' red for the winter months, then this is it. Alternatively, trade down a few pounds in money and a few kilos in brawn, and marvel at the best value Zin on the planet – 2002 Ravenswood Vintners Blend Zinfandel (£6.99, **Asd**, **Boo**, **Maj**, **Saf**, **Tes** and **Wai**).

£8.99 **Tim Adams Shiraz**, **2002**, Clare Valley, South Australia (**Tes**). I foolishly thought that Tim's 2001 was as good as this wine could ever get. I spoke too soon – the 2002 is extraordinary. The lift, quality, definition and precision of this wine is frightening. Not content with this pepper and blackberry masterpiece, he did it again in 2003 (due on our shelves in the late autumn). If you want a fail-safe, crowd-pleasing, first-class dinner party wine, which will inevitably make your guests jump to their feet and applaud, this is it. It won't surprise you that 'Bonecrusher' Adams is also a Grenache wizard – 2001 Tim Adams The Fergus (£9.99, **Australian Wine Club**) is a lusty troubadour, yearning to be heard.

£9.79 **Spice Route Pinotage**, **2003**, Swartland, South Africa (**Boo**). Dense, powerful, inky fruit, a Christmas cake nose and a macerated-plum palate – this is a heroic wine with incredible presence and a sensational finish. Initially flamboyant, then mellow, and finally smugly satisfying – all in one mouthful. Not bad, hey?

£9.99 **Clos de los Siete**, **2003**, Tunuyan, Argentina (**Wai**, **Bacchanalia**, **Peter Green**, **Harrods**, **Henderson**, **Great Northern Wine**, **Wimbledon** and **Winecellars**). I tasted one of the very first bottles of the 2003 Clos de los Siete in the country and it is every bit as serious as the debut 2002 vintage. Michel Rolland (winemaking consultant to the rich and famous) and six other investors are responsible for this imposing new wine, and it bears a lot of his trademark flavours. There is a mass of extracted, dark fruit, charcoal-ember nuances, sweet, tight-grain oak and heady spices. The blend of Malbec, Merlot, Syrah and Cabernet gives the core fruit a lot of complexity, and it will age like clockwork.

£9.99 **Domaine des Garennes**, **2001**, Minervois, France (**M&S**). This excellent Minervois is made from a blend of genteel Syrah, cheery Grenache and swarthy Carignan. The main thrust here is one of dark, intense blackcurrant, blackberries and dark chocolate. There is intensity, power and a liberal dusting of pepper and spice, too. There is no doubt you can smell that this is a BIG wine, and it is. When you've tired of swirling the wine around your glass, have a sip and you'll see that every nuance on the nose is amplified on the palate. This is a truly glorious and totally complex red wine.

£9.99 **Glaetzer, The Wallace**, 2002, Barossa Valley, South Australia (**Odd**). The Wallace is a Shiraz/Cabernet/Grenache blend and it is less muscular than you might expect for a Barossa Valley wine. The plummy fruit is moderately spicy and surprisingly well mannered, finishing in a lithe, languid aftertaste. It is ready to drink now but will definitely hold well for five years to come, by which time I expect it'll be an absolute dream. Buy the Wallace when you are feeling mellow and you need a wine to match your mood.

£9.99 **Jack & Knox, The Outsider Shiraz, 2002**, Riebeeck, South Africa (**Odd**). Crash helmets on, seatbelts fastened, countdown begins… This is one of the wines of the year. The Outsider looks cool, tastes unbelievable and embodies all that is gripping about South African winemaking today. The steeped blackcurrant, bruised-plum and cherry fruit is incredible. The spice and woodsmoke is mesmerising, and the sheer density and length of flavour is a wonder to behold. Yeehah!

£9.99 **Les Hauts de l'Enclos des Bories**, 2001, Minervois La Livinière, Languedoc, France (**www.tesco.com**). At ten pounds this is a very smart wine, indeed. It is densely packed with phenomenal fruit and yet it is not in any way too heavy or tannic. The ripeness and balance between the cherry, blackcurrant and plum flavours and the chocolate, spice, pepper, lavender and thyme nuances is a joy.

£9.99 **Neffiez, Cuvée Baltazar, 2002**, Coteaux du Languedoc, France (**Thr**). This is the Ray Winstone of top class French Syrahs. On first impressions, you think it would

BLOCKBUSTER

kneecap you if you put a foot wrong, but once you've softened it up a little you stand a very good chance of being lifelong friends. Just one tip – decant this, it is a beast!

£9.99 **Quinta de la Rosa Tinto, 2001**, Douro, Portugal (**Bentalls**, **Boo**, **Flying Corkscrew**, **Fortnum & Mason**, **Selfridges** and **Wine in Cornwall**). The sheer quality and density of black-fruit flavour in this wine is tremendous. The core is like crushed, super-ripe, velvety-smooth blackcurrants infused with sweet spices and black liquorice. It is wonderfully rich and multi-layered, and it must be one of the finest and most balanced Portuguese wines I have ever tasted. Oh, and it is already drinking perfectly.

£9.99 **Rupert & Rothschild Classique, 2002,** Franschhoek, South Africa (**Rodney Densem**, **Handford**, **Harrods**, **Mill Hill**, **Philglas & Swiggot, Roberson**, **Saf** and **Villeneuve**). The name says it all – this is a classic and a Rothschild is involved! It is made from Cabernet, Merlot and there is a whisper of Pinotage to top it off (so perhaps a Cape classic, then, and not a French one!), and it is a beautifully balanced wine. The 2002 has charm, harmony and more than a little elegance. Once again, South Africa turns up the heat with cracking value-for-money wines.

£9.99 **Twin Wells Shiraz, 2001**, McLaren Vale, South Australia (**M&S**). Benchmark, blackberry-, iodine-, plum- and pepper-stuffed McLaren Vale Shiraz costs a lot more than a tenner normally. This is another one of Bruce Tyrrell's excellent wines and if you want to nail the flavour of this world-class region in one glass, this is the way to do it!

BLOCKBUSTER

78   red

£9.99 **Two Hands Angels Share Shiraz**, 2003,
Barossa Valley, South Australia (**Cooden**, **Great Northern
Wine**, **Henderson**, **Luvian's**, **Nidderdale**, **Philglas & Swiggot**,
www.sainsburyswine.co.uk, **Sommelier**, **Taurus Wines** and
Vin du Van). This is a young wine but it is already showing
some serious class and depth of fruit. The spice, intensity
and breadth of flavour is stunning and, I am sorry, but this
bloke ain't givin' the Angels any of his share!

£10.29 **Penfolds Bin 28 Kalimna Shiraz**, 2001, South
Australia (**Maj**, **Odd**, **Som**, **Tes**, **Thr** and **Unw**). With
awesome intensity and plum, blueberry, cedar and allspice
effortlessly mingling on the palate, this is my favourite
Bin 28 in years. At a tenner this is not only stunning value
for a drinking wine, it is also a bargain for a bottle that
will age like clockwork for a decade and come out positively
beaming. Across the board Penfolds has made 2001 its most
impressive vintage for years.

£11.69 **Neil Ellis Vineyard Selection Cabernet
Sauvignon**, **2001**, Stellenbosch, South Africa
(**Welshpool Wine**). This is a single vineyard release that
we only see in tiny quantities in the UK, but it is well
worth tracking down since it is a very smart wine indeed.
Rich, full and darkly blackcurranty, it is a medium-weight
model with considerable intensity, as opposed to being an
overly alcoholic, sun-drenched New World wine. There is
class and complexity here, with stunning oak and excellent,
fit, refreshing tannins. Welshpool Wine is the retail arm
of Neil Ellis' UK agents, so this price is a total and utter
bargain.

BLOCKBUSTER

£11.99 **Peter Lehmann, The Futures Shiraz, 2002,**
Barossa Valley, South Australia (**Adnams, Boo, Odd** and **Vin du Van**). Last year's Top 250 announced the arrival of The Futures. The stunning 2001 is still out there, but I want to alert you to the arrival of the awesome 2002. It is two pounds more – it had to be, the 2001 was, and still is, remarkably inexpensive for the degree of expertise in the glass – and it is even better – which is, frankly, unbelievable. I tasted it alongside a barrel sample of its big brother Stonewell – the 1998 vintage of which is the best wine Ian Wigan has made to date (£29.99, **Bibendum, Odd, Vin du Van** and **Wai**) – and it was certainly not ⅓ of the wine. My scores were only a point apart – with Futures, on that day, in the lead! So, take the plunge, buy a case, stick it in your cellar and drink it in five years time. You will chuckle when you recount to your pals that it only cost twelve quid!

£11.99 **Quinta do Crasto, Old Vines Reserva, 2001,**
Douro, Portugal (**Sai**). The Old World fights back with this prune, creosote and loganberry cocktail. This is a masterful wine with a commanding presence and a superhero finish. Let's get ready to rumble.

£12.49 **Fox Gordon, Eight Uncles Shiraz, 2002,**
Barossa Valley, South Australia (**Odd** and **Vin du Van**). Natasha Mooney is an extraordinarily talented winemaker (she made my favourite vintages of E&E Black Pepper Shiraz) and this is the first outing in the UK for her new label Fox Gordon – it is a triumph. Pinpoint accurate Barossa Shiraz with oodles of class, texture and a never-ending finish – epic.

BLOCKBUSTER

£12.99 **Warwick Trilogy**, **2001**, Stellenbosch, South Africa (**Handford**, **Playford Ros**, **Raeburn**, **Frank Stainton** and **SWIG**). Trilogy is a wine that I have followed for many years. It used to be the trailblazer for Bordeaux styles from the Cape, but now there is a lot more competition. Interestingly though, Warwick is still setting the standard for the rest and working extremely hard to reward its faithful followers with stunning wines. 2001 Trilogy is a star wine and so is its sibling 2001 Warwick Three Cape Ladies (£11.99, **Handford**, **Frank Stainton** and **SWIG**), which bolsters the blend with Pinotage.

£13.60 **Crozes-Hermitage**, **Cuvée Gaby**, **Domaine Colombier**, **2001**, Northern Rhône, France (**Jeroboams & Laytons**). The density of fruit and pepper on the nose is almost sneeze-worthy. Gaby is a top flight Syrah and this is the definition of Crozes. A great taste off would be to pit this wine against Knappstein Enterprise Shiraz. In a trice you would discover the difference between the flavour of Syrah in the Old and New World.

£13.99 **Majella Cabernet Sauvignon**, **2001**, Coonawarra, South Australia (**Cooden**, **OFW**, **www.sainsburyswine.co.uk**, **Sommelier** and **Noel Young**). This is first-class Aus Cabernet and it really shows what can be done with attentive viticulture and inspirational winemaking. 2001 Majella Cabernet is a near-perfect wine. It is thirty or so pounds cheaper than some of its peers and yet it has more vitality and regional expression than I could possibly wish for in any one bottle. You are a lucky person if you snare some of this wine. Bravo Prof.

BLOCKBUSTER

£14.99 **Craggy Range Gimblett Gravels Block 14 Syrah**, **2002**, Hawke's Bay, North Island, New Zealand (**Amps**, **Best Cellars**, **D. Byrne**, **Andrew Chapman**, **Cheers**, **Constantine**, **Corkscrew**, **Great Grog**, **Inspired Wines**, **Noble Rot**, **Waitrose Inner Cellar** and **Noel Young**). This sexy Syrah with its 100% French oak spiciness is my top NZ Syrah of the year. It is extraordinarily dark, massively peppery and as sleek as a Bentley Continental GT. And just to make matters even more impressive, the funky 2002 Craggy Range Gimblett Gravels Merlot (same stockists and price as the Syrah) is my favourite Merlot. Winemaker Steve Smith is doing something right, to say the least! In fact, every wine in the Craggy cellar is a lesson in complexity, balance and control, and I urge you to hunt these wines down.

£14.99 **Knappstein Enterprise Shiraz**, **2001**, Clare Valley, South Australia (**Bibendum** and **Odd**). Andrew 'The Ox' Hardy has pulled out all the stops for 2001 Enterprise Shiraz. It has extremely spicy fruit on the nose, with warm tar, cloves, blackberries and smouldering ember nuances, and the compelling palate is deep, dark and potent. Beam me up!

£14.99 **St. Hallett Old Block Shiraz**, **2000**, Barossa Valley, South Australia (**Bibendum**, **Oz Wines**, **Sai** and **Tes**). Many other estates dropped the ball in 2000 but this legendary wine is terrific. The Old Block vineyard is the reason behind the staggering consistency of quality and, if anything, in weaker years it tempers the massive power in the vines and allows us to drink the wine earlier – not that we need an excuse!

£14.99 **Serrata di Belguardo, 2001**, Tenuta di Belguardo,
Maremma, Tuscany, Italy (**SWIG, Wimbledon** and
Winecellars). Maremma is the hot new place in Tuscany
and the Mazzei family, who have owned the awesome
Chianti estate Fonterutoli since 1435, are there in force.
Sporting Leonardo's polyhedron on the label, this is a
Cabernet/Sangiovese/Merlot blend. It is every inch a 'super-
Tuscan' despite the fact that it is actually the 'second' wine
of the estate (the great Tenuta di Belguardo is the first at
£40). I would save £25 and have a pop at my chosen wine,
as it possesses everything you could want considering its
excellent vintage and incredible pedigree. Dark, macerated
black fruit, high-tone oak, balsamic, liquorice, thyme and
leather all meld together with da Vinci-like precision. This
is a colossal wine.

£14.99 **Yalumba MGS, 2002**, Barossa Valley, South Australia
(D. Byrne, **Carringtons, Fine & Rare** and **Handford**). Black
ink, cracked pepper and a massive whack of bonfire, all
overlaying the deepest, darkest mass of intense blackberry
fruit seen on the planet – hurrah for Mourvèdre, Grenache
and Shiraz, the three musketeers of the red grape world!
And, despite all this power, you can drink it now.

£15.29 **Penfolds Bin 389 Cabernet Sauvignon/
Shiraz, 2001**, South Australia (**Maj, Odd, Sai, Saf,
Selfridges, Tes** and **Thr**). After a short period in the
doldrums, 389 is back to ramming speed with the heroic
2001. This wine will age and develop exponentially over
the next two decades. It is a tour de force from winemaker
Peter Gago and his dedicated team.

BLOCKBUSTER

£16.95 **Quinta do Portal Touriga Nacional**, 2001, Douro, Portugal (**Simon Charles**, **Great Northern Wine**, **Great Western Wines**, **Charles Hennings**, **Michael Jobling**, **Thos. Peatling**, **Villeneuve** and **The Wine Man**). If this isn't Portugal's finest red of the year, I don't know what is. Portal's Touriga reeks of class and breeding, and really challenges Spain and Italy's reds at the twenty-pound mark. Not only that, but it looks the business, so if you know any fans of huge, intense, deep, dark reds with oodles of charm and heroic length, make their day and buy them this bottle.

£17.99 **Kevin Arnold Shiraz, Waterford**, 2002, Stellenbosch, South Africa (**Berry Bros.**, **Fortnum & Mason**, **Hoults**, **OFW** and **The Vineyard**). This is the flagship wine from Waterford estate, and winemaker Kevin Arnold throws his heart and soul into its production (and therefore gets his name on the label). It is profound, briary, peppery and spicy, and there is even a wonderful lick of seaweed to add yet another dimension to the broad Shiraz repertoire of flavours. This is a honed, athletic wine with supple tannins and plush oak, and it is able to hold its own on the dining room table with top Aussies and Northern Rhônes alike.

£18.99 **Best's Bin 'O' Shiraz**, 2000, Great Western, Victoria, Australia (**Cooden Cellars**, **Handford**, **Peake** and **Roberson**). Viv Thomson's iconic wines beg to be bought, tasted and treasured. This Bin 'O' Shiraz comes from venerable old vines and is nothing short of history in a glass. Australia's true aristocracy.

£19.99 **Frog's Leap Zinfandel, 2002**, Napa Valley, California (**Fortnum & Mason**, **Harvey Nichols**, **Oxford Wine** and **Noel Young**). The addition of tiny quantities of Petite Sirah, Carignan and Gamay to this breathtaking Zin give it yet more spice, liquorice and herb flavours, adding to the already dense mass of blueberry fruit. This bottle is pure, impressive and single-mindedly committed to its task of blowing your socks off. 2001 Frog's Leap Cabernet (£25.00, **Fortnum & Mason**) is another wine from the big red barn that proves that Napa and, in this case, the Rutherford district make world-class wines.

£21.99 **Ulithorne Frux Frugis Shiraz, 2002**, McLaren Vale, South Australia (**OFW**). The 2001 vintage made TWL last year and this 2002 is, perhaps, even finer. It is like the 2001's engine was taken out, fine-tuned and then slotted back into place a year later. Frux Frugis is every inch a heroic wine. If you are a fan of top-flight Australian wine then this is a very hard bottle to beat. The 2002 recently won a place in the 100 Best Australian wines on www.expertwine.com. It is a cult wine with a non-cult price tag – reserve your bottles today. You will not regret acting on this platinum-plated tip off.

£23.00 **Tim Adams, Aberfeldy Shiraz, 2002**, Clare Valley, South Australia (**Australian Wine Club** and **Oz Wines**). Aberfeldy is always a mighty wine but in 2002 it has tremendous class as well. Coming from 98-year-old vines, this special creation has a very long and happy life ahead of it (at least fifteen years). The only problem is that you have to fight for some stock, as production is

BLOCKBUSTER

understandably limited. I am a massive fan of huge red wines but only when they have layers and layers of complexity and the all-important balance between fruit, alcohol, tannin and oak. This wine has it all, very few do.

£29.95 **Vino Nobile di Montepulciano, Asinone, 2000**, Poliziano, Tuscany, Italy (**Edencroft, Valvona & Crolla, Wimbledon** and **Winecellars**). This is an astonishing wine with a cornucopia of spice, power, blackberries and plums on the palate, and a truly amazing, near-heart-stopping finish. I will not bang on about Asinone because I could write a thousand words and there is only one point that I need to make – I marked it a perfect 20/20 in my notes, and this only happens three or four times a year. Don't forget to look out for 2002 Rosso di Montepulciano (£8.99 **Sai**) – it is a spectacular introduction to this wine.

£32.95 **Amarone della Valpolicella Classico, Allegrini, 2000**, Veneto, Italy (**Andrew Chapman, Bennett's, Harrods, Hedley Wright, Lea & Sandeman, Moriarty, Philglas & Swiggot, Reid Wines, Selfridges, Valvona & Crolla** and **Villeneuve**). The balance of intense fruit sweetness, meaty, plump fruit and tangy, liquorice tannins is a joy. I love this style of wine but rarely drink it as you have to get the food, the occasion and the friends right, in order to make the most of a wine of this magnitude. I can't help with the guest list but I can with the menu – make sure you eat a full-on game dish (duck, venison or boar) with roasted vegetables and fresh pasta, and a large chunk of cheese to follow.

BLOCKBUSTER

£5.99 **Brown Brothers Late Harvested Muscat, 2003**, Victoria, Australia (**Boo**, **Maj**, **Mor** and **Saf**). Ignore the price – just buy this wine and taste it. You will be blown away. This is a 'full' bottle and it would stretch to ten glasses at a dinner party, which makes it one of the finest-value wines on the planet (60p a glass). The fruit is pure and grapey, and the quality level is so high that this unassuming wine is head and shoulders above virtually every other Muscat de Beaumes-de-Venise at three times the price that I can think of – phenomenal.

£5.99 half bottle, **Brown Brothers Orange Muscat & Flora, 2003**, Victoria, Australia (**Asd**, **Coo**, **Maj**, **Peckham & Rye**, **Sai**, **Tanners**, **Unw** and **Wai**). A double top for Brown Bros. – not surprising since they make some of the most influential, superb and cracking-value sweeties in the world. This juicy, orange-segment-scented Muscat is a remarkable wine. Year in, year out, it hits the spot. The ethereal nose, and honey and fruity caramel palate knock people flat. Have a glass of this in hand and chocolate pudding will never have tasted so good.

£6.99 half bottle, **Stella Bella Pink Muscat, 2004**, Margaret River, Western Australia (**Odd**). Made by the Suckfizzle team of Janice Macdonald and Stuart Pym, this frivolous, fizzy, cherry-scented, off-dry wine is the ultimate choccy or strawberry pud wine. A half bottle will serve six (or two if you're naked) so it is only a pound or so a head. You'd never forget the person that serves this to you, so get in first and be the hostess with the mostess.

£8.99   50cl bottle, **Coteaux du Layon Chaume,
Domaine des Forges, 2002**, Loire, France (**Wai**).
Forges is a classic Loire sweetie with a decadent, runny
honey nose and wonderful, near-tropical palate. This Chenin
Blanc is not cloyingly sweet, as the level of acidity is
enough to leave your palate feeling refreshed after every
sip. It is superb with fruit-based puddings and also a dream
with rich pâtés and terrines. Plan your dinner party
carefully and top and tail it with this wine.

£8.99   50cl bottle, **Paul Cluver Weisser Riesling Noble
Late Harvest, 2003**, Elgin, South Africa (**Bedales,
Croque-en-Bouche, Nectarous, Premier Cru, The Wine Mill**
and **Wine Society**). Paul Cluver's awesome Riesling is the
best of its kind in South Africa and easily one of the finest
in the New World. It is lusciously honeyed and fabulously
exotic, decadently potent and, as you'd expect, the acidity
is utterly gorgeous, cleaning up the palate after every sip.

£9.99   **Moscato d'Asti Moncucco, 2003**, Fontanafredda,
Piemonte, Italy (**SWIG, Wimbledon** and **Winecellars**). Asti
has never been so chic. The bottle, flavour and aura
surrounding this brand-new cuvée is fascinating and, at a
teeny 5.5 per cent alcohol, you can drink this frothy, grapey
elixir by the flagon. Try it with English strawberries and
Scottish raspberries, and you will be in heaven. Gone are
the days of vulgar Asti Spumanti, welcome to the future of
Asti – chic, cultured and ever so enviable.

£9.99   half bottle, **'T' Chenin Blanc Noble Late
Harvest, 2001**, Ken Forrester, Stellenbosch, South

Africa (**Caves de Pyrene**). 'T' is named after Ken Forrester's enchanting wife Teresa and I can see why – it is completely gorgeous. As you already know, Ken is a Chenin Blanc expert and this lustrous variety is a dab hand at making epic sweeties (see the Coteaux du Layon above). This South African version is extremely tropical and has moments of mango, kiwi, mandarin and brandy snap, all brought into line with a plunge pool of refreshing acidity on the finish. This and the Cluver Riesling above are South Africa's two finest sweet wines – and they are both under a tenner!

£13.99　half bottle, **De Bortoli, Noble One**, **2001**, Riverina, New South Wales, Australia (**Berry Bros.**, **Lea & Sandeman**, **O.W. Loeb**, **Odd**, **Unw** and **Wine Society**). This is an icon. It was labelled 'Sauternes' in the old days and it is this style that Noble One is emulating. It is a botrytised Semillon with more honey, orange blossom, class and breeding than many of Bordeaux's finest. If you haven't tasted it before, you are in for a very pleasant surprise. A comparable Sauterne would be three times the price!

£13.99　half bottle, **I Capitelli**, **2002**, Roberto Anselmi, Monteforte, Veneto, Italy (**Luvian's**, **Selfridges**, **SWIG**, **Valvona & Crolla**, **Wimbledon Wine**, **Winecellars** and **Noel Young**). This is a 'passito' (dried grape) style of Soave, made by dashing, sports car fiend Roberto Anselmi. He does make full bottles (£25.99) but I'm sure you won't need one, as there is enough honey, lemon meringue pie and toffeed pineapple fruit in this half bot to please any army. It is a sensational wine with enough class to hold its own against any pud you could throw at it.

toffeed tarts

£5.03 **Tesco Finest Manzanilla**, **NV**, Jerez, Spain (**Tes**).
I always choose a dry sherry in the Top 250 and, rather than
going for a famous brand this year, I have picked this
inexpensive wine. It is a fabulous piece of work with a salty
tang and unrivalled palate-cleansing properties.

£5.99 **Waitrose Solera Jerezana Rich Cream
Sherry**, **NV**, Spain (**Wai**). Four years in a row! What
more can I say? This is a stupendous wine and it's perfect for
sticky cakes, steamed puds, toffeed tarts and nice girls, too.

£6.99 half bottle, **San Emilio PX**, **Emilio Lustau**, **NV**,
Jerez, Spain (**Boo**). This is the wine that covers all of the
'fortified' bases in one go. It is dark and brooding like port.
Sweet, but not too cloying, like Madeira. Classy and elegant
like expensive Sherry. And yes, it is Sherry, but not any old
one. This is a PX or Pedro Ximénez, the wildly wicked,
raisin- and caramel-scented wine. Drink this bargain- priced
brew with Christmas pud and you'll not know what's hit you.

£10.99 **De Bortoli Show Rutherglen Liqueur
Muscat**, **NV**, Victoria, Australia (**Berry Bros.** and **Unw**).
This is a 'full'/75cl bottle of liqueur Muscat and it is a ripper.
One sip and you'll transport your palate to the moon and
back. This ridiculously intense wine is crammed with coffee,
fat plum, boozy raisin and caramel flavours. It is rich and
heady as it slides over your palate but still finishes dry on
the aftertaste. This is what you want in your hip flask on a
cold wintry walk. Better still, have an ice-cold shooter
glassful with an espresso after lunch and you'll feel
invincible for the rest of the day.

£8.99 50cl bottle, **Raven Special Reserve Port**, NV, Quinta do Noval, Portugal (**Bentalls**, **Corks**, **Great Grog**, **Mill Hill**, **Mitchells**, **Som** and **Unw**). There is a fashion at the moment for designing spanky looking port bottles in an effort to attract a younger audience. This one's a beauty, there is not doubt, but I don't taste the bottle, I taste the wine inside. It just so happens that this port is utterly lovely, silky smooth and just the sort of wine that would please everyone after a relaxed, gastronomic evening.

£9.49 **Blandy's Duke of Clarence Rich Madeira**, NV, Portugal (**Asd**, **Coo**, **Maj**, **Mor**, **Odd**, **Roberson**, **Saf**, **Sai**, **Som**, **Stevens Garnier**, **Thr**, **Unw** and **Wai**). I know this wine very well – I have been its intimate friend for over fifteen years. The Duke of Clarence (I kinda wish it was a Duchess) is a reliable pal. You can always depend on this wine because it tastes the same day in, day out – on Thursdays, in Reykjavik, when you're tired and emotional, or just feeling downright celebratory. It is, of course, best-enjoyed late at night with your closest friends when the toffeed, ripe, nutty, raisiny fruit, with its ample sweetness and clean, tart finish, wows you.

£11.99 **Flagstone, The Last Word 'Port', NV**, South Africa (**Odd**). It's Bruce Jack again (he is so greedy this year!), and his tribute to the 'port' style. It's no surprise that this is a totally awesome, fruit-driven number with blackcurrant, prune, raisin, cocoa, fig, chocolate and a frenzy of berry sweetness. The momentary flashes of otherworldly flavours make this a 'Baz Luhrmann does fortified' style of wine (including all of the dance moves and zany music). I could easily see myself sipping it in front of the telly with a large box of Green and Black's choccies and bursting into song.

£9.99 **Taylor's Late Bottled Vintage Port**, **1999**, Portugal (**Asd**, **Boo**, **Maj**, **Mor**, **Odd**, **Sai**, **Saf**, **Som**, **Tes**, **Thr**, **Unw** and **Wai**). Last year's 1998 vintage LBV, which is still dotted around the shelves, was a Top 250 wine. Taylor's LBV is a star wine and one of the best of its kind in the world. This 1999 is more fragrant and juicy than the 1998, with a medium-weight palate and less overt tannin and brutish structure. It is more of a caring, sharing style and I like it a lot. All of the classy Taylor's nuances are there but this time the wine is easier to get to know and much more relaxed. I would keep any 1998s you still have in your cellar and drink this harmonious vintage first.

£9.99 50cl bottle, **Vinho Licoroso**, **Quinta de Cabriz**, **NV**, Dão, Portugal (**FWW** and **Philglas & Swiggot**). Somewhere between port and a pudding wine, this is a very sexy, smooth, sultry glass indeed. I think that sipping it with devilishly expensive chocolates would be a real treat and, come to think of it, chocolate puddings would be wickedly accurate as well.

£11.04 **Tesco Finest 10-year-old Tawny Port**, **NV**, Portugal (**Tes**). If you fancy a whirl with a tawny port, then start here. Made by the famous Symington family (owners of Grahams, Dows, Warres and Smith Woodhouse), this is a creamy, toffee, plum and raisin wine with a smooth, welcoming palate.

£13.99 **d'Arenberg Fortified Shiraz, 2001,** McLaren Vale, South Australia (**Bibendum, D. Byrne, Odd** and **Noel Young**). Another luxurious, after dinner smoocher, this is another kind of porty wine but it has its roots firmly embedded in monstrous Aussie Shiraz territory. The black fruit has oodles of charm and length, and there is a wicked twist of spice (and pepper) on the finish. This is a challenging and undoubtedly rewarding wine for the committed canoodling enthusiast. You can find cheeky half bots if you can't hack a whole one.

£10.99 **Lustau East India Rich Oloroso Sherry, NV,** Spain (**Wai**). If you want to finish off a posh evening with a mellow, classy, fortified wine, then look no further than this excellent bottle. It will pour twelve godly glasses and reward the drinker with a caramel, nut- and raisin-scented elixir that goes brilliantly with coffee and chocolates. But, if you chill it down, it is stunning with sticky toffee pudding or traditional fruitcake.

£13.95 **Quinta do Infantado, Late Bottled Vintage Port, 1998,** Portugal (**Bennett's, Liberty** and **Valvona & Crolla**). Infantado is a small producer with a big but covert reputation. This 1998 LBV is a cracking bottle with dark, brooding, plum and blackcurrant fruit, and a massive inky finish. You are getting a ton of flavour for the money and if you are a serious port fan, this is a name to get to know.

£16.99 **Taylor's 10-year-old Tawny Port, NV,** Portugal (**Asd, Boo, Fortnum & Mason, Maj, Mor, Saf, Sai, Selfridges, Thr** and **Unw**). This has always been the model by which all other tawny ports are gauged, and it's easy to see why. This is more intense than the Tesco Tawny, so choose this if you are a tawny old hand, or a graduate of the other wine.

£18.99 50cl bottle, **Antique Pedro Ximénez, Fernando de Castilla, NV**, Jerez, Spain (**Corks, Hoults, Sommelier** and **Valvona & Crolla**). If Lustau PX is for setting the scene, Fernando de Castilla PX is the unforgettable finale. This weird, dark, mysterious, mahogany-hued wine is hypnotic, ever-so-slightly-hallucinatory and unbelievably intoxicating. Happy, smiley and, dare I say it, giggly, this is a dreamy, smooth, coffee, raisin, walnut and Christmas spice wine. Many PX wines do this trick on the tongue, but Fernando de Castilla's version does it to every molecule in your body. This is like liquid Connolly leather, only more amazing on the nose and more luxurious to the touch. One sip and you are in its power – you have been warned.

A–Z OF FOOD
AND WINE
COMBINATIONS

INTRODUCTION

Over the last few years I have always been delighted when people walk up to me at wine tastings or in shops and say just how crucial this chapter is to their gastronomic lives. It can be a nightmare trying to match wine to food accurately, and if you are entertaining at home, or out and about, there is always a pressure to 'get it right'. I realise that not everyone shares the same taste in wine (and food for that matter), but after having worked as a wine consultant to restaurants for fifteen years now, I have written more wine lists and trained more wine waiters than I care to mention. I have been fortunate to work with a broad range of cuisines, too, and I can safely say that I've encountered a panoply of tricky dishes. Finding a worthy selection of bottles from which the customer can select a wine of their choice is sometimes easy, but occasionally you find a stubborn ingredient or a fussy drinker and the test is all the more exciting. I love it when we come to a result and get even more pleasure when the table orders another bottle of that wine! This is the immensely gratifying side of food and wine matching, and that is precisely what this chapter can do for you.

Your task, and believe me it is a thrilling one, is to make the final selection of which bottle(s) to uncork. Bear in mind your own personal palate, and that of your friends, when making this choice, and also consider how much you want to spend, as there are many occasions when less is more. The first step is to find the dish, then read through my recommendations. Now you have a choice. Either zoom through this year's Top 250 and find the exact bottle you need – quick, easy and you'll be drinking one of the best wines in the world. Just hunt by style and price and you'll be there in a trice. Alternatively, peruse the Gazetteer section and make a shopping list of several producers in the category of wines you need. Then flick through the Merchants pages and phone around to a few of your neighbourhood specialists and ask them to rise to the challenge. Or, if you are feeling brave, just head out of your front door, book in hand, and wing it. This is the way to gain confidence and, if you play your cards right, you could well find a real surprise on the shelves. Whatever you decide, I wish you the best of luck and happy drinking.

You can always grab a few bottles of a multi-purpose, multi-talented style of wine. Some names pop up in this chapter more often than others – Sauvignon Blanc, the crowd-pleasing, refreshing, dry, white grape is always a winner and definitely a safe place to go if you are worried. As is the juicy, smooth, black-fruit-driven, New World Cabernet/Merlot blends – try to keep a few bottles of these styles of wine at home in readiness for unexpected guests or impromptu cooking. It is also worth pointing out that Beaujolais, once one of the most ridiculed styles of wine in France, is incredibly versatile in the kitchen. It appears over twenty-five times in this chapter and, with the recent, amazing 2003 vintage in France, it is a style of wine you mustn't miss this year!

The other day I opened several bottles of the aptly named 2003 Sunday Morning Pinot Gris from Victoria, Australia, for a group of friends at home. We had prepared a monster buffet lunch, which included dishes as disparate as salade Niçoise, duck liver pâté, English cheeses, good old-fashioned pork pies, sushi, tomato and mozzarella salad, cold rare roast veal with tuna and capers, quiche Lorraine, potted shrimps and courgette fritters. This bizarre list of my favourite dishes seemed a bridge too far for any one white wine, but it occurred to me that the freshness and spice on the nose, and initial hit of citrusy fruit would cut through any of the fishy-based dishes, while the richness and texture of the floral, near-exotic palate would be perfect with the charcuterie, pâté, pork pie and veal, and the whack of zesty, palate-refreshing acidity would slice through quiche, cheese and any sauces or dressings. All in all, the class and complexity of this screw-capped white (so no chance of a grotty corked bottle and no need for me to sniff every new bottle that was opened) was exactly what we needed.

My pals were delighted with the wine, but amazed when I revealed that the price of this celestial bottle was only £7.99 (see the Top 250). For me this fun exercise encapsulated the whole point of food and wine matching. I hope you have some similar triumphs over the coming year.

APÉRITIF WINE STYLES

Pre-dinner nibbles like *dry roasted almonds*, *bruschetta*, *cashews*, *canapés*, *crostini*, *crudités*, *olives* and *gougères* (heavenly cheese puffs served with style in Burgundy and Chablis) are designed to give your palate a jump-start and get your juices flowing before a feast. It is crucial at this stage of the proceedings not to overload your taste buds with big, weighty, powerful wines. Save these for later and aim for refreshing, taste-bud-tweaking styles that set the scene, rather than hog the stage: Champagne is, not surprisingly, the perfect wine if you're feeling flush but, if not, sparkling wines from the Loire (Saumur), the south of France (Limoux) or Crémant de Bourgogne (Burgundy) would do the job. Italy offers up superb, dry, palate-enlivening fizz in the form of Prosecco, from Veneto, or some more serious sparklers from Franciacorta, Trentino or Alto Adige. I never really drink the Spanish fizz Cava unless I'm in Barcelona, but there are a few worthy versions to be found in the UK. The authentic Champagne-taste-alikes come from the New World. These are usually very good value, too – New Zealand, Australia (particularly Tasmania) and California are the places to go to find awesome quality. Fino or manzanilla sherries are wonderful palate cleansers, particularly with salty dishes, despite being perpetually 'out of fashion'. The least expensive option (and often safest, particularly if you are eating out) is a zesty, uplifting, palate-sprucing dry white wine. Even a moderately expensive one is often half the price of a bottle of Champs and there are thousands of these around, so go for it. There are loads of first-class examples in this book. Stay with unoaked styles and keep the price under control, and then step up the pace with the next bottle, when the food hits the table. If the choice is poor (a short restaurant wine list or a poorly stocked off licence) then grab a neutral, dry, inexpensive white wine and pep it up with a dash or two of Crème de Cassis (blackcurrant liqueur). Spend up on the cassis, as it will go a long way, and make a Kir. Use the same liqueur to turn a dry, sparkling wine or inexpensive Champagne into a glitzy Kir Royale.

STARTERS AND MAIN COURSES

Anchovies Strongly flavoured whether they are fresh or cured, these hairy fish (whether you like 'em or not) need dry, unoaked, tangy, acidic whites or juicy, bone-dry rosés. Head to Italy, Spain or France and keep to a low budget – a fiver is all you need. There are a few worthy rosés from the New World, but watch the alcohol level, as they can be a little high (stay under 14% vol for safety). Dry sherry is also spot on, but consider what is in the rest of the dish.

Antipasti The classic Italian mixed platter of *artichokes, prosciutto, bruschetta, olives, marinated peppers* and *aubergines* enjoys being romanced with chilled, light Italian reds like Valpolicella and Bardolino, or clean, vibrant, refreshing whites like Pinot Grigio, Pinot Bianco, Frascati, Greco, Est! Est!! Est!!!, Orvieto, Verdicchio or Gavi.

Artichokes Dry, unoaked, refreshing whites are best here, especially if you are going to dip the artichokes in *vinaigrette* (see 'Vinaigrette'). Alsatian Sylvaner, Pinot Blanc, lighter Riesling, Loire Sauvignon Blanc or Aligoté from Burgundy are perfect partners, as are the Italian whites listed above for 'Antipasti'. If you want to head to the New World, then keep it angular and edgy with South African Sauvignon Blanc or Argentinean Torrontés.

Asparagus Because of its inbuilt asparagusy characteristics (see my tasting note on page 163-4), Sauvignon Blanc is the ideal match here. New World styles like Chilean (Casablanca), Australian (Adelaide Hills) or New Zealand Sauv (Marlborough) have tons of flavour and would be better suited to asparagus dishes that have *hollandaise*, *balsamic vinegar* or *olive oil* and *Parmesan*. Old World styles, like those from France's Loire Valley (Sancerre and Pouilly-Fumé) are great if the dish is plainer. Northern Italian whites like Pinot Bianco or Pinot Grigio, as well as South African Sauvignon Blanc (somewhere between New Zealand and Loire in style) would also do the job brilliantly.

Aubergines If served grilled, with *pesto* or *olive oil*, *garlic* and *basil*, you must identify the most dominant flavours in the dish. In both of these recipes they are the same – garlic and basil – so tackle them with dry Sauvignon Blanc or keen Italians like Verdicchio, Fiano or Falanghina. Plain aubergine dishes are fairly thin on the ground as these glossy, sleek, black beauties are often used within vegetarian recipes (for example, *ratatouille* or *caponata*). If cheese or meat (*moussaka*) is involved, those flavours take over from the aubergines, so light, youthful reds are required. Southern Italian or Sicilian Primitivo, Nero d'Avola or Aglianico, southern French Grenache-based blends, Chilean Carmenère, Spanish Garnacha or Aussie Durif are all good matches. Just make sure they are not too ponderous or alcohol heavy. If the dish is hotter or spicier, or the aubergines are *stuffed*, you will need a more feisty red, but don't be tempted by anything too weighty (avoid tannic red grapes like Cabernet, Pinotage, Nebbiolo, Zinfandel and Shiraz). *Imam bayildi*, the classic aubergine, onion, olive oil and tomato dish, is a winner with juicy, slightly chilled Chilean Merlot, youthful, bright purple Valpolicella, spicy Sardinian Cannonau or black-fruit-imbued Italians – Barbera d'Alba, Montepulciano d'Abruzzo or Morellino di Scansano.

Australian The masters of fusion Down Under manage to juggle the freshest of land and sea ingredients, and weave into them the best of Asia's spices and presentation. This beguiling and thoroughly delicious style of cuisine is a real hit worldwide, as the cooking is virtually fat free and packed with zesty, palate-enlivening flavours. It is no surprise that in trendy Sydney, Adelaide, Perth and Melbourne restaurants they reward their palates with finely tuned Clare and Eden Valley Rieslings, fresh, grapey Verdelhos, zippy, perky Adelaide Hills and Tassie Sauvignon Blancs and assorted Pinot Gris, Semillon/Sauvignon blends and keen, fresh, oak-balanced Chardonnays. Not all Aussie reds are huge and porty, with the vogue for more aromatic wines coming from McLaren Vale, Nagambie Lakes, Great Western, Canberra or Frankland (Shiraz), Tasmania, Mornington, Geelong or Yarra (Pinot Noir) and cooler Margaret River, Orange or Coonawarra (Cabernet) really hitting form. It is no wonder they are all so fit and healthy down there, with such glorious local produce, awesome wines and inspired chefs!

Avocado If the avocado is *undressed*, you need light, unoaked whites, in particular Loire Sauvignon Blanc, Muscadet or fresh, cheap, clean Italians. If *dressed* with *vinaigrette* or with *Marie Rose sauce* (in a prawn cocktail), richer Sauvignon Blanc (NZ and the Cape), Pinot Gris (smart Italians and New Zealand) or Australian

Verdelho and Riesling are spot on, as are young, white Rhônes and Alsatian Pinot Blanc. *Guacamole*, depending on its chilli heat, needs cool, citrusy, dry whites to douse the palate.

Bacon This usually pops up as an ingredient in a dish and not often as the main theme, unless you've had a heavy night and need a miracle cure – *bacon sarnie*! If you feel like a glass of wine to accompany this classic bread and pig delight, or your *full English breakfast* (I know I do), then chilled red Côtes-du-Rhône or Cru Beaujolais would be a joy. If you are brave (or foolish, or both) try it with a sparkling Shiraz from Down Under. If you are using grilled *pancetta* or *lardons* in a salad, remember that the salty flavour and/or the smoked taste could suggest a move away from a salady, light white wine to a juicy, fresh red. Red Burgundy is heavenly with *bacon and eggs*, if a little ostentatious.

Barbecues The unplanned, off the cuff, ever-so-slightly dangerous (999) nature of the English barbecue, combined with unlimited platters groaning with meat, spicy marinades and intense, smoky sauces, ensures an informal (often comical) and always flavour-packed occasion. Shoot for good value New World gluggers (white or red), as long as they are assertive, juicy and fruit-driven. Lightly oaked Chardonnay, Chenin Blanc or Semillon for whites, or inexpensive Zinfandel, Merlot, Carmenère, Cabernet Sauvignon or Shiraz for reds all work. Don't be afraid of chilling both the whites and reds for maximum effect. Chile, Argentina, Australia, South Africa and New Zealand are the likely candidates for your guest list.

Beans With *baked beans* you simply need fruity, berry-driven reds, as the tomato sauce flavour is dominant and tends to take over. Any youthful reds with refreshing acidity, such as those from the Loire,

Spain, South Africa, South America or Italy, should work well. Remember to keep the price down – it's not worth spending over a fiver for a *beans-on-toast* wine, unless you are a little loopy or rudely loaded! Not surprisingly, anything goes with *green beans*, as they are the least flavoursome of vegetables. You'd have to mince along with a light, dry white to let a green bean truly express itself. *Tuscan bean salad* demands a slightly chilled, light-bodied red or a fresh, zingy white to cut through the earthy flavours. If you throw some beans into a stew (Mr Taggart), such as *cassoulet* or any of a wide variety of Spanish dishes, then Grenache-dominant wines from the south of France (Fitou, Corbières, Faugères or Minervois), or Garnacha-based wines from Spain (Navarra, Terra Alta, Priorato, Campo de Borja or Tarragona) will easily deal with the beanie ballast. *Black bean sauce* requires a few moments meditation. The curious, gloopy texture and intensity of dark sweetness must be countered by huge, juicy, mouth-filling, velvety smooth reds – Zinfandel is the only red grape brave enough. *Refried beans*, either in *tacos* or other *Mexican* dishes, have a fair degree of earthy sludginess that needs either rich whites like a bright New World Chardonnay (Chile, South Africa and Australia make the best value) or fresh, fruity reds. I would try Bonarda, Sangiovese or Tempranillo from Argentina as a starting point, then head over to Chile for some Carmenère or Merlot if you have no joy. My favourite bean is the noble cannellini, the base for all great bean-frenzy soups. What should you uncork? Sorry, but you'll have to wait with spoon, glass and corkscrew at the ready for the 'Soup' entry.

Beef There are so many different beef dishes, so it is lucky that the rules are not too tricky. Reds, predictably, are the order of the day, but it is the size and shape of them (the wines, not the cows) that determines just how good the match will be. *Roast beef* (or *en croûte/beef Wellington*) served up for Sunday lunch requires a degree of respect. When you gather around the table do, by all means, push the boat out. It is at times like these when old-fashioned gentleman's claret (red Bordeaux) really comes into its own. Don't ask me why, but elegant wines such as claret, Bandol, erudite northern Rhônes – Hermitage, Crozes-Hermitage, Cornas, St-Joseph or Côte-Rôtie – or even Italy's answer to an Aston Martin V12 Vanquish, the Super-Tuscans (see the stellar list in the Gazetteer), are simply magnificent with this king of beef dishes. As you'd expect, not one of these wines is remotely affordable (nor is the car, mind you). They are all special occasion wines, so if you are looking to shave a few pounds off, I would recommend heading to the top Cabernets from Australia's Margaret River (Western Australia) or Coonawarra (South Australia), or Sonoma or Napa regions in California. You've guessed it, these are again fairly dear, but these reds will give you the richness and complexity that you are craving. If you are on a strict budget, then don't change regions, just buy cleverly – not all wines from Bordeaux are exorbitantly priced. Try the less famous sub-regions like Côtes de Castillon, Bourg, Blaye and Francs, and go for a good vintage (see my Vintage Table on page 232-3). These wines can really hit the spot. Hearty Southern Rhône or Languedoc reds would also do very well. Most Aussie (try Clare Valley and McLaren Vale in particular), South African, Chilean and Argentinean Cabernets or Cab/Shiraz blends around the tenner mark offer charm, complexity and competence, especially if you stick to my recommendations.

It is at this price point that the New World leads the pack. But even if you drop down to a fiver you can still have fun, just remember to stick to hotter climate wines, as claret and red Rhônes at this price can be pretty dire.

One question worth asking is – 'how do you like your beef cooked?' If you are a keen carnivore and a fan of *rare* beef, you can safely drink a younger, more tannic red wine, as these harder tannins balance perfectly with juicy, rare meat, slicing through the flesh and making your mouth water. If you like your beef *well done*, then go for an older wine with smoother, more harmonious tannins. *Stews, casseroles* and *meat pies* need richer, more structured reds, particularly if a meaty, stock-rich gravy is involved. Cabernet Sauvignon, Syrah (Shiraz), Pinotage, Piemontese (northern Italian) reds, Zinfandel and Malbec are but a few of the superb, hunky, chunky grapes to go for. Look for wines from South Africa, Australia, California and Argentina. Southern Rhônes like Gigondas, Lirac, Cairanne, Rasteau or Vacqueyras will be superb, as will Provençal or Languedoc reds made from a similar blend of swarthy red grapes. Portuguese wines are worth considering with rich beef dishes – the red wines from Dão and the Douro Valley are still woefully under-priced and mightily impressive. Cahors in southwest France also deserves a listing, as it is a perfect beef partner. *Bollito misto,* the Italian stew made from beef and just about everything else you could possibly think of, demands local wines – Teroldego and Marzemino, from Trentino in northern Italy, would be an inspired place to kick off, as would smart Valpolicella, Barbera and Dolcetto. *Boeuf bourguignon*, as the name suggests, usually pressgangs the help of red Burgundy. But please don't cook with anything expensive – save your money for the 'drinking' wine and cook with a simple generic bottle (Beaujolais or Bourgogne Rouge). *Steak and kidney pie* loves manly, rustic reds with grippy acidity and chunky tannins. These wines slice through the gravy and often-sturdy kidneys – Madiran and Cahors from France, Malbec from Argentina and New World war-horses, like South African Pinotage and Syrah, and Aussie Shiraz also enjoy this challenge. *Cottage pie,* with carrot, celery, onions and minced beef rarely requires anything more challenging than an inexpensive, fun lovin' red. You could even try your hand with Eastern Europe (although don't expect me to road-test this for you), or southern Italy or Sicily (safer) and then go crazy and buy two bottles. A heroic *Beef stroganoff* also demands rusticity in its dancing partner, so gather some southern Rhônes together (Sablet, Cairanne or Vacqueyras); even a straight Côtes-du-Rhône from the right domaines can be a joy (see the Gazetteer page 183). *Hungarian goulash* would be wonderfully authentic if a Hungarian red wine joined it. Nuff said! But if you want to play a bit safer, head to Rioja, Navarra or Toro (Spain) or Chilean Cabernet Sauvignon. Straight *steak* has a more direct, meaty flavour than a stew, so finer wines can be dragged out of the cellar (or local merchant). Wallow in Chianti, Brunello di Montalcino, Ribera del Duero, Californian Merlot, Zin or Cab, top-end Cru Beaujolais, Crozes-Hermitage, St-Joseph (both Rhônes), and South African, Argentinean and New Zealand Cabernet Sauvignon or Shiraz. Watch out and don't OD on *Béarnaise sauce*, which, though great with steak, can clog up the taste buds (and the waist band) a little. With *steak au poivre*, the pungent, pulverised peppercorns make themselves known in each and every mouthful, so look for meaty (and peppery) wines like northern Rhône reds (Syrah) or their cousins from further afield – Shiraz from Australia or South Africa. *Burgers*, heaven in a bun (homemade of course, not mechanically reclaimed!), often served with ketchup, bacon, cheese or relish (or all of the above), need fruity reds like Italian Dolcetto or Barbera, Spanish Garnacha, young Rioja Crianza, juicy Californian Zinfandel, South African Pinotage, Chilean or South African Merlot, Australian Petit Verdot or Shiraz blends. Once again, go for younger wines if you like your burger rare, and older, smoother wines if you are at the well-done end of the spectrum. *Chilli con carne* is a difficult dish to match with wine. As with burgers it is necessary to search for fruitier styles like Aussie Merlot, or Negroamaro or Nero d'Avola from southern Italy and Sicily. *Steak tartare* is a strange one, as I'm still not sure whether I actually really like it, but I must admit it works terrifically well with very light reds and rosés – Tavel (southern Rhône) and other Grenache-based rosés (try Spain or Australia) are perfect, as are snooty Pinot Noirs like Sancerre red or rosé. If you fancy splashing out, then rosé Champagne is the ultimate combo (admittedly a touch poncey), but go easy on the capers, if they are served alongside. *Cold, rare roast beef salad* and other cold beef dishes need fresh, light reds with low tannins – Beaujolais, Valpolicella, red Loires (either Cabernet Franc or Gamay) or Argentinean Tempranillo or Bonarda would all work. Pinot Noir is also a treat with this style of dish – Burgundy, Central Otago (NZ), Tasmania, Yarra Valley and Mornington (Oz). The only occasion when you are allowed to break the red-wine-with-beef rule (there has to be one) is with *carpaccio* (raw/rare) or *bresaola* (air-dried). These wafer-thin sliced beef dishes can handle whites. Any dry, apéritif-style Italian white or light Montepulciano-style red would be spot on.

Cajun see 'Mexican'.

Capers
Sauvignon Blanc, from almost anywhere, or very dry Italian whites like Soave (Veneto) or Greco, Fiano or Falanghina (Campania) are very good matches, as they can cut through the peculiar, green, vinegary tanginess you experience when you burst open and crunch on a caper. (For more suggestions see 'Apéritif'.)

Caviar
I know it is a sin, but I adore decent caviar. Sevruga or Oscietra (not Beluga – ridiculously decadent) are my faves and Champagne is definitely the call of the day. Avoid rosé styles, though (they always taste metallic with caviar in my experience), and there is no need for popping prestige cuvées (£50 plus) unless you're

desperately trying to impress (or are a tasteless lottery winner – congrats). If you want to keep the budget down, and there is nothing wrong with that, then Sancerre, Pouilly-Fumé (Loire) or tighter South African and New Zealand Sauvignons are all stunning combos. These styles also work if caviar is used in a sauce, but look to the main ingredient as well as the caviar for guidance.

Charcuterie A selection of charcuterie (*assiette de charcuterie* to be precise including *saucisson, salami, ham* etc.) contains many diverse flavours along a similar textural theme. I love smart rosés and top quality (slightly chilled) Beaujolais or Loire Gamay. Light to medium Italian reds, like Valpolicella, Morellino di Scansano, Montepulciano d'Abruzzo or Aglianico from the south would also be good matches (take a few degrees off these, too). If you favour whites, then stick to firm, rich white grape varieties like Riesling or Pinot Gris, which usually manage to harness at least as much flavour intensity as the reds anyway. Do watch out for pickles, gherkins, cornichons or caperberries, as excess vinegar will guarantee that you'll not be able to taste the next mouthful of wine! My advice is to shake your gherkin first (does that sound a little too kinky?), endeavouring to knock off as much vinegar as possible before eating. (For *chorizo* and *spicy salami*, see 'Pork'.)

Cheese (cooked) There is a full cheese-board section at the end of this chapter, so flick on for non-cooked cheese nibbling. *Cauliflower cheese* (*leek Mornays, cheesy pasta* dishes etc.) and straight *cheese sauces*, depending on the strength of cheese used, need medium- to full-bodied whites such as New World Chardonnay, Chenin Blanc and Semillon. For reds, you must join the quest for fresh acidity and pure berry fruit. This hunt should lead you to the delicious wines from the Loire (Saumur-Champigny,

Chinon or Bourgueil) or Chilean, Australian or South African Merlot, Italian Cabernet Franc, Lagrein, Dolcetto or Freisa, or youthful Rioja, Navarra, Toro or Campo de Borja reds from Spain. *Fondue* needs bone-dry whites (or bloody good lager!) to cut through the waxy, stringy, molten cheese. If you are a perfectionist then you'd be trekking off, crampons ahoy, in search of the inoffensive but, in all honesty, fairly dull wines from Savoie – Chignin-Bergeron, Abymes, Crépy or Apremont. However, if you are after pleasant-tasting, accurate-but-not-ridiculously so wines, then well-balanced, fully ripe (as opposed to upsettingly lean and enamel-challengingly acidic) styles like entry level Alsatian Pinot Blanc, Riesling and Sylvaner, and fresh Loire Sauvignon Blanc and Chenin Blanc would be ideal. You could even try dry Portuguese whites and various northeastern Italian single varietals like PG or PB. *Raclette* would love to be partnered with light red Burgundies or Cru Beaujolais. With *cheese soufflé*, one of the true gems in the cooked cheese repertoire (chez Jukesy Towers especially), you can really go out on a limb. Argentinean Torrontés, or any aromatic dry whites like Muscat (Alsace), Riesling (from Alsace or Clare Valley/ Adelaide Hills/Eden Valley/Frankland in Australia) or even lighter Gewürztraminer (Tasmania or Alto Adige in Italy are worth a punt) would be delicious. If the soufflé has any other hidden ingredients remember to consider them before plumping for a bottle – with *smoked haddock soufflé* you'd be wise to follow the fish. *Mozzarella*, with its unusual milky flavour and otherworldly texture, is well suited to Italian Pinot Bianco, Pinot Grigio, good Vernaccia, Arneis, Gavi and Verdicchio. Yes, these are all Italians! *Grilled goats' cheese* is equally at home with Sancerre (remember the best goats' cheese hails from Chavignol, Sancerre's finest village) and all other Sauvignon Blancs from around the world (South Africa would be my first choice). Lighter reds also work, particularly if you are tucking into a salad with some ham joining in the fun. Goats' cheese is pretty forgiving when it comes down to it, but avoid oaked whites and heavy reds.

Chicken Chicken is very accommodating – loves whites and reds. But be careful, as it is a touch fussy when it comes to the precise grape varieties. Chardonnay is chicken's favourite white by far, with Riesling coming in a close second. Pinot Noir is the bird's favourite red (it's every bird's favourite red, surely?), with Gamay claiming the runner up spot. This means that a well-educated, classy chicken loves every village in my beloved Burgundy region, and who can blame it? Lighter dishes such as *cold chicken* or *turkey* are fairly versatile, so try al fresco-style wines (see 'Picnics'). *Cold chicken and ham pie* works well with lighter reds and sturdy rosés from the southern Rhône, Beaujolais and the Sancerre (Loire Valley). If you are feeling adventurous then try chilled Beaujolais-Villages – it's a super red match. *Poached chicken* can handle the same sort of wines but with a little more weight – both Old and New World Pinot Noir work here. White wine companions include lighter New World Chardonnay or French Country Viognier and Marsanne and Roussanne blends. Possibly my favourite dish of all time, *roast chicken*, follows this theme once again, but takes it a stage further. Finer (by that I mean more expensive) red and white Burgundy, elegant, cooler climate Australian or Californian Chardonnay and Pinot Noir, and top flight Beaujolais (again) are all wonderful matches. *Coq au vin* also works well with red Burgundy, but you can scale the wine down to a Chalonnais, Hautes-Côtes or Bourgogne rouge (from one of my reputable producers, of course) – none of these should cost more than a tenner. *Chicken casserole* or *pot pie* ups the ante even further and it enjoys a broader wine brief. Medium-weight Rhône reds and New World Grenache-based wines, as well as mildly oaky Chardonnays, are all in with a shout. *Chicken* and mushroom pie, *fricassee* and other chicken dishes with *creamy sauces* call out to Chardonnay and beyond – dry Riesling from Germany, Alsace (France), or Clare Valley, Eden Valley, Frankland or Tasmania (Australia), Alsatian Tokay-Pinot Gris and funky Rhône whites. New World Pinot Noir (from California, New Zealand and Tassie and Victoria in Oz) is the only red variety to feel truly at home here. OK, so far things have been fairly straightforward, but I am now going to throw a few obstacles in front of our friend, as *chicken Kiev* changes the rules completely. Full, rich and even part-oak-aged Sauvignon Blanc or Sauvignon/Semillon blends are needed to take on the buttery/garlic onslaught – white Graves (Bordeaux) and California does this well with their Fumé Blancs, as does Margaret River in Western Australia, but watch this space as this style is starting to be made all over the world. Not content with this hurdle, *coronation chicken*, depending on who is making it (I like a lot of poke in the sauce), can also have a bit of a kick, so dry Riesling from New Zealand or Clare Valley/Eden Valley in Australia would be worth unscrewing. Lastly, *barbecued chicken wings* can be nuclear-hot and, in my experience, beer is usually a better bet. If, for some reason, you would like to try this dish with a bottle of wine, then a clean, inexpensive New World Chardonnay with a touch of oak won't let the side down.

Chilli *Enchiladas, chimichangas, fajitas, chilli con carne, dragon's breath pizzas* and any other scarily fiery Mexican dishes all ping under the weight of a hefty dose of chillies. Thirst-quenching, chillable Italian red grape varieties like Primitivo, Nero d'Avola, Frappato or Negroamaro, or juicy New World Bonarda, Durif, Cab Franc and Merlot are needed to cool you down and rebuild your taste buds. If you need a bottle of white then New World Chardonnay or Semillon, thoroughly chilled, will have enough texture and body to handle the heat. I love Clare Valley Riesling with chilli-laden seafood or chicken dishes, but keep the price sub-tenner.

Chinese The perennial problem when matching wine to Chinese food is that one invariably feels drawn to share your dishes with your mates and therefore you end up tasting every dish on the table, mixing flavours wildly. Sweet-and-sour dishes career into spicy ones, stir-fried dishes hurtle into crispy chilli ones, while poor old plain-boiled food struggles for a break in the non-stop palate action. John Woo would be proud but your taste buds are crying, so this means Chinese-friendly wines must be multi-skilled, pure, fruit-driven offerings with lashings of all-important, crisp acidity. Tannic, youthful reds and oaky, full-bodied whites are completely out of bounds. White grape varieties to consider (in unoaked form) are Sauvignon Blanc, Riesling, Semillon, Pinot Gris, Greco (southern Italy), Verdelho (Australia) and bone dry Gewürztraminer. Reds are a little more difficult, as there are only a few truly juicy varieties, but New World Merlot, Argentinean Bonarda and cheaper Californian Zinfandels are all good bets. It is no surprise that Antipodean wines work well with this style of cooking as Asia is on their doorstep.

Chutney see 'Pâté' and 'Pork'.

Duck *Roast* or *pan-fried* duck is often served with fruit or fruity sauces, so you need to balance this with a fruity wine. Reds are de rigueur here – New World Pinot Noir, good quality Beaujolais, Italian Barbera or Negroamaro, Australian Chambourcin, lighter Californian Zinfandel and any other super-juicy, berry-drenched wines would do the business. *À l'orange* swings the colour firmly to white, but full-flavoured, juicy wines are still the vogue. Alsace or top Aussie Riesling, Alsatian Tokay-Pinot Gris, or Southern French and Rhône Viognier all have enough richness and texture to crack this dish, as do top-end northern Italian white blends. With *cherries*, village-level red Burgundy (utilising the beautifully cherry-scented red grape Pinot Noir), top notch Barbera from Piedmont, smart, new wave Reserva-level Rioja and medium-weight but classy Zins from California are all excellent. The more robust *confit de canard* demands meatier reds with backbone, grippy acidity and tannin to cut through the sauce and fat, like those from Bandol in Provence, Languedoc Roussillon or the southwest of France – Madiran or Cahors for example. For an unlikely but first-class combo, give *crispy aromatic duck* a whirl with chilled Chambourcin of Durif from Australia, or juicy, fruit-driven Californian Zinfandel – they are a dead-cert.

Eggs For *quiches*, *soufflés* or *light, savoury tarts* consider the main flavours (ham, cheese, herbs etc.) and their impact on the dish. Also, think about what you are eating with it. Once you have nailed these flavours, unoaked or lightly oaked Chardonnay is a fair starting point – Chablis is the classic, but northeastern Italian Chardonnays would also be spot on. New World unoaked Chardonnays are now creeping through, too. *Omelettes*, *frittata* and *savoury pancakes* follow the same rules. However, for *oeufs en meurette* (the legendary Burgundian dish of poached eggs in red wine with lardons) a red wine is definitely called for – mid-priced Beaujolais or a fresh, young red Burgundy would be accurate. For *fried* and *poached* eggs, look at the other ingredients involved. If combined with a salad utilising stronger-flavoured ingredients, try Beaujolais, but if you'd rather go white, then Alsatian Riesling or a top Pinot Blanc. For *quails' eggs*, see the Apéritif wine styles. Finally, *eggs Benedict* has an awful lot going on, from the muffin base, via the bacon or ham and ending with the gloopy, wickedly rich hollandaise. Youthful Côtes-du-Rhône is a classic combination.

Fish The flavour of fish depends not only on the sort of fish you are cooking but also, crucially, on how it is cooked. The general rule is the milder the flavour, the lighter the white wine, and the richer the flavour, the heavier the white wine. Fish cooked in red wine is one of the few exceptions to this white-dominated section, as here a light, fresh red would simply meld better with the sauce. From Bianco de Custoza and Soave (Italy), Austrian Grüner Veltliner, Menetou-Salon and Sauvignon de Touraine (Loire), white Burgundy (Mâcon, Rully, Pouilly-Fuissé, Meursault and so on), fine Californian Chardonnay, zesty Jurançon Sec, heady Australian or New Zealand Pinot Gris, plump Marsanne or whip-cracking Hunter Valley Semillon, to any aromatic Riesling or Viognier – the opportunities are endless. Just remember that poaching and steaming are gentler, non-taste-altering ways of cooking, while grilling, searing, frying and roasting all impart distinctive charred or caramelised nuances to the fish. Also consider what you are cooking the fish with; check through the recipe for strongly flavoured ingredients, such as lemon, capers, balsamic vinegar, flavoured olive oil and pungent herbs. Often, the finer the piece of fish, the more money you should chuck at the wine. *Dover sole*, *lemon sole*, *turbot* and *sea bass*, at the top of my Premier-fish-league, are all pretty pricey, but if you are that committed to a dish you should endeavour to complete the picture by splashing out on a serious bottle of white Burgundy. Failing that, for well under a tenner you could pick up a top South African Chardonnay, Australian Semillon, Adelaide Hills/Eden Valley/Clare Valley/Frankland Riesling or Chardonnay, Riesling from Alsace, posh Lugana or Gavi from Italy, dry white Graves (Bordeaux), white Rhône wines or trendy Spanish Albariño or Godello to go with these fish. *Halibut*, *John Dory*, *sea bream*, *skate* and *brill* all enjoy these styles of wine, too, while *swordfish*, *monkfish* and *hake* can take slightly weightier whites (or even a fresh light red, such as

Beaujolais). *Salmon* (poached or grilled) also likes Chardonnay, whether it is from the Old or New World, but steer clear of oaky styles. *Trout* likes Riesling and the all-time classic Chablis. But, for an especially wicked combo, try to track down the unusually scented French Country wine, Jurançon Sec. *Fish cakes*, especially proper ones with a high salmon content, go wonderfully with dry Riesling, richer Sauvignon Blancs or fresh Semillons, particularly if you are keen on a generous spoonful of tartare sauce. *Red mullet* has more than enough character to handle rosé wines, making a beautiful pink partnership between plate and glass. *Kedgeree* is trickier, as the combo of smoked haddock, cayenne, parsley and egg may make you lean towards red. But don't, as rapier-like acidity is needed to slice through this dish and I'm sure you know which white grape does this best – Sauvignon Blanc (mind you, you shouldn't be drinking wine at breakfast anyway!). Sauvignon is also the grape to enjoy with *fish 'n' chips* (*cod*, *haddock* or *plaice*) because it can handle the batter and, to a certain degree, the vinegar (but go easy), and it shines with *fish pie* – poshest partnership being the Loire all-stars Pouilly-Fumé or Sancerre. If you fancy a trip to the New World, then Marlborough in New Zealand has to be the starting point for fans of this zesty grape, with South Africa being next and Australia's Margaret River giving the best Sem/Sauv blends. *Fish soups* and *stews* need more weight, and one of the finest matches is white Rhônes made from Marsanne and Roussanne, or Viognier. Aussie Marsanne or Pinot Gris would also be a great option. *Sardines* require masses of perky acidity to cut through their oily flesh; once again Sauvignon Blanc is the winner (don't forget Muscadet), but Italian Pinot Grigio, Arneis, Verdicchio or Gavi, Spanish Albariño, French Aligoté and even light reds, like Gamay, would be smashing. *Canned tuna* just needs unoaked, dry white wine. However, *albacore*, the finer, paler version, is more delicately flavoured so take care not to swamp it. The Italian trio, Lugana, Bianco di Custoza or Soave Classico, would do this job inexpensively and with the required style. *Fresh tuna*, seared and served rare, desperately craves juicy, fresh, light reds and chilled rosés (you could sneak a Sauvignon in, if you wish). *Brandade de morue* (salt cod), with its garlic and oil components, can stand up to whites with a little more soul. Albariño, from Galicia in Spain, is a perfect choice. However, Penedès whites and even light rosés are all within its grasp. *Herrings, kippers* and *rollmops* all have a more robust texture and aroma thanks to the curing process. Once again, dry whites and rosés work well, but steer clear of oaked whites, as the pungent barrel nuances will overshadow the subtleties of the dish. *Smoked eel* is often served with crème fraîche, and cream is always a little problematic for wine, but look to Austrian Riesling or Grüner Veltliner, top end Italian Pinot Grigio or bone-dry, world-class Riesling, and almost any dry wine from Alsace. These will all relish the challenge. *Smoked salmon* is perfect with Gewürztraminer, whether it is from Alsace, Oz or Chile. Just make sure you buy a bone-dry, not off-dry version. The scent and tropical nature of Gewürz works amazingly well, but so does Viognier and even Canadian Pinot Blanc. Don't forget Champagne or top-end Tasmanian or Californian sparkling wine, particularly if serving blinis topped with smoked salmon and caviar. *Smoked trout* or s*moked mackerel pâté* is a challenge – fishy, smoky and creamy flavours all in one dish. Hunter Valley Semillon, Adelaide Hills Sauvignon Blanc and Tasmanian Pinot Gris (all Aussies), southern French Viognier, lighter Alsatian Riesling and Pinot Blanc are all perfect matches. Lastly, *curries* or *Asian* fish dishes often sport spices, such as turmeric, ginger and chilli, so turn to two of our favourite saviour white grapes for a solution – New World Sauvignon Blanc's supreme confidence and Australia's mind-blowing array of Rieslings.

Frogs' legs Aim for smooth, mildly oaked Chardonnay from Burgundy (Chablis), Australia, South Africa or New Zealand. Consider what you've cooked these cheeky blighters in and tweak your wine choice accordingly – if *garlic butter* is involved, stick to Sauvignon Blanc. Good Luck and keep the lid tight on the pan.

Game All flighted game, including *pheasant, quail, guinea fowl, woodcock, teal, grouse, snipe, wild duck* and *partridge* adore the magisterial red grape Pinot Noir. So red Burgundy would always be my first choice, with California, New Zealand, Tasmania, Victoria and Oregon somewhere behind the leader. The longer the bird is hung, the more mature the wine required (this can mean ten- or even twenty-year-old bottles). I have enjoyed red Bordeaux, Super-Tuscan, northern Rhône, Spanish wines from Ribera del Duero or Tarragona and many other top reds with this heady style of cuisine. But it is important to aim for complex reds with layers of fruit and a bit of age, and this inevitably means spending up. *Jugged hare*, often uses port and/or redcurrant jelly in the recipe, so a pretty feisty red wine is needed. New-style Piemontese reds made from Nebbiolo or Nebbiolo/Barbera blends would have the stuffing, as would more structured Australian Shiraz (McLaren Vale, Langhorne Creek or Barossa Valley), Zinfandel from California or South African Pinotage. One slightly cheaper and worthy source of full-bodied red is the Douro Valley in Portugal. Not only would you have a beefy wine, but it would also be in perfect synergy if you've used port in the recipe. *Rabbit*, as well as being a less athletic version of hare, is also less pungent and has lighter-coloured flesh so, although big reds are essential, they don't need to be quite as muscular as those suggested for hare. The classic combo of *rabbit with mustard and bacon* has some pungent flavours on board, so aim for fairly swarthy bottles with feisty tannins and a youthful, purple hue – Chianti, Carmignano, Vino Nobile di

Montepulciano (all from Tuscany), Bandol (from Provence), Lirac, Rasteau, Vacqueyras, Cairanne and Gigondas (from the southern Rhône), Argentinean Malbec, South African Cabernet and Shiraz, and smarter Chilean Cabernet blends would be spot on. *Wild boar* favours rich, brooding red wines and, depending on the dish, you could choose any of the aforementioned reds but, this time, add the two finest of all Italian wines – Brunello di Montalcino and Barolo. The only problem is you might need to take out a bank loan to buy a bottle. *Venison* loves reds, and any bottle in this section would do, including top Australian Cabernet Sauvignon and some of the better New Zealand Hawke's Bay Cabernets and Syrahs. Finally, served cold, *game pie* behaves like cold chicken and ham pie (see 'Chicken'). If served hot, open any wine suggested for steak and kidney pie (see 'Beef').

Garlic *Roast* garlic tends to emasculate fine wines so, if you are partial to shoving a few bulbs in the oven, keep the wine spend down and follow the main dish. *Garlic prawns*, *mushrooms* and *snails* all need aromatic, bone-dry Sauvignon Blanc. If you fancy being ahead of the pack and ever so patriotic then try dry English white wines. Watch out for *Aïoli (garlic mayonnaise)* because you'll get a shock if your wine isn't feisty enough. Once again, Sauvignon Blanc can provide solace, but you will have to find a bot with a lot of character and vivacity. (For *chicken Kiev* see 'Chicken'.)

Goose The best wines for roast goose lie somewhere between those suited to game and those for chicken. In short, this means lighter red Burgundy (and global Pinot Noir) in the red camp, and big, rich Chardonnays and Rieslings in the white.

Greek see 'Mezze'.

Haggis Traditionally accompanied by a wee dram of whisky but, if it could speak for itself (and some do) it would plump for a rich, textured, aromatic white wine. Depending on your palate, you could choose a broad, luscious New World Chardonnay at the rich end, or a scented, white Côtes-du-Rhône at the lighter end. If you really want to go over the top, try a Grand Cru Alsace Riesling or Tokay-Pinot Gris, or a Condrieu from the northern Rhône.

Ham Smart Cru Beaujolais, Chilean Merlot or Carmenère, youthful Navarra or Rioja, Italian Nero d'Avola, Montepulciano or Negroamaro and youthful, inexpensive South African Merlot or Pinotage all have the essential juiciness to complement a glorious ham. The golden rule is to avoid any tannic or heavily acidic reds – stick to more mellow styles. There is a splinter group for whom heady whites also work – busty Viognier and lusty Chardonnay would do. *Parma ham and melon, prosciutto, jamón Serrano* and *pata negra* all like dry German Riesling, many of the aromatic whites from Trentino, Alto Adige and Friuli (northern Italy), and Verdejo or lightly oaked Viura from Rueda (Spain). *Honey-roast ham* needs mouth-filling, textural, bone-dry whites like 'dry' Muscat, Viognier, Verdelho and Riesling. Search for these in Alsace, Australia, the Rhône Valley and from the vast array of terrific French Country wines (and grab some ripe figs to eat alongside). *Ham hock* with lentils or boiled Jersey potatoes and beetroot or peas is a treat with posh, dry rosé, and there are a fair few out there, so head to Tavel in the southern Rhône or to richer examples of Sancerre rosé or Grenache rosés from McLaren Vale in Oz. *Smoked ham* has a fairly strong aroma and lingering flavour, so Tokay-Pinot Gris and young Vendange Tardive level Rieslings from Alsace would be exact, as would older Aussie Rieslings. If you favour red wine then choose a Merlot, a Cabernet Franc (from Australia or the Loire) or a

Beaujolais, and chill it a degree or two to perk up its finish. *Gammon steak* (sling the grim addition of pineapple or peaches) makes a neat partnership with oily, unoaked whites. All Alsatian wines and most dry German Rieslings would be delicious, as would the world-class Rieslings from Australia's Clare Valley, Eden Valley, Tasmania and Frankland. Semillon rarely gets the call up for a specific dish, but Aussie versions (Hunter Valley) and dry white Bordeaux (both with a smattering of oak) are simply stunning with it, too.

Indian My induction into matching Indian food with wine is now complete. These days I would describe it as a full-time passion. When I designed and wrote the wine list for the re-launch of top London Indian restaurant, Chutney Mary, it was clear to me that unoaked or mildly oaked whites were to be the driving force in my selection. Smooth, juicy rosés were also essential, as were overtly fruit-driven reds, avoiding any that were noticeably tannic. The surprise came when I made the final selection and found that Italy, Australia, South Africa and New Zealand had claimed the lion's share of the list. There were a few wines from other countries but virtually no classics like claret, Burgundy or Rhône. Shock horror! This just proves that, depending on the style of cuisine, a wine list can be balanced, eclectic and hopefully thoroughly exciting, without relying on France. The grape varieties or styles of wine that go particularly well with Indian food are: whites – Pinot Grigio, Verdicchio, Sauvignon Blanc, Pinot Bianco, Fiano, Torrontés, Riesling, Viognier, Verdelho, light Gewürztraminers and Albariño; reds – Valpolicella, Beaujolais (Gamay), Grenache (and Spanish Garnacha), Negroamaro, Pinot Noir, Nero d'Avola, Zinfandel, Barbera, Lagrein and Merlot. Other styles that work well include rich rosé, Prosecco, Asti (with puddings), rosé Champagne, Aussie sparklers and good-quality ruby port.

Japanese *Sushi* is a strange one to drink wine with, as surely green tea or sake (but not for me!) would be more appropriate? However, sparkling wines and Champagne are a treat with the best sushi, especially bone dry cuvées – 'Ultra Brut' or 'non dosage'. Not surprisingly, the ever-ready Sauvignon Blanc grape is there, waiting in the wings to save you and the bill. You could always look to zesty, unoaked Italian whites for more joy – Vernaccia, Arneis and Gavi are all ideal. Perky Pinot Gris and Riesling from Australia and New Zealand are also a bloody good choice. *Teriyaki* dishes are a nightmare to match wine to, as the sweetness and fruitiness in the glossy soy and saké glaze is incredibly flavour dominant on the palate. Zinfandel or rich Pinot Noir from California, super-ripe Chambourcin, lighter, modern Shiraz or Merlot from South Australia, and Nero d'Avola or Negroamaro from Sicily would just about manage this scary challenge. You will always be offered a blob of nuclear green goo with your sushi called wasabi. I'm afraid wasabi is a stealthy, committed and silent wine assassin – thank God it's green so at least you can see it sneaking up on you.

Junk food What should you drink with a hamburger, cheeseburger, chicken nuggets, bargain bucket of fried off-cuts or any of the other palate-abusing, mass-produced, fast-food delicacies? A high-sugar, monstrously carbonated soft drink, of course, for that all-encompassing explosive gut/nauseous cold-sweat feeling that you look forward to enjoying ten minutes after thundering this demonic cuisine down your cakehole. If you are seriously considering opening a bottle of wine (what are you doing?), you'll have to wrestle this toxic creation back into its day-glo polystyrene container and drag it back to your lair. OK, now you've got to warm it up again – do you bother? Course not, you're either starving or worse for wear, or both. But what should you uncork? Chilean Carmenère, Aussie Shiraz/Cab, Kiwi Sauvignon Blanc or South African Chenin/Chardonnay (just keep the price down, you don't want to regret opening it in the morning). If you are well organised you'll always keep an 'emergency' white in the fridge and red in the cupboard for times like these. That way you can't muck up and open a serious bottle by mistake. Either way, while you are guzzling Dante is rewriting furiously, inventing yet another circle of hell for your internal organs to slumber in. When you wake up, join a gym, lapse the membership in a few months, and I'll see you at the chippy on Saturday night.

Kidneys Lambs' kidneys tend to absorb a fair amount of the flavour from the ingredients in which they are cooked so follow them. Mustard is often used, so keep the reds firm, chunky and with a lick of crunchy, palate-refreshing acidity – Chianti, Morellino, Lagrein, Barbera (all Italian), Rioja, Toro, Calatayud, Navarra (all Spanish), Languedoc and the Rhône Valley (both French) would all be worthy of consideration. (For *steak and kidney pie* see 'Beef'.)

Lamb Red Bordeaux is, strictly speaking, the classic combination with *roast lamb* or *lamb chops*. However, reds from nearby Bergerac or Madiran and, further afield, Burgundy, South Africa's smarter Pinotage and Shiraz, California's Merlot, Australia's Shiraz and Cabernet blends, Spain's Rioja, and Argentina and Chile's Cabernets and Merlots are all in with a shout. Keep the wine firmly in the middleweight division and you will do well. You could, of course, go bonkers on the price or stick within a tight budget, as lamb is less particular than, say, beef or game. The way it is cooked, though, should definitely influence your final choice. If cooked *pink*, the range of suitable wines is enormous (any of the above). If *well done*, then a fruitier style of red should be served, so head to the New

World countries, as lamb tends to dry out and it needs resuscitation. Watch out for gravy and mint sauce, as an abundance of either could test the wine. *Lamb pot roast* and *casserole* tend to be a little richer in flavour than a chop or roast lamb because of the gravy. Again, don't spend too much on the wine, as authentic Languedoc or southern Rhône reds will do fine. *Shepherd's pie* is incredibly easy to match to red wine. In fact, just open whatever you feel like – if it's red and wet, it will be spot on. Plain *lamb shank* is another relatively easy dish to match to red wine, with inexpensive European examples from Portugal, Spain, Italy and France all offering enough acidity and structure to cut through the juicy, mouth-watering meat. *Moussaka*, with cheese, onion, oregano and aubergines, is altogether different. Lighter, fruit-driven reds such as New World Pinot Noir, inexpensive workhorses from Toro, Alto Duero or Campo de Borja in Spain, or cheaper South American reds will work well. *Stews* like *navarin* (with vegetables), *Irish stew*, *cassoulet* or *hot pot* all have broader shoulders when it comes to reds. Beefier southern French examples from Fitou, Corbières, St Chinian, Madiran, Faugères, Minervois or Collioure would be perfect. From further afield, Malbec from Argentina or Carmenère from Chile, as well as medium-weight, scented Aussie Shiraz (McLaren Vale, Pemberton or Yarra Valley), would also suit these dishes. *Cold roast lamb* follows the same rules as beef and, to a certain extent, ham in that fruity, light reds and juicy medium- to full-bodied whites work pretty well. Beaujolais, served cool, but not cold, is a great partner, while Chardonnay in any of the following guises would augment the dish – medium-priced white Burgundy, Chardonnay from Margaret River, Adelaide Hills or Yarra Valley (Australia) or Nelson or Marlborough (New Zealand), or lighter South African and Chilean styles. Lastly, *kebabs*, one of lamb's most exciting and gastronomically enlightening incarnations whether you've lovingly marinated and skewered the meat yourself or just adoringly watched it being shaved off that brontosaurus-sized mass of meat in a kebab shop. I suspect you'd struggle to balance a kebab and a glass of wine while stumbling down the street after a late-night gig. But on the off-chance that you make it home before tucking into the nuclear-hot dish, then a glass of big brand, sub-fiver New World Chardonnay or Semillon/Chardonnay would be a welcome break between mouthfuls, and not something you'd be too upset about having opened in the cold light of a new day.

Liver *Calves' liver with sage* (an old-fashioned but ever-so-tasty dish) needs medium-weight reds with fairly tight acidity. The texture of medium rare liver is relatively delicate, but the flavour is rich and dominant, and the acidity cuts through this intensity with style. Loire reds made from Cabernet Franc are your first port of call; Saumur-Champigny, Chinon, St Nicolas de Bourgueil and Bourgueil are all relatively inexpensive (sub-tenner) and a perfect match. Personally I wouldn't look any further, but if you need a larger choice then head to Northern Italy. Valpolicella, Teroldego from Trentino, Lagrein, Marzemino and Cabernet (Franc or Sauvignon – sometimes Italians don't specify which you're getting) all have the required fruit richness with the balancing acidity, freshness and grip needed for this task. *Liver and bacon* needs a touch more spice, but not much more weight, in a red wine, so move to a warmer part of France or Italy (i.e. head further south). Red Bordeaux and Chianti would be ideal, but this is likely to push the price up a few pounds.

Meat *Balls* (see 'Pasta'), *pies* (see 'Beef') and *loaf* (see 'Terrines').

Mexican *Fajitas, enchiladas, tortillas, quesadillas, tacos, burritos* (my tummy is rumbling as I write this) – loaded with chilli and salsa

– lead to the consumption of copious quantities of lime-stuffed (why?) beer, which has excellent thirst-quenching properties but bugger all flavour. If you are partial to a glass of wine, you must go in search of ripe, fruity, chillable red grapes like Nero d'Avola, Negroamaro and Primitivo (from southern Italy), Carmenère and Merlot from Chile, inexpensive Zinfandel from California and Cabernet or Merlot cheapies from Oz to cool you down and smooth out your battle-scarred palate. As for whites – they are likely to get bashed up no matter what you choose – find inexpensive, New World, mildly oaked Chardonnay or Semillon (or a blend of the two), chilled down sub zero, that allow you to taste the food and then the wine in turn, without suffering from too much chilli or refried bean reflux. Interestingly, *Cajun* cooking follows a similar pattern to Mexican food when it comes to wine styles, as cayenne, paprika, oregano, garlic and thyme all cook up a storm and need to be tempered with similarly juicy whites and reds.

Mezze (or *Meze*) This is the chance for dry Greek whites to shine, and there are enough out there of sufficiently high quality really to hit the mark. If you are unable to track them down, then try dry Muscat, Pinot Blanc or Sylvaner from Alsace, New Zealand Sauvignon Blanc or Argentinean Torrontés. You could always try to find dry Muscat from Australia, Spain or Portugal. Albariño from northern Spain and good old Vinho Verde from Portugal also work. Greek reds still lag behind the whites in terms of overall quality – some cheapies are fine, if a little coarse, but I would avoid spending more than a tenner as you will be hard-pushed to justify it. I would head off to Italy or Spain instead.

Mixed grill A vital part of every man's cooking repertoire, mixed grill is the dish of choice for superheroes the world over. You need a rich, robust red and there is nothing more macho than a feisty southern Rhône (see the Gazetteer for top performers) or its New World counterpart, a 'GSM' blend (Grenache, Shiraz and Mourvèdre in any combo – I have yet to see a label boasting MSG!) from Australia.

Moroccan/North African The most important factor to remember when matching this intriguing style of food with wine, is the level of spice involved in the dish. Then you can do one of two things – either choose fresh, clean, neutral whites which sit in the background and let the food do most of the talking, or go head to head with the flavours and drink a stunning aromatic white. Spain, Italy and France are the most obvious, and geographically closest ports of call and, within these three great wine nations, my favourite aromatic white styles would be Albariño (from Galicia in north-western Spain), Viognier (south of France) and Ribolla Gialla, Traminer, Erbaluce, Tocai, Lugana and richer Pinot Grigios (northeast and northwest Italy). Other Italian whites that would be a little more intense and competitive with the food are Grillo from Sicily, Falanghina, Fiano and Greco from Southern Italy. Reds that work well are Rioja or similar-style Tempranillo/Garnacha blends (Spain), chilled and ripe Côtes-du-Rhône (France), and Nero d'Avola, Aglianico, Frappato or Primitivo (southern Italy and Sicily). If you want to go down the neutral route, choose Beaujolais as a red, or Alsace Pinot Blanc or Loire Sauvignon Blanc as a white. If you feel the need to stray further from the Med, aim for more Sauvignon Blanc, this time from Chile or South Africa, for its herbal, lime-juice characters, and Barossa Valley Bush Vine Grenache (South Australia) for its pure red-berry fruit and herbal, smoky nose.

Mushrooms Although mushrooms traditionally form an integral part of a vegetarian's diet, I am delighted to forgo my carnivorous tendencies if mushrooms form the backbone of an evening's cooking. It is the inbuilt 'meatiness' in field mushrooms or the intensity, flavour and texture of wild mushrooms that really does it for me. Clearly the mushroom family is a diverse one and you can cook them in every way imaginable, so this is a pretty long entry. When matching wine to mushrooms, ignore the fact that they are fungi and look at the task they are employed to do in the dish. *Baked* or *grilled* mushrooms usually retain their essence, moisture and flavour, and cellar temperature reds (i.e. chilled a touch) should allow them to express themselves. Make sure that you choose relaxed, open reds with low tannins – simple Grenache blends, Gamay or Pinot Noir, for example. *Creamy sauces* are always difficult; if you overdo the cream, a robust, oaked Chardonnay or Semillon is needed, but if the cream features only in a supporting, 'whisked in' role, then refreshing red grapes such as Merlot and Barbera would be superb. *Mushroom omelettes* and *mushroom tarts* are both classic examples of how a mushroom can hold its own in the egg world – here, again, light, fruit-driven reds must be mobilised. *Wild mushrooms* can be intensely scented, gamey and foresty, so look to my 'Game' entry and trade down in terms of muscle and expenditure. *Mushrooms on toast* are ever so fashionable again (hoorah) – good news, as there is nothing better for setting the palate up for a main course. This is one of the easiest dishes to make at home and, even if you splash out on fancy bread and top shrooms, it is still a dead cheap dish. Wine-wise, look to the main course you are preparing and downsize the style a touch for your starter wine. If you are having a double serving as a stand-alone dish, then try Barbera or Dolcetto from northern Italy, for their truffley, black cherry aromas and flavours. *Stuffed mushrooms* depend on what they are stuffed with. I know that sounds obvious but cheesy or veggie ones work well with light reds. If you lose the cheese, rich whites are in with a shout – medium-sized Chardonnays and Rieslings are ideal. For *mushroom risotto* see 'Risotto'.

Mustard Make sure you turn up the volume on any red or white wine if you are contemplating a mustard sauce/dressing or an accompanying dish with a mustardy theme. You do not need to go too far in terms of size or style, but a notch up in quality and flavour is needed to accommodate the mustard intensity – this will probably mean you'll have to spend a pound or two more on your bottle.

Olives See 'Apéritif Wine Styles' if you are restricting your intake to pre-dinner olives. But, if you're cooking with olives, say in a lamb recipe (one of the classic food and food combos!), take care not to pour in the liquor (water, brine or oil), as it is very pungent (and often not of the highest quality) and can cast too strong an influence over the final taste of the dish. This, of course, would affect your wine's chances of happiness. As usual, the trick is to look to the main ingredient in the recipe and make sure that your chosen wine can be enjoyed alongside a sliver of olive (munch on one and taste the wine). *Tapenade* is a funny old thing – totally unfriendly when it comes to wine (unless you find refuge in dry sherry), so it is best to go for very dry whites from cooler-climate regions, for example Frascati, Gavi, Soave, Lugana, Greco, Falanghina, Grillo and Vernaccia (all Italian), or Sauvignon de Touraine, Cheverny, Muscadet, Bergerac Sec, Jurançon Sec or Pacherenc de Vic Bihl (all French).

Onion As a stand-alone dish, onion is at its best in a classic *French onion tart*, and Alsatian Riesling is the only true wine to drink with this noble offering. If you must stray from this advice (and risk a visit from the wine police) Clare Valley Rieslings from South Australia would work beautifully. Occasionally you see *caramelised* *onions* offered as a side dish – watch out. They are often intensely sweet (of the same order as a treacle tart) and, although you can moderate this by combining mouthfuls with the other elements of your meal, they are a real danger to a glass of dry wine so don't eat them with anything serious. My advice is to eat enthusiastically and sip cautiously. For *French onion soup* see 'Soup'.

Oysters see 'Seafood'.

Paella Not worthy of its own listing really, except for the fact that it is such a cacophonous mix of ingredients. The answer is that chilled, ripe Cabernet Franc (red Loire), Albariño or Godello (Spanish white grapes) or French Grenache-/Spanish Garnacha-based light reds and rosés all do well in a crowd-pleasing way.

Pasta *Naked* pasta tastes pretty neutral, which is why it is never really served on its own. The trick with pasta and wine matching is to consider what you are serving over, under, around or in it. Stuffed styles such as *cannelloni, agnolotti, cappelletti, tortellini* or *ravioli* can contain veg, cheese, meat and all sorts, so think inside out and select accordingly. *Spinach and ricotta tortellini* soaks up juicy Italian reds like Freisa, Dolcetto and Barbera from Piedmont, and young, simple Chianti, Franciacorta, Bardolino and Valpolicella. *Seafood* pasta dishes, including the all-time favourite *spaghetti vongole* (clams), love serious, crisp Sauvignon Blanc (from anywhere), decent Frascati (over £5 if you can find it!), Soave (again, break over the fiver barrier), Lugana, Fiano di Avellino, Verdicchio, Greco di Tufo and Vernaccia di San Gimignano. *Meatballs, spaghetti Bolognese, lasagne* and *meaty sauces* all respond to juicy reds. Keep the budget down and head for expressive, fruit-driven examples that work in harmony with the dish, as opposed to trying to dominate it.

Consider all of Italy, many New World regions, but steer clear of overly alcoholic wines (read the label and stay under 13.5%) and, although heretical, anything bright and juicy made from Tempranillo or Garnacha from Spain would also be delicious. *Roasted vegetables* often pop up in pasta dishes allowing you to choose between richer whites and lighter reds. *Pesto* may be a classic pasta combo but it is remarkably argumentative on the wine front. Oil, pine nuts, Parmesan and basil seem innocent enough, but combine them and you are forced into lean, dry whites for safety. Go to the famous Italian regions of Friuli, Alto Adige or Veneto as your guide. Sauvignon Blanc is grown up there, so at least you can rely on that stalwart grape but, otherwise, Pinot Grigio, Riesling, Picolit, Tocai Friulano and Pinot Bianco are all good bets. *Red pesto* is a different beast altogether. This time go for light red wines and keep their temperature down (15 minutes in the fridge) to focus the fruity flavours. *Cheesy* and *creamy sauces* tend to be more dominant than the ingredients bound therein, so Bardolino and Valpolicella (both from Veneto), Dolcetto, Freisa and Barbera (all from Piedmont), Montepulciano (from Marche) and medium-weight Chianti (from Tuscany, but you knew that!) are all accurate. If, for some reason, you want to stray from Italy's idyllic shores (I wouldn't – there is so much choice and the wines are cheap and widely available) then there is plenty more to be found; medium-weight reds and dry whites are everywhere. Just remember not to overshadow the dish, particularly with higher-alcohol wines. For *tomato sauce*, see 'Tomato'. For *mushroom sauce*, see 'Mushrooms'.

Pâté Regardless of its main ingredients, pâté is, perhaps surprisingly, keen on white wines. The only reds that really work are featherweights such as Beaujolais and Bardolino. In the white world, you need to hunt down fruity, aromatic wines from any decent estate in my Gazetteer. The crucial character you are searching for in these wines, in terms of taste, is a degree of sweetness. All styles from technically dry (but still ripe and fruity – Riesling, Gewürztraminer, Muscat, Chenin Blanc and so on) up to genuine sweet wines can be considered. Pâté is usually served as a starter, so pouring a sweet wine at the beginning of the meal might seem a little about face. But if you are serving pudding or cheese later on in the proceedings (plan this carefully beforehand), you can happily open a bottle of sweet wine, serve a few small glasses for starters and finish it off later. Many sweet wines are sold in half (37.5cl) or 50cl bottles, so if it's a small gathering, anything up to six, you'll not waste any wine. *Chicken liver pâté* favours dry to medium-dry German Riesling, Alsace Riesling, Pinot Blanc or mildly sweet white Bordeaux styles (Loupiac or Saussignac) and older Aussie Rieslings (Eden and Clare Valleys). *Country pâté*, a clumsy catch-all term that often hints at a coarser texture pâté of indeterminate origin, again likes light white wines with a degree of sweetness (or a pint of bitter). If you are pushed into choosing from a short wine list or are confronted with an undernourished off-licence, then play safe, buy a dry white and hope for the best. But if you have the luxury of choice, then Alsace is a great region to start with. Riesling and Tokay-Pinot Gris are the plum picks here. Head to the New World and you'll find Riesling in abundance in Australia, while Chilean Gewürztraminer is an unusual but rewarding style. With *duck pâté* and *foie gras* (*goose liver*), we are firmly in sweet wine territory – Sauternes, Loire and Alsace sweeties, Aussie botrytised Riesling and Semillon, or, on a tighter budget, Monbazillac, Ste-Croix du Mont, Loupiac, Cadillac and Saussignac, Sauternes' taste-alike neighbours. If you have never tasted this heady food and wine combo, you are in for a very pleasant surprise indeed. *Parfait*, the smoother, creamier, whipped-up version of pâté, tends to reveal its covert brandy ingredient more than a coarse pâté, so make sure your sweet wine is rich enough to cope with this. If you don't want to sip a sweet wine, then nearly sweet whites from Alsace also work. Vendange Tardive (late-picked) wines offer richness without cloying, sugary sweetness and will appease the non-sweet wine fans. Grapes to consider are Tokay-Pinot Gris, Gewürztraminer and Riesling. *Smoked salmon* pâté and other *fish* pâté incarnations are well served by dry aromatic whites (see 'Fish'). One thing to remember with pâté dishes is that occasionally *chutney* (or *onion confit/marmalade*) is served on the side, giving an intense, sweet fruit or veg explosion of flavour, which may confuse the wine. Alsatian Vendange Tardive wines, mentioned above, have tons of spice and richness of fruit and they will simply cruise through these added flavours – drier wines will choke. I have already talked about *gherkins* and *capers* in the 'Charcuterie' section, so keep them well under control.

Peppers Fresh, crunchy, raw peppers crackle with zingy, juicy, healthy flavours. It should come as no surprise, then, that Sauvignon Blanc (from almost anywhere) is the best grape for them – 'capsicum' is actually a classic tasting note for this variety. It is a marriage made in heaven, but if you want to try something different, then dry Chenin Blanc from South Africa or Italian Pinot Grigio would also be splendid. *Piemontese peppers* are a favourite Saturday lunch dish of mine, and with the olive oil, garlic, black pepper and tomato ingredients, dry whites are required, especially if the traditional anchovy fillets are criss-crossed on top of the shimmering tomatoes. Assertive Sauvignon Blanc is the best option, although Verdicchio, Orvieto, Greco, Fiano and Gavi (or a less expensive, Cortese-based Piedmont white) would be appropriate. A *stuffed pepper* depends more on the stuffing than the pepper itself, so look to the filling for ideas. Generally speaking, meat or cheese stuffing goes well with light Italian reds. *Peppers marinated in olive oil* love any dry white wines – for consummate accuracy Italian is best, so find some Soave, Frascati or Friuli single varietals such as Pinot Grigio, Pinot Bianco, Traminer or Sauvignon Blanc. For *gazpacho* see 'Soup'.

Picnics You simply must find screwcap-sealed bottles for picnics. There are so many out there these days and the benefits are numerous – there is no need for a corkscrew, you can reseal the bottle with ease and you also don't have to worry about anyone knocking it over. Your first port of call for all-round picnic-matching skills has to be rosé. It is multitalented when it comes to all manner of cold food dishes, and if you chill the bottles down ice cold before departure, it will drink like a fresh white early on, and as the day hots up (global warming and all), it will behave more like a red. This should cunningly coincide with your move through the courses, from crudités and dips, via smoked salmon, to rare roast beef and finally some good cheese. Other varieties that enjoy *al fresco* food are Sauvignon Blanc for whites and Beaujolais for reds. Once again, chill all your wines right down prior to departure and, to enjoy them all at their best, drink them in order from white, via rosé to red, and bring some ice if you can.

Pigeon see 'Game' but spend less!

Pizza I adore pizza and, if prepared well, there is nothing to touch it for taste bud satisfaction. Heroic pizzas rarely allow white wines enough space to be heard. However, I suppose a simple *vegetable* or *seafood* pizza might need a weedy, dry white wine. Assuming you have a tomato (or red pepper – much tangier) base and some mozzarella cheese on top, the real point of a pizza is the unlimited number of toppings that you sling on – mushroom, onion, anchovy, caper, olive, beef, ham, egg, pepperoni and, crucially, chillies. A real man's pizza has these and more, so you will have to find a feisty red and cool it down. My all-Italian pizza wine line-up includes: whites – Arneis, Soave, Bianco di Custoza, Verdicchio, Pinot Bianco, Pinot Grigio and Orvieto; chillable reds – Sardinian Cannonau, Freisa, Barbera and Dolcetto from Piedmont, Marzemino and Teroldego from Trentino, Bardolino and Valpolicella from Veneto and Chianti, Montepulciano d'Abruzzo, Morellino di Scansano, Sangiovese di Romagna, Primitivo di Puglia, Nero d'Avola di Sicilia, Negroamaro and Aglianico all from further south. If you insist on drinking non-Italian wines with pizza, you might just find you are the victim of far more than your normal share of corked wines (just call me Mystic Matthew).

Pork The noble porker has so many different gastronomic guises that I have given the gallant sausage its own section. And, no doubt, *pâté* and *terrine* lovers are delighted that these two dishes also warrant their own headings. I have also dealt with *charcuterie*, *cassoulet*, *bacon*, *full English breakfast* and *ham* in other sections. Here I endeavour to cover the porcine dishes not otherwise mentioned. First in this section, then, is the princely *pork pie* and its less exciting, ever-so-slightly oddly coloured, asteroid cousin, the *Scotch egg*. A good pork pie is a real treat and, while I'm sure that a pint of real ale is the ideal partner, a glass of Cru Beaujolais is also a perfect fit. The Scotch egg somehow crops up in pubs and picnics more than at the dinner table (not really surprising, would you want one hibernating in your fridge?) and real ale is the only sensible choice – but you wouldn't be putting a foot wrong by ordering a juicy Merlot either. If you like a dollop of Branston or Piccalilli on the plate, then expect the wine to be sent into a tailspin. *Chorizo* and *salami* fall into the aforementioned 'Charcuterie' section, but remember that the spicier the salami, the greater the need for cool red wine. A plate of chorizo is excellent with dry sherry – manzanilla and fino are the two best styles. Next on the agenda, *spare ribs* – whether drenched in barbecue sauce or not, they are prehistoric fare, so cave-man reds are needed to slake your thirst. Juice and texture are the essential ingredients, so head to the New World in search of Argentinean Sangiovese, Malbec, Bonarda or Tempranillo, Chilean Carmenère or Australian Cabernet/Shiraz blends. Californian Zinfandel would also work well, although it might be disproportionately expensive for the dish. *Rillettes*, which can also be made from duck or rabbit, expose one of pork's lighter sides. This mild, oddly fondanty, savoury dish is often served as part of a plate of cold meats. White wine is called for, with Pinot Blanc, Sylvaner and Riesling from Alsace all working well. As usual, Aussie Riesling will find this a doddle, too.

I have left the big daddy to last – *roast pork*. There are a number of ways to serve this so, when it comes to matching it to wine, the brief is fairly open. One thing is certain – if you are going to serve a red, make it light (Pinot Noir is best). Pork is far more excited by white wine, particularly if there is apple sauce moored alongside. Classy, unoaked Chardonnay from Chablis or Burgundy would be exact, although New World Chardonnays can hack it as long as they are not too overtly oaky. Riesling (dry and luxurious), Condrieu (the super-dear northern Rhône Viognier), Vouvray (make sure it says 'sec' – dry – on the label) and southern Rhône whites (thin on the ground but a lot of bang for your buck) are all worth a substantial sniff.

Quiche (and posh tarts?) see 'Eggs'.

Rabbit Rabbit *rillettes* love a little more scent and exoticism in their wines than pork rillettes, so Marsanne, Roussanne and Viognier from anywhere in the world (Rhône is your starting point, maybe California or Victoria in Australia next) or Pinot Blanc and Riesling (the richer styles from Alsace) would be mouth-wateringly spot on. All other bunnies, see 'Game'.

Risotto Generally, the richness and texture of a risotto needs to be 'cut' with the acidity of a clean, dry white wine, but what else have you folded into your risotto? It is these magic ingredients that matter the most when finding the perfect wine to counter the creamy, cheesy (if you've whacked a spot of grated Parmesan and butter in with the stock) rice. Light reds can work with *wild mushroom* risotto but, even with this, I prefer scented, cool, classy whites. *À la Milanese*, with saffron, can force a light, dry white into submission unless it has enough fruit and 'oomph' – Arneis or Gavi from Piedmont are worth a go, as is Riesling from a good Australian or Alsatian producer. *Chicken and mushroom* risotto likes Chardonnay and lighter Pinot Noirs, just as a non-risotto dish might. *Primavera* favours fresh, zingy, green whites – Sauvignon Blanc anyone? For *seafood* risotto see 'Seafood'.

Salads A huge subject that just needs a spot of common sense. Basic *green* or *mixed* salad without dressing is virtually tasteless, as far as wine is concerned, but be careful if it's dressed – particularly if vinegar is involved because this changes all the rules. People will tell you that light whites are always best with salad, but you are hardly going to order a glass of white to accompany your *pousse and shallot* salad after having downed a rare steak and chips. Just chomp through the salad, having a break in the red, and then bring it back into view when you've finished. Don't worry, the salad is a palate cleanser and knows that it is not the main show. *Seafood* salad enjoys the white wines that go well with seafood (obvious, I know, see 'Seafood'); *Niçoise* likes tangy Sauvignon Blanc, Sauv blends and neon green Margaret River Semillons (Australia); *chicken* salad works well with Rhône whites and middle-weight Chardonnays; *feta* salad, not surprisingly, is perfect with dry Greek whites; *French bean and shallot* salad likes lighter, inexpensive Alsace Tokay-Pinot Gris and Pinot Blanc; *tomato and basil* salad is best matched with rosé or anything fresh, dry, keenly acidic, white and Italian; *Caesar* salad, if made properly, is great with Sauvignon Blanc or Gavi; *Waldorf* salad needs softer, calmer white grapes like Pinot Blanc and Sylvaner (Alsace), or South African Chenin Blanc; *pasta* salad can get a little stodgy, so uplifting, acidity-rich, dry whites are essential. Every country in the wine world makes salad-friendly wines, even the UK, where the better dry white grapes like Bacchus, Reichensteiner and Seyval Blanc, in the right hands, can be a joy (you know where to look!).

Sausages (Meaty ones, please, no fish or veggie!) Any sausage dish, including *toad-in-the-hole* and *bangers and mash*, needs manly, robust, no messin' reds. Cahors, Garnacha blends from Tarragona, Shiraz or Cabernet from Western Australian, Victoria or McLaren Vale, Malbec from Argentina, any Languedoc or southern Rhône reds, Barbera from northern Italy, Primitivo from southern Italy, and Chinon or other red Loires are all suitable. Zinfandel, Merlot and Cabernet from California would also be awesome, as would a bottle of plain old claret. Hurrah for sausages and their global compatibility with red wine! They're not fussy and nor should you be.

Seafood Muscadet, Cheverny, Menetou-Salon, Sauvignon de Touraine, Quincy, Pouilly-Fumé and Sancerre (all white Loire wine), Chenin Blanc (South Africa), Albariño (Spain), Lugana, Verdicchio,

Soave and Pinot Grigio (Italy) and any buttock-clenchingly dry, unoaked New World whites are all perfect with seafood. *Squid* and *octopus* both need very dry whites with aromatic fruit like Sauvignon Blanc, northern Italian or Penedès (Spain) whites, and resinous Greek whites if the dish is served in its ink. The curious, bouncy texture of both squid and octopus does not embrace wine in the same way fish does, so concentrate on the method of cooking and the other ingredients to help you make your final choice. *Crevettes grises*, or the little grey/brown shrimps, eaten whole as a pre-dinner nibble, are stunning with Muscadet or Sauvignon Blanc from the Loire, Australia or New Zealand. *Crayfish* and *prawns* are a step up in terms of flavour and dry English whites, simple, dry Riesling, and Sauvignon or Semillon/Sauvignon Blanc blends are all lovely. If you are a *prawn cocktail* fiend (bring it on), then decent Sauvignon Blanc (no need to spend over £8) is dry and sharp enough to wade through the livid pink Marie Rose sauce. *Lobster*, the noblest of all crustaceans, served cold or in a salad, should tempt you to delve into the deepest, darkest corners of your cellar and uncork the finest whites. Burgundy (no upper limit), Australian (ditto) and Californian Chardonnay (only the best – not too oaky) and Viognier (from its spiritual birthplace in Condrieu, in the northern Rhône) will all set you back a fortune but, hey, you've already bought lobster, so go the extra yard and finish the job properly. *Lobster thermidor* is not my favourite dish, as I feel that lobster loses its magical texture and elegant flavour when served hot, but you can easily uncork richer (but less expensive) whites like Aussie Semillons or South American Chardonnays. If you feel like a slice of lobster class, but for a slightly reduced price, then *langoustines* (or *bugs/yabbies* if you're mad for crustacea and on hols in Australia) are the answer. Lobster-wines are perfect here, but just adjust the price downwards by a few quid or more. *Dressed crab* is a fabulous dish and, once again, Loire whites like Muscadet (only £4–£5 for a good bottle) are spot on. Dry whites such as Ugni Blanc from Gascony, Jurançon Sec and 'village' Chablis are also excellent, but Sauvignon Blanc is again probably the pick of the grapes (it always is). Don't just look at the Loire, though, as the white wines from Bordeaux and Bergerac often have a fair slug of Sauvignon in them and, of course, Sauvignon is grown all over the world. *Mussels* probably do best in *gratin* or *marinière* form when dry Riesling, Barossa or Hunter Valley Semillon, New Zealand Pinot Gris and New World Sauvignon Blanc are all worthy contenders. *Scallops* require a little more weight in a white wine (mildly oaked Sauvignon Blanc, for example – Fumé Blanc from California). They can even handle a spot of light red (chilled). *Scallops sauté Provençal* (with tomatoes and garlic) and *scallops wrapped in bacon* are wicked with smart rosé. *Scallops Bercy* (with shallots, butter, thyme, white wine, parsley and lemon juice) are superb with top Sancerre or Pouilly-Fumé – spend up, it will be worth it. *Oysters* are traditionally matched with Champagne – but not by me. I prefer a simple dry white like Muscadet, with its salty tang, or a 'village' Chablis or Sauvignon de St-Bris. A *plateau de fruits de mer* involves all of the above, plus *whelks* (yuk) and *winkles* (mini-yuk), and really only needs a first-class bottle of Sauvignon de Touraine or Muscadet. You'll thank me because, after you receive the bill for this mountainous platter of seafood, you'll be delighted to spend a fraction of that on a bottle of chuggable wine. Finally, s*eafood risotto* – here dry Italian wines including decent Frascati, Vernaccia di San Gimignano, Arneis, Verdicchio Classico, Greco and Fiano, along with South African Sauvignon Blanc and Chenin Blanc make a rather delicious combination. Remember that Chilean Sauvignon is often cheaper than both South African and New Zealand versions, so if you are having a big risotto party then look here for a volume purchase. For *clams*, see 'Pasta'.

Side dishes see 'Vegetables'.

Snails Oh yeah! See 'Garlic'.

Soups Dry sherry is often quoted as soup's dream date. But it seems a little ludicrous to crack open a bottle of fino every time I fancy a bowl of broth. And, what's more, it isn't always the best wine for the job, as the soup dynasty holds a diverse collection of individuals – no one wine can expect to cover all of the flavours. *Minestrone*, with its wonderful cannellini bean base, and *ribollita* (the stunning, next-day minestrone incarnation, re-boiled with cabbage and bread thrown in for extra body) like to keep things Italian, with Teroldego or Marzemino from Trentino and Valpolicella being superb candidates. If you want to hop over the mountains to France, then simpler southern Rhônes (a well-made C-de-R would do) make a refreshing and accurate alternative. *Spinach and chickpea* soup goes well with bone-dry whites like those from Orvieto, Frascati, Greco, Verdicchio (Italy), Penedès or Rueda (Spain), or Sauvignon Blanc from New Zealand, South Africa or Chile. *Vichyssoise* (chilled leek and potato soup) needs creamy, floral whites, such as simple Alsatian Riesling, South American or French Viognier, or light, white Rhônes. *Lobster* or *crayfish bisque* has a creamy texture coupled with a deceptive richness, so dry sherry could conceivably make an appearance here. If you don't fancy that, then youthful white Burgundy is best. *Bouillabaisse with rouille*, the serious fish, garlic, tomatoes, onion and herb broth with floating toasty crostinis topped with garlic, chilli and mayo, is a mighty dish and yet it only needs very simple whites like our old favourites Muscadet and Sauvignon de Touraine. *Consommé* is a definite dry sherry dish (at last). *Gazpacho* (chilled *tomato*, *cucumber*, *onion*, *pepper* and *garlic* soup) likes nothing more than

Spanish new-wave (unoaked) Viura or cheeky Verdejo from Rueda. *Mushroom* soup is another dry sherry candidate (you might use some in the recipe), while *French onion* soup goes well with dry Riesling from Alsace or South Australia. *Oxtail* demands hearty reds – rustic, earthy inexpensive southern French bruisers like St Chinian or Minervois are ideal. *Lentil and chestnut* and *lentil and bacon* soups both crave dry sherry (this time trade up from a fino to an amontillado, for complexity and intensity), while *clam chowder* is basically a fishy soup with cream (and sometimes potato), so Sauvignon Blanc, Chenin Blanc and all seafood-friendly whites are perfect. *Vegetable* soup can be dull but it can also be excellent; either way, rustic reds at the bottom of the price ladder are needed. *Tomato* soup is a strange one. Always avoid oak. I favour light reds or dry whites – Gamay (Beaujolais or Loire) or Sauvignon Blanc (Pays d'Oc, Loire, South Africa or Chile) all do the job admirably.

Sweetbreads With *butter and sorrel, sauce ravigote* (mustard, red wine vinegar, capers and tarragon) or *sauce gribiche* (like ravigote but with chopped hard-boiled eggs and parsley as well), sweetbreads demand aromatic, decadently textured, self-confident whites. Alsatian or South Australian Riesling (Clare or Eden Valley) with a bit of age would be my first choice. If you can't find any, then try creamy, oily, nutmeg- and peach-scented Rhône whites. All of these are dear, but there's no way around this quandary, as this is a demanding sector of the food repertoire. *Ris de veau aux morille*s (veal sweetbreads with a very rich, creamy wild mushroom sauce) needs the most intense Rhône whites or Alsatian Rieslings.

Tapas Sherry and dry white wines, preferably Spanish and avoiding oak, are perfect partners for these addictive Spanish snacks.

Terrines A terrine is a more robust, often hearty, pâté, generally served in slices. So what's good enough for a pâté is often perfect with terrine. One of the classics is *ham and chicken*, which loves white Burgundy or elegant, non-French, mildly oaked Chardonnays. Another white Burgundy lover is *jambon persillé*, the sublime parsley, jelly and ham dish. This is not surprising as it is a Burgundian recipe in the first place. I would dive in with a youthful, inexpensive Bourgogne Blanc from a reputable Domaine, or head south to Rully, Mercurey, Montagny or a crisp Mâconnais wine for a match. Beaujolais, Alsatian Gewürztraminer, Riesling and Tokay-Pinot Gris love *rabbit*, *hare* and *game* terrines, particularly if there are prunes lurking within. *Fish* terrines follow the lead of fish pâtés and mousses with Sauvignon Blanc, Riesling, clean, fresh Chardonnays like Chablis, Fiano di Avellino from Campania in Southern Italy and finally the enigmatic Spanish stunner, Albariño.

Thai Along the same lines as Vietnamese and other 'Asian but not overly so' styles of cuisine, it is best to look to the main ingredient and then concentrate on appropriate southern hemisphere, fruit-driven wines. Likely candidates are: Australian or New Zealand Riesling, Viognier, Semillon, Verdelho, Pinot Gris and Sauvignon Blanc. New World sparkling wines in general work well, as do dry Muscats from Portugal and Pinot Gris, Torrontés or Viognier from Argentina.

Tomatoes Strangely, tomatoes are pretty fussy when it comes to wine matching (see 'Soup'). Pinot Noir works well but, generally, New World versions perform better than their Old World counterparts, as they often have more fruit expression and lower acidity. Other reds, like Sicilian Nero d'Avola, Aglianico, Primitivo (all southern Italy) and any juicy, warm-climate Merlot or Zinfandel are accommodating. When *raw*, as in a salad, rosé is a good choice.

A *tomato sauce* demands dry, light whites and Italy is the best place to look for these, as they are often ripe and cheap. *Ketchup*, while delicious, is so sweet and vinegary that it gives wine a hard time, so use sparingly on your burger if you like drinking fine wine. Drench it if you're gunning down a cheap glugging red.

Truffles Foresty, feral and musky – yum! Choose similarly scented wines to match this unusual life form – Burgundian Pinot Noir, Piedmont's magnificent Nebbiolo and Barbera, and Syrah (French and serious, please). If you want to cook chicken or fish with truffles, then vintage Champagne (or go crazy and find some vintage rosé Champs) or top Alsatian Riesling would be spectacular.

Turkey The thing to watch out for with *roast* turkey is the cranberry sauce factor. Often a fresh, young Crianza Rioja or juicy New World Pinot Noir complements this outlandish red-fruit flavour. At Christmas, Rioja is again a winner as mountains of cocktail sausages, bacon, sprouts and the rest take the flavour spotlight away from the turkey. If you are feeling very brave, totally ahead of your time, or just a little barking, sparkling Shiraz from Australia (you can get a superb example for as little as £7) would be fantastic, celebratory and original. Otherwise, see 'Chicken'.

Turkish I have already covered lamb kebabs (with lashings of chilli sauce) in the 'Lamb' section but, essentially, Turkish food is best with Greek wines (endeavouring to be non-political) as the cuisine styles are linked and the resinous, aromatic whites and purple, earth- and violet-scented reds are spot on.

Veal There are some mightily good dishes in this section, but sadly there is no hard and fast rule as to what to follow on the wine front, so read carefully. In general, veal prefers to keep the company of grown-up white wines and classy, lighter reds. *Saltimbocca*, the terrific veal, sage and prosciutto dish, needs a wine to 'jump in the mouth'. Pinot Nero (Italian Pinot Noir) would be fine, but is hard to find and often a little dear. If your search is unsuccessful, try another unusual wine – Trincadeira from Portugal would be an inexpensive and inspirational substitute. *Vitello tonnato*, a phenomenal dish of contrasting flavours, using thinly sliced, braised veal and served cold, drizzled in a sauce made from marinated tuna, lemon juice, olive oil and capers, is one of the world's most sumptuous starters. Taking the tuna and anchovy (used in the braising stage) as your lead – fresh, sunny, seaside whites like Verdicchio, Greco and Vernaccia work especially well. *Wiener schnitzel*, fried veal in egg and breadcrumbs, can often taste a little on the dry side, so what else is on the plate? If there is nothing of enormous character to deflect your mission, give it the kiss of life with a juicy, mildly oaked Chardonnay. *Blanquette de veau*, the French classic with a creamy sauce, is definitely a white wine dish. Again Chardonnay will do, but for perfection go for Viognier, Roussanne or Marsanne blends from the Rhône or Victoria in South Australia. *Osso bucco*, veal shin with wine, tomatoes, parsley, garlic and zesty gremolata, is a lighter, yet more heady stew than most, and Tasmanian, Yarra Valley, Adelaide Hills (Aussie), New Zealand or Oregon Pinot Noir would be great, as would huge, full-on Chardonnays from anywhere in my Gazetteer.

Vegetables Vegetables (served on their own, or as an accompaniment) taste, on the whole, relatively neutral. But, depending on how they are cooked, they can require a moment or two's thought. Any *gratin* (baked with cheese) or *dauphinoise* (thinly sliced potato baked with cream and garlic) dish needs light reds or firm, self-confident whites. *Beetroot* is a tad tricky, but Alsatian whites generally have the texture and flavour to make it through. *Cabbage, leeks, spinach, parsnips, cauliflower, sprouts, courgettes, carrots, peas* and *potatoes* are usually innocent so don't worry about them, but *gnocchi* (plain or flavoured with spinach) needs juicy, fruit-driven wines with perky acidity to cut through their texture and lubricate the palate. *Marinated* vegetables and *polenta* love Italian whites – Pinot Grigio, Soave, Verdicchio etc. *Lentils* often dry the palate out and rustic, earthy reds are essential. Look to French Country wines for an endless supply of candidates or to Chile and Argentina for Malbec or Syrah/Shiraz. *Corn on the cob* is a dead ringer for New World Sauvignon Blanc. Open a bottle and, with some wines, you may actually detect a canned sweetcorn aroma! *Celeriac* is a stunning accompaniment to a dish and it has a pretty strong aroma and flavour, so make sure your wine is up to it.

Vegetarian If you are a strict vegetarian or vegan, look at the label (usually the back) on the wine bottle, as most organic and vegan associations have stickers or a logo to let you know the contents and production techniques of the wine. If you are still unsure, ask your wine merchant.

Vinaigrette A passion killer for wine, vinegar is strongly flavoured and makes any wine taste flat for a few seconds. This can give your palate an annoying stop-start sensation, which is a little like someone switching the light on and off every so often. Dressing made with lemon juice and oil is more wine-friendly and healthier.

Vinegar See above! Balsamic vinegar seems to be more accommodating than most, perhaps as you tend to use less, and it is more winey in depth and flavour.

Welsh rarebit Make sure you always finish on a good note! Whether you make these toasties for late night nibbling or as a traditional savoury for after pudding, you deserve a meaty little rustic red swimming alongside. Anything from the south of France, southern Italy or Spain would be a delicious match. Make sure it is not too dear, and if you are really snookered pop over to Australia for a chunky, inexpensive Shiraz.

PUDDINGS

It seems to me that port drinking has taken something of a hit of late in the after-dinner drinking stakes. Many of my friends now prefer to end a meal on a sweet wine, as it enlivens the palate and wakes you and your taste buds up. For my part, there is nothing better than finishing off dinner with a glass of sweet wine, particularly if it accompanies a tasty pudding. Read on for a comprehensive list of my favourite puddings and their dream wines. Thankfully there is only one rule to remember when matching wine to sweet dishes – you must make sure the wine is at least as sweet as the pudding, otherwise it will taste dry. Most wine shops have a few sweet wines lurking on the racks, but sadly not as many as one would like. You may have to find a decent independent merchant to get a good selection of sweeties so check out the 'Directory' on page 203 for a merchant near you. But also run through my Top 250 for a serious list of sweet wines that between them cover every dish in this decadent section.

Almond tart Despite its heavenly flavour and fantastic texture, this dish needs careful handling on the wine front, as an overbearing sweet wine would crush the delicate almondy nuances. Lighter, youthful sweeties like Muscat de Beaumes-de-Venise, Muscat de Rivesaltes, Moelleux (sweet) Loire whites and Jurançon Moelleux would all be spot on. Stick to these styles if your almond tart has fresh fruit on top. *Bakewell tart*, while perhaps not as elegant as a fresh fruit tart, likes these sweeties, too, but you'd be well advised to go for a little more age on a sweet Loire wine.

Apple

Strudels, pies, fritters and *crumbles* all enjoy varying degrees of nutty, cinnamony, buttery pastry and burnt, brown sugar flavours. These overlay the intrinsic fruitiness of the filling and, therefore, demand a richer, heavier style of pudding wine than you might expect. Having said that, we are still in the foothills of sweetness! German Riesling (of at least Auslese status), late-picked Muscat or Riesling from Australia, classic French Sauternes (don't spend too much) or New World botrytised Semillon and lighter, youthful Hungarian Tokaji (a lower number of Puttonyos) are all runners. *Baked apples* (assuming they are served warm/hot) ought to have ice-cold, light, fresh German or Austrian Riesling (Spätlese or Auslese level) and clean, light Muscats. This will give your palate a marvellous and invigorating sauna then plunge pool sensation every time you take a sip. If they are served cold, don't bother with wine. See below for *tarte tatin*.

Apricot

A sensationally accurate apricot match is Vendange Tardive (late-picked) Condrieu (from the northern Rhône) for *apricot crumble*. Unfortunately this wine is extremely rare and exceedingly expensive (best to buy it on hols in the Rhône), so where else should you look? The answer is sweet Jurançon (Moelleux), bursting with tropical quince and peach flavours, or Monbazillac or Saussignac – a friendlier-priced Sauternes-style offering from southwest France.

Bananas

Raw – don't be silly, wait until lunch to open a bottle! *Banoffee pie*, the hideous love child of sticky toffee pudding and schoolboy banana jokes, can only be tamed by the most outrageous of sweet wines – Hungarian Tokaji (I wouldn't waste it), Australian liqueur Muscat (this will slow you down) and Malmsey Madeira (I might even turn up if this was served). With comedy *banana splits*, the candied sprinkles, shaky shaky things and ice cream flavours are more dominant than the neutered banana, so watch out on the wine front. I personally wouldn't serve wine at a kiddie's birthday party, unless the adults are desperate – OK, so you are desperate, grab some Aussie liqueur muscat.

Berries *Black*, *goose*, *blue*, *rasp*, *Chuck* (bad joke), *logan*, *huckle*, *straw*, *Halle* (good joke), *mul*, *cran*, *bil* and his amour *damson* bounce around in many different recipes. Whether they are served *au naturel*, in a juicy *compote*, or cooked in a *summer pudding*, they all love the talented sweet wine superhero Semillon and his trusty sidekick Muscat. Track down these grapes from France – Sauternes, Saussignac, Monbazillac, Loupiac and Cadillac all fall neatly into the Semillon camp; while Muscat de Rivesaltes, de Beaumes-de-Venise, de Frontignan and de Lunel all advertise Muscat on the label, so are easier to spot on the shelves. Aussie late-picked Muscats are all great and inexpensive, but watch out for liqueur Muscats, as they are wildly different and will destroy a delicate *fruit purée*.

Biscuits/Biscotti (and proper shortbread) Vin Santo is the top choice for the biscuit family. Sweeter Madeira styles and cream sherry also work very well, counter-pointing the crumbly texture, butter and fruit or nut ingredients well. None of these wines need be served in large quantities (unless you are particularly thirsty!), as they are all sipping styles. Sauternes (heady, sweet white Bordeaux) or New World botrytised Semillon (exactly the same style but better value) come in a worthy second. Other lighter biscuits enjoy the company of simple sweet wines – I would still stick to Semillon – or Chenin Blanc-based French versions.

Brandy snaps God, I love brandy snaps (thank goodness for Ma Jukesy, as I haven't a snowball's chance in hell at making them myself). Once again, try Australian liqueur Muscat, you'll love it – just try to stop when you've got through the first batch and bottle, otherwise you'll be drunk and fat in one easy move.

Bread and butter pudding You need wines with a bit of power and acidity for a traditional B & B pudding (so I am told – not my scene, you see). Weightier Muscat-based wines are just the job – Moscatel de Setúbal from Portugal and Moscato or Passito di Pantelleria from the volcanic island off the south of Sicily would be a delight. Take it steady, though, as these are addictive, gloriously moreish and hugely alcoholic. Buckle up for a late night.

Cakes What's wrong with a cup of Darjeeling? Well, quite a lot, really, when you could be enjoying an elegant glass of cream sherry or a schooner of Aussie liqueur Muscat with *coffee* cake, Bual or Malmsey Madeira with *Dundee* or *Battenberg*, Maury or Banyuls with *brownies* or a traditional *fruitcake*, or demi-sec Champagne with *Victoria* or *lemon sponge*. For the perfect sugar hit try *doughnuts* and ice cold Asti, drunk between the checkout and the car park at your local supermarket!

Cheesecake Whether it is cherry or any other style, the 'cheesiness', not the fruit, controls the choice of wine. Botrytised Semillon and Riesling from the New World, Coteaux du Layon and other sweet Loire wines, Austrian Beerenauslese, and Alsatian Vendange Tardive Riesling and Tokay-Pinot Gris all work. The trick is to keep the sweetness intense and fruit-driven, without resorting to heavyweight styles of high alcohol/fortified wines.

Cherries In *pie* form, cherries behave like berries and prefer the company of mid-weight sweet wines. Cherries served with *chocolate* in a *marquise* or *Black Forest gâteau*, though, can handle a much richer wine. Try Amarone, the wickedly intense red wine from Veneto in Italy, Maury or Banyuls from Roussillon (France) or really juicy Californian Zinfandel for a bizarre match. Your guests might think you're a course late with the red, but it works, honest.

Chocolate A deluxe *choccy cake* can, if it's not too intense, retreat into lighter Muscats and botrytised Rieslings. Chocolate *mousse*, *petits pots au chocolat* and chocolate *soufflé* all head towards Orange Muscat, with its wonderful pervading aroma and flavour of orange blossom. This is one of the finest food and wine combinations of all, as orange and chocolate are natural partners (why do you think Terry is so chuffed?). Australia and California make two examples that I know of, so well done Brown Bros and Andrew Quady respectively, your places in choccy heaven are guaranteed. If these wines are too hard to find, then you could even twist my arm to open a bottle of Asti Spumante! Chocolate *pithiviers*, the single most decadent dish in the pudding repertoire, needs unctuous fortified wines with a touch of burnt nuttiness – Banyuls or Maury (Roussillon, France), liqueur Muscat and liqueur Tokay (Australia). Match any of these ridiculously insane dishes with the following list of galactically serious wines – Passito di Pantelleria (for its mind-boggling orange zest aroma), Tokaji, black Muscat (space-age – careful, get ready for re-entry), liqueur Muscat, PX (short for Pedro Ximénez, the boozy, black, teeth-rottingly sweet turbo-sherry), botrytised Semillon from the New

World, Maury and Banyuls (the mega, port-like sweet Grenache wines from the south of France) and, finally, young, punchy, underrated, tawny port.

Christmas pudding During the festive period, it is useful to have a wine that lasts well once opened – you've got to make it all the way from Christmas Eve to New Year's Day, after all. Top-quality tawny port and liqueur Muscat or Tokay from Australia, as well as heady Malmsey Madeira, all fit the bill. You can squeeze twelve glasses out of a bottle without short-changing anyone. Not bad, hey, and these are not expensive wines by any stretch of the imagination. See my 'Top 250' for worthy versions.

Cinnamon rolls A heavenly creation – but ever so wicked. You need considerable levels of sweetness and toffeed aromas in the wine to cope with the intensity of sugar. Vin Santo, Hungarian Tokaji, liqueur Muscat and old oloroso sherry would be stunning. Old-fashioned *lardy cakes* are, sadly, hard to find these days, but if you do, then stick to Malmsey Madeira – it fits with the image as well as being a great flavour combination.

Crème brûlée As I only like the top, crunchy, caramelised bit, as opposed to the silky, creamy bit, I have asked some pals which wine is the best match. The general consensus is that you need to aim somewhere between my almond tart and cheesecake wines. As Loire sweeties, made from Chenin Blanc, appear in both sections, they must be spot on – Coteaux du Layon, Vouvray Moelleux, Bonnezeaux (pronounced 'Bonzo') and Quarts de Chaume are your choices. You could always look for some South African Chenin Blanc sweet wines, as the grape is widely planted down there and they are stunning value for money.

food and wine

Crème caramel Sadly this is another pud that you won't get me near (I've got a texture problem – too slippery), but I have it on good authority that light, delicate sweeties are required. German Auslese Rieslings from the Mosel and youthful, fairy-light Muscats are apparently spot on.

Crêpes Suzette Clairette de Die, the little-known sparkling wine from the Rhône, or Asti (Italy's frothy Moscato) would be cheap but worthy options, with demi-sec Champagne being the grown-up and expensive choice.

Custard As soon as you start waving custard around on, say, a spotted dick, you are giving your palate much more to think about. Intense creaminess craves acidity in a wine. With custard being the ultimate in eggy creaminess, the big guns like Malmsey Madeira, liqueur Muscat and Tokaji must be let out of the cellar.

Doughnuts see 'Cakes'.

Fruit *Raw* fruit of any kind has a much lighter flavour than you would expect when pitted against a sweet wine. So stay with dainty Asti, German or Austrian Spätlese Rieslings, demi-sec Champagne, fresh, clean Muscats, Italy's Recioto di Soave, Spain's Moscatel de Valencia or very light, young Sauternes. Oh, if you fancy a *lychee*, then find a sweet Gewürztraminer, as it has remarkable lychee characteristics on the nose and palate. *Poached* fruit, like *peaches* or *apricots*, picks up sweetness from the added sugar and can be pretty intense, so tread carefully. You may need a rich Coteaux du Layon from the Loire to see you through.

Fruitcake see 'Cakes'.

Gingerbread A wonderful creation that, along with *ginger cake* and *ginger biscuits*, is made even better when accompanied by a glass of good-quality cream sherry or Malmsey Madeira.

Gooseberry fool A heavy, oleaginous sweet wine would trample this refreshing, palate-tweaking pudding. What you need is young, botrytised Semillon, like Sauternes, Saussignac, Monbazillac or Loupiac, or Asti or demi-sec Champagne. Try to keep the price down as more expensive wines will usually taste finer and more intense. Or grab a bottle of fresh, young, Riesling Auslese (Mosel, Germany) for a fruit-cocktail-style, grapey flavour – it will also be much cheaper.

Ice cream If you want to play safe then *vanilla, chocolate, rum and raisin, coffee, toffee* and *cookie-dough* ice creams all love Pedro Ximénez (PX), the intensely coffee-and-raisin-drenched sweet sherry. You could always try sweet liqueur Muscats from Australia as well. If you have a *fruity* ice cream or *sorbet*, just leave it alone – you need a few minutes without a flagon in your hand occasionally. If you want to ignore me – go crazy and experiment, but you're on your own.

Jam tart You have to find a very sweet wine. This is the only rule, as you can't get sweeter than jam. Icewine (made from pressing grapes that have frozen on the vine) from Canada might be a relatively inexpensive way of tackling this dish. Other than that, you are looking at a monstrous price tag (with Trockenbeerenauslese from Germany) and, you have to ask, is the tart worth it?

Jelly Light, sweet German Riesling should not interfere too much with jelly. Hang on. Stop right where you are – are you seriously thinking about drinking wine with jelly?

Lemon meringue pie German Riesling would work well here, but make sure it's sweet but not too cloying. Recioto di Soave (Italian) or youthful sweet Loire Chenin Blanc (Coteaux du Layon) would also handle this citrus theme well. The good thing is that these styles of wine are relatively inexpensive and pretty easy to come by. *Tarte au citron*, my preferred choice in the lemon/pastry arena, is also stunning with Coteaux du Layon.

Meringue On their own, meringues are virtually tasteless and often a bit dusty, so if served with fruit (*pavlova*), it is the fruit that you need to worry about – see 'Fruit'.

Mince pies I generally follow the Christmas pud/Christmas cake lead of rich, sweet Madeira, youthful tawny port and blindingly brilliant Australian liqueur Muscats. It will save you another trip to the shops and all of these brews are big enough to wrestle with a four star brandy butter.

Pastries Belonging in the same school as tarts and cakes, I am not really convinced you need a wine recommendation for this family of buns and so on. Are you really going to crack open a bottle of wine for a *pain au chocolat*? If you are in the mood though, then don't let me stop you – Coteaux du Layon, Muscat de Beaumes-de-Venise, Saussignac and Monbazillac are France's best efforts. Botrytised Riesling from Australia and New Zealand, or sweet Muscat from California might also work well. Otherwise, try a German Spätlese Riesling but remember to keep the price down – and wait for midday!

Peach melba Botrytised Riesling does the peachy thing well, as you should be able to detect peach notes in the wine – head Down

Under or to Germany. Alternatively, a late-picked Viognier from the Rhône would be stunning, but they are hard to come by and mightily dear. If all else fails, grab a bottle of Sauternes, as it is the most multi-talented of all sweet wines.

Pecan pie A great dish which craves the company of Australian wines. Not sure why but this is exactly the right fit and you should search for a liqueur Muscat of Tokay. If this sounds like a little too much globe-trotting, stick with a posh Malmsey Madeira.

Pineapple upside-down pudding This deserves a mention as one of the classic and most irresistible menu items of all time. The caramel and pineapple team up to form a supremely exotic partnership and smart Sauternes would give a real result here. If you are keeping an eye on expenses, then Australian botrytised Semillon would also work wonders.

Plum crumble Of the crumble family, plum is up there with blackberry and apple (essential Jukesy fodder) as one of the mightiest. A degree of concentrated sweetness is needed here, so head off to Canada for decadent Riesling Icewines, Hungary for sexy Tokaji, or Italy for heroic Vin Santo.

Rhubarb crumble A relative lightweight next to the plum crum, rhubarb crumble takes it easy on the wine front. Exotically sweet Riesling from just about anywhere has rhubarby notes on the nose and palate, so this is the one and only grape to follow with rhubarb–based puddings (including *fool*, *compote* and *ice cream*).

Rice pudding Still nothing to add since last year's lack of note! I haven't eaten rice pudding since school, and don't intend to.

Rum baba By the very nature of the beast, a rum baba has a bit of a kick to it. Underneath the mild, genial exterior, a sweet-wine-thumping freak is itching to get out. Rum baba is the Hannibal Lecter of the pudding world and you have to go for a fortified wine to stand a chance of survival. Our SWAT team are tawny port, Bual or Malmsey Madeira and liqueur Muscat – night sights on… go get 'em boys.

Sorbet see 'Ice cream'.

Steamed puddings I am a devout fan of steamed puddings. The greatest syrupy, toffeed, old-fashioned ones (*spotted dick*, *treacle sponge* and *suet pudding* included) deserve the most regal sweet wines. I don't care that suet is a beastly ingredient and that these recipes don't involve any tricky cooking techniques. To me they are culinary utopia. All of these wines have been mentioned before but, they all do the business so here we go – top-flight botrytised Semillon (from anywhere), decadent Madeira, Tokaji (spend up by as many puttonyos as you can afford), Vin Santo (see the Gazetteer) and liqueur Muscat (from any one of the top Victorian or South Australian specialists in Australia).

Strawberries Top quality strawberries love Asti and Moscato d'Asti (Italy), demi-sec Champagne and Clairette de Die (Rhône, France). These are all fizzy or frothy, with the faintest touch of grapey sweetness.

Tarte au citron see 'Lemon meringue pie'.

Tarte tatin This is another of the greatest dishes of all time. I haven't put it into the apple section, and not because these days tatin is made with pear and all manner of other fruit (and savoury ingredients), but because the tatin method of cooking is the influencing factor. The rich, toffee/caramel gooeyness is what preoccupies the palate and, for that reason, honeyed Loire sweeties like Coteaux du Layon are right on the button. New World botrytised Semillons would be great, as well, and Sauternes would be a real treat.

Tiramisù A strangely unappetising dish, in my opinion, as coffee, mascarpone, chocolate and brandy are frighteningly odd bedfellows. If you must eat this sickly dish, stay accurate with Vin Santo (to knock out the flavour) or Marsala (to knock you out).

Treacle tart Treacle tart, particularly if you have included lemon zest in the recipe, is not as stodgy as you might expect. You could try Sauternes but, if in any doubt, Hungarian Tokaji, Vin Santo or youthful liqueur Muscat would probably be safest.

Trifle The grand old English creation adorning vicarage sideboards up and down the country, must be delighted to have so many options on the wine front. German Riesling Beerenauslese is my top choice but any sweet Riesling would be lovely. Likewise, Sauternes and the family of worldwide sweet Semillons all love this dish. If you are going to pour in a bit of booze (sherry is traditionally used), a good quality cream sherry is probably best. Whatever you choose, I'll have a glass of pud wine please and politely refuse the trifle.

Zabaglione Passito di Pantelleria, from an island off Sicily, is the only wine to accompany this creamy concoction – unless the Marsala you use in the recipe is of sufficient drinking quality. If it is, then you can cover two bases with one wine – and that must be the epitome of food and wine matching.

CHEESE

The old 'red-wine-with-cheese' adage is downright wrong. When pondering which wine to drink, keep an open mind as, surprisingly, almost anything goes – white, red, sweet, dry and fortified. Try to keep your cheese board simple to limit the number of flavours and, therefore, wines needed – and watch out for chutney as its pungent flavour tends to trip wines up. I have listed the main categories of cheese and mentioned, within each, some of my favourite examples.

Fresh cheese (*Cream cheese, feta, ricotta* and *mozzarella*) These usually pop up in salads or simple cooking, and their flavours are not dominant, so drink what you fancy. Whites would be best and make sure they have some cleansing acidity on board.

Natural rind cheese (*Goats' cheese – Crottin de Chavignol, Sainte-Maure de Touraine, Saint-Marcellin* and *Selles-sur-Cher*) Sauvignon Blanc from the Loire Valley in France is the benchmark with goats' cheese, and the stunning wines from Sancerre are the pick of the crop (Chavignol is one of the finest wine villages in Sancerre and the home of the famous Crottin de Chavignol cheeses). If you're caught short, though, any dry, fresh, unoaked white would be OK. If you feel like drinking red, then Loire Cabernet Franc or Gamay work perfectly well.

Soft white cheese (*Camembert, Brie de Meaux, Pavé d'Affinois, Chaource, Bonchester, Pencarreg, Explorateur, Boursault, Gratte-Paille* and *Brillat-Savarin*) Once again, Sauvignon Blanc works terrifically well here. Although, if you want more palate 'oomph', head to Marlborough in New Zealand, Elim in South Africa or Adelaide Hills in Australia. Remember that the richer the cheese, the bigger the white, so Chardonnay can be considered, too. For reds try Pinot Noir (either red Sancerre or lighter red Burgundies), fresh young Syrah/Shiraz from the Rhône or McLaren Vale in Oz, and rosé Champagne. Gratte-Paille and Brillat-Savarin traditionally go well with youthful, inexpensive claret – stick to my favoured wines in the Gazetteer section or Top 250.

Washed rind cheese Milder examples like *Chaumes*, *Port Salut* and *Milleens* need nothing more than dry, fruity reds – light Loire examples, or Bordeaux or New World Merlots. Smellier cheeses, including *Epoisses*, *Chambertin* and *Langres*, really enjoy white Burgundy (from Chablis in the north all of the way down to Mâcon in the south), Alsace Riesling or Tokay-Pinot Gris, and other controlled (i.e. not too oaky) Chardonnays from further afield. *Munster* loves Alsatian Gewürztraminer and *Vacherin Mont d'Or* loves red Burgundy, Beaujolais and lighter red Rhônes.

Semi-soft cheese This covers a huge selection of cheese. Try the following combinations: *Livarot* – Alsatian Tokay Pinot-Gris; *Maroilles* – Roussanne or Marsanne from the Rhône; *Pont-l'Evêque* – Viognier, also from the Rhône; *Raclette* – (assuming you are reading this halfway up a mountain in the Alps, you lucky thing) anything from the Savoie region, red or white; *Gubbeen* – Pinot Blanc or Sylvaner from Alsace; *Edam* – whatever, it's not fussy (light whites and reds); *Morbier* – Rhône whites; *Fontina* – light, Alpine Gamay or Valpolicella; *Reblochon* – this outstanding cheese likes much richer Gamay (smart Cru Beaujolais) and also red Burgundy; *Saint-Nectaire* – another heroic cheese, particularly the wild, farmhouse version, likes the same again, plus meaty red Côtes-du-Rhônes; *Tomme de Savoie* – Rhône whites or lighter reds; *Bel Paese* and *Taleggio* – Lombardy whites such as Lugana and reds like Dolcetto and Franciacorta.

Hard cheese The largest category of all, ranging from mild, via medium and strong, to extra-strong cheeses. As a starting point get an idea of the strength and age of your chosen cheese (a small taste in the shop is recommended) and this will help your wine selection. Cheeses in this group are, among others – *Cheddar, Gruyère, Cheshire, Parmigiano-Reggiano, Pecorino, Cornish Yarg, Double Gloucester, Lancashire, Caerphilly, Gouda, Beaufort, Manchego, Cantal, Etorki, Comté, Emmenthal, Jarlsberg* and *Mimolette*. From wines for mild cheese all the way to wines for the extra strong: whites – Alsace Pinot Blanc, Chablis, Jurançon Sec, white Burgundy, white Rhônes, New World Semillons and, lastly, New World Chardonnays; reds – Loire reds, Chilean Merlot, Côtes-du-Rhône, spicy Italian reds like Primitivo, Old World Cabernet from Bordeaux or Margaret River (Australia), Shiraz from Frankland, Barossa Valley, McLaren Vale and Clare Valley (Australia), Vino Nobile di Montepulciano and Chianti (Italy), and Zinfandel (California); fortified – port (tawny, LBV and vintage), Madeira, Banyuls and Maury (both from France), and old oloroso sherries.

Blue cheese For *Stilton* look no further than rich, nutty Madeira, tawny port, LBV or vintage port; *Roquefort* and *Fourme d'Ambert*, in contrast, prefer sweet Sauternes, Monbazillac or Saussignac; *Dolcelatte* is a bit of a lightweight and, because of its unusual sweet flavour and texture, I leave it alone (can you tell I can't bear it?); *Gorgonzola* likes Amarone della Valpolicella; *Chashel Blue* needs sweet whites; and *Beenleigh Blue*, on account of its birth nation, needs a pint of authentic, lumpy, hazy scrumpy cider (always end on a rum note!).

GAZETTEER

GRAPE VARIETIES

Before I kick off with the hot list of my favourite wineries in the world, I have compiled a short Albariño-Zinfandel of the most important white and red grape varieties you will come across in the course of drinking through my Top 250. These tasting notes should give you an idea of some of the flavours you will find in the wines.

WHITES

Albariño/Alvarinho (Al-ba-reen-yo/Al-va-reen-yo)

A good example can have a peachy aroma like Viognier, and a floral, spicy palate like Riesling. They always have a bone-dry, refreshing finish, often with a touch of spritz.

Aligoté (Al-ee-got-ay)

Aligoté produces dry, lean apéritif styles of wine designed for drinking within the first year of release.

Chardonnay (Shar-dun-ay)

Ranging in style from fairly colourless, neutral and characterless to wildly exotic, rich and golden – you can detect honey, butter, freshly baked patisserie, hazelnuts, vanilla, butterscotch, orange blossom and fresh meadow flowers in full-on Chardonnays.

Chenin Blanc (Sh-nan Blon)

Chenin is an underrated grape that makes clean, zippy, dry, apéritif wines, medium-dry, food-friendly styles and rich, honeyed, succulent peach-flavoured sweeties, dripping in unctuous, mouth-filling richness.

Gewürztraminer (Guh-vurz-tram-inner)

'Gewürz' has the most distinctive aroma of any grape variety. Pungent lychee, spice and rose petal cavort on the nose, and are usually accompanied by oiliness on the palate and a long, ripe finish. It also has the unusual knack of often smelling sweet but tasting dry.

Manseng (Man-seng)

Both Gros and Petit Manseng wines have a complex nose of quince, peach and lemon curd and a citrusy, floral palate accompanied by a shockingly firm, crisp finish. Although pretty rare, they are also used to make celestial sweet wines with juicy finishes.

Marsanne (Marce-ann)

Plump, rich, vaguely floral, peachy and always oily, Marsanne makes rather hefty, foody wines and likes to be blended with the more elegant grape Roussanne.

Muscat (Mus-cat)

Muscat wines vary from the lightest, fizziest soda-siphon of grapey juice, to the deepest, darkest, headiest liqueur that looks like a rugby player's liniment. Muscat is the only grape variety that in its simplest form actually smells and tastes 'grapey'.

Pinot Blanc/Pinot Bianco (Pee-no Blon/Pee-no Bee-an-cko)

Almost all made worldwide is unoaked, dry and relatively inexpensive, and tastes vaguely appley, creamy and nutty.
Most is dull but every now and again a delicious one comes along.

Riesling (Rees-ling)

One of the truly great white varieties, Riesling produces a vast array of wine styles, from bone-dry apéritifs, through structured, foody beauties, via long-lived, complex and off-dry stunners, and ending up at heart-achingly beautiful sweeties. Rhubarb, petrol, honey, honeysuckle and spice are there in varying degrees throughout this cornucopia of guises.

Roussanne (Roo-sann)

Generally lean, leggy and hauntingly aromatic with hints of apricot and honey. When on top form, Roussanne takes well to oak barrels and can provide a welcome chang for Chardonnay drinkers.

Sauvignon Blanc (So-veen-yon Blon)

'Sauv' Blanc is an up-front, brazen, aromatic, happy-go-lucky style, with an asparagus and elderflower scent, and refreshing, zesty, dry, citrusy fruit. Sauvignon is the definitive apéritif grape variety.

Sémillon (Sem-ee-yon)

The dominant aromas in dry Sémillon are honey and lime juice, and sometimes creamy vanilla and toasty oak elements creep in, depending on the style. But Sémillon also makes incredible, unctuous sweet wines, tasting of tropical fruit, honey, honey and more honey.

Tokay-Pinot Gris/Pinot Gris/Pinot Grigio (Tock-eye Pee-no Gree/Pee-no Gree/Pee-no Gridge-ee-oh)

The flavour of Tokay-Pinot Gris is somewhere between that of Pinot Blanc and Gewürztraminer. The distinctive nose of this grape is one of spice, fruit and honey. It does not have the rose-petal, perfumed element of Gewürz, and tends to be drier, like Pinot Blanc. Italy's Pinot Grigio is more akin to Aligoté, as it usually makes a light, spritzy, dry, apéritif style of wine.

Viognier (Vee-yon-yay)

In the best examples, Viognier offers a mind-blowing perfume of peach kernels, wild honey and apricot blossom, followed by an ample, curvaceous body with plenty of charm and a lingering, dry aftertaste.

REDS

Cabernet Franc (Cab-er-nay Fronk)

Often used in a blend with Cabernet Sauvignon and Merlot, Cabernet Franc lends an aromatic dimension to a red wine. It has firm acidity, oodles of black fruit flavours and usually brings violets and green, leafy notes to the nose.

Cabernet Sauvignon (Cab-er-nay So-veen-yon)

Age-worthy Cabernet Sauvignon forms the backbone of many sturdy, lusty reds. Its hallmarks are deep colour, blackcurrant flavour, with occasional cigar-box or cedarwood notes and, when on top form, a smooth, velvety, dark-chocolate texture and flavour.

Gamay (Ga-may)

Gamay is a jolly fellow, that makes underrated, early-drinking wines ranging in taste from chillable, frivolous, summery, strawberry juice concoctions to wintry, foody, black cherry and pepper styles.

Grenache/Garnacha (Gre-nash/Gar-natch-ah)

Grenache is usually blended – with Syrah (Shiraz) among others. It is a meaty, earthy, red- and black-fruit-drenched variety, often with high-ish alcohol and a garnet hue. It sometimes picks up a wild herbal scent not dissimilar to aromatic pipe smoke.

Malbec (Mal-beck)

This brutish grape is inky black in colour and loaded with macerated black fruit flavours and earthy spice, often enhanced by a dollop of well-seasoned oak. Malbec is one of the biggest, brawniest red varieties on the block. Also known as Cot in Cahors.

Merlot (Mer-low)

Merlot is a juicy grape, with supple, smooth, silky, blackberry, plum, red wine gum and fruitcake flavours. It happily flies solo but loves the company of Cabernet Sauvignon in a blend. As Merlot is usually oak aged, the fruit flavours are often accompanied by a touch of sweet wood-smoke barrel nuances.

Mourvèdre/Monastrell/Mataro (More-veh-dr/Mon-ah-strell/Mat-are-oh)

This rich, plum- and damson-flavoured variety is often made into powerful, earthy, long-lived wines. It is not the most charming variety in its youth, but ages gracefully, picking up more complex aromas and flavours along the way. It also likes to be blended with Grenache and Syrah.

Nebbiolo (Neb-ee-olo)

A tough grape that often needs five years in the bottle to soften to drinkability. A great Nebbiolo can conjure up intense plummy flavours with leathery, spicy, gamey overtones and a firm, dry finish.

Pinotage (Pee-no-tahge)

Pinotage is an earthy, spicy, deeply coloured grape with tobacco and plums on the nose, crushed blackberry fruit on the palate and a hearty, full, savoury finish. A speciality of South Africa.

Pinot Noir (Pee-no Nw-ar)

When on form, the Pinot Noir nose is often reminiscent of wild strawberries, violets and redcurrants, with a black cherry flavour on the palate. There can be a degree of oakiness apparent, depending on the style. As these wines age, they may take on a slightly farmyardy character as the colour fades from dark to pale brick red.

Sangiovese (San-gee-o-vay-zee)

This grape has red and black fruit flavours (mulberry, cherry, plum, blackcurrant and cranberry) on the nose with a whiff of fresh-cut herbs and leather for good measure. Famous for making Chianti, there is usually an oaky element tucked into the wine, and it always has an acidic kick on the finish.

Syrah/Shiraz (Sirrah/Shirraz)

Syrah invokes explosive blackberry and ground-pepper aromas with vanilla, smoke and charred-oak nuances. In the New World, big, inky-black Shiraz (the Syrah synonym) has high alcohol and a mouth-filling prune, chocolate, raisin and spice palate.

Tempranillo (Temp-ra-nee-yo)

Ranging in flavour from vanilla and strawberry early-drinking styles, to dark, brooding, black cherry reds, Tempranillo is Spain's noblest red grape, and the main variety in Rioja and countless other noble Spanish wines.

Zinfandel (Zin-fan-dell)

'Zin' tastes like a flavour collision between turbo-charged blackberries and plums, a handful of vanilla pods and a fully stocked spice rack. These wines generally have luxurious, mouth-filling texture and often pretty scary alcohol.

WINE REGIONS OF THE WORLD

In this crucial chapter I have taken my lifetime's tasting notes and whittled them down to the very best bodegas, châteaux, domaines, estates, tenutas and wineries. This year, as I have tasted so many wines, it took me an age to update and overhaul this roll call of stunning wine producers. Every entry has had to fight for its place in this elite list, and this year it's the biggest yet – a good sign that more people are making better wine than ever before.

If a favourite winery of yours is missing, it is either because I haven't tasted their wines yet or, sadly, they have not quite made the cut. Please do drop me a line if you have a hot tip (see address on page +++) and I will track down the wines and have a go for next year's edition. Every year I start off with a huge number of estates and then I prune them down ruthlessly to a more manageable list of only epic wineries. I avoid any that churn out so-so, average wines and also those who have made one-hit-wonder wines, in favour of the top quality, talent-rich, hard-working estates whose wines have set my palate alight with wonder and enthusiasm. These are the producers you can rely on day in, day out, when you are shopping for home drinking, eating out in a restaurant, travelling the globe on business or holiday, or buying a gift for a wine-savvy pal.

Occasionally you'll spot a producer or winery whose name is in bold. These are specially selected estates that are truly outstanding and every wine in their entire portfolio is first class. If a producer is both in bold and has a £, it means that its wines are on the expensive side (£25 plus). These plutonium-plated names are the money-no-object wines, for those of you with a no-upper-limit mentality. This doesn't mean that every wine they make is out of reach – far from it. Their flagship wine may be dizzily dear, but their other labels may still be brilliant and significantly cheaper, so do take note. The bold estates without a **£** make more affordable wines (somewhere between £5 to £25), so keep an eye out for them – this is where I do virtually all of my everyday drinking.

AUSTRALIA

I have been to Australia three times in the last year and on each occasion I was amazed at the breadth, quality and variety of wines on offer. There is a drive and determination about Australian winemakers that is both invigorating and, at times, unnerving. They are continually striving to make better and better wines – the passion and fervour with which they attack this target is mesmerising. I don't see this hunger for improvement and development anywhere else in the world. Cooler climate wines are emerging with finesse and elegance, and the big, overblown, oaky Chardonnays of the past seem like a hangover that is fading wonderfully away. Big, porty Barossa Valley reds are even fine-tuning and getting fitter. Fizz is finding its feet and aromatic wines are nothing short of stunning. You can now drink world class Cabernet, Shiraz, Chardonnay and Riesling at under a tenner from this winemaking utopia. There has been a recent wave of Aussie-knocking in the wine press and presumably this is because they are number one and so they're a soft target. The most successful category in the UK market, driven by a handful of massive brands, must be worth a dig or two, surely? It is always easy to take a pop at large companies but if you look at the average quality of, say, Jacob's Creek or Hardy's entry level ranges, you would be hard pushed to find better quality–price ratio wines anywhere else in the world.

Australia has a new target in its export armoury – the USA is just about to overtake the UK as the number one market for Australian wines worldwide. Their average retail price is much higher than ours, as supermarket deals fuel the majority of our Aussie buying. This must change – we should all trade up immediately to seven–ten pound wines. This is where the true quality is found and where the UK wine drinker should be concentrating. It is important for the UK to be offered the best wines in the Aussie portfolio because, when America starts to ramp up its sales, there is a danger that we'll miss out. I have already heard more than one Australian wine company MD talking about pulling out some of their lines from the UK, as the buyers and customers don't seem to want to spend more and the Americans can't get enough.

This would be a great shame. We, arguably, made the market in the first place and our European tastes have helped to fashion the 'new' Australian wine scene. Now that the Australian wine industry is way past its adolescent stage and is starting to mature at an alarming rate, we must continue to surf this wave of stunning wine. I am pushing as hard as I can to spread the word about the gems I have found down under. Please use this Gazetteer to further your wine knowledge and palate development – there is an entire world of wine to be discovered in Australia and this is the definitive list. These wineries will not let you down.

WESTERN AUSTRALIA
The top producers are – **Alkoomi**, Amberley, Ashbrook Estate, **Brookland Valley**, **Cape Mentelle**, **Cullen**, **Devil's Lair**, Evans & Tate, Ferngrove, **Frankland Estate**, **Houghton**, Howard Park, **Juniper Estate**, **Leeuwin Estate**, Millbrook, **Moss Wood**, Picardy, **Pierro**, Plantagenet, **Suckfizzle Augusta (Stella Bella)**, **Vasse Felix**, Voyager, West Cape Howe, Wignalls and Xanadu.

SOUTH AUSTRALIA
The top producers in each region are:
Clare Valley – Cardinham, Clos Clare, Crabtree, Eldredge, **Grosset**,

Jeanneret, Jim Barry, **Kilikanoon**, Knappstein, **Leasingham**, **Mitchell**, **Mount Horrocks**, Neagles Rock, O'Leary Walker, Pauletts, **Petaluma**, **Pikes**, Reilly's, Sevenhill, Skillogalee, Taylors (Wakefield in the UK), **Tim Adams** and **Wendouree £**.

Barossa Valley – Barossa Velley Estate, Burge Family Winemakers, Charles Cimicky, **Charlie Melton**, Craneford, Elderton, **Fox Gordon**, **Glaetzer**, Grant Burge, **Greenock Creek**, **Haan**, **Heritage**, Kaesler, **Orlando (Jacobs Creek)**, Penfolds, **Peter Lehmann**, Rockford, **St Hallett**, Seppelt, Thorn-Clarke, Tin Shed, **Torbreck £**, Turkey Flat, **Two Hands**, Two Fold, **Veritas**, **Willows**, Wolf Blass and **Yalumba**.

Adelaide Hills – Ashton Hills, **Barratt**, Chain of Ponds, **Geoff Weaver**, **The Lane**, Lenswood Vineyards, Nepenthe, **Petaluma**, **Shaw & Smith** and **Starve Dog Lane**.

Eden Valley – Henschke, Irvine, **Mesh** and **Pewsey Vale**.

Coonawarra – **Balnaves**, Bowen, **Brand**s, Highbank, **Hollick**, Jamieson's Run, **Katnook**, Ladbroke Grove, Leconfield, Lindemans, **Majella**, **Parker**, **Penley**, **Redman** and Wynns.

McLaren Vale – d'Arenberg, Chalk Hill, **Chapel Hill**, Clarendon Hills, Coriole, **Fox Creek**, Geoff Merrill, **Hardy's**, Hastwell & Lightfoot, Kangarilla Road, **Kay Brothers Amery**, Koltz, **Linda Domas**, **Mitolo**, Noon, Pertaringa, Pirramimma, Richard Hamilton, Rosemount (McLaren Vale), Simon Hackett, Tatachilla, **Wirra Wirra** and Woodstock.

Adelaide Plains – Primo Estate.

Miscellaneous – **Heartland** (Limestone Coast/Langhorne Creek) and Zonte's Footsteps (Langhorne Creek).

NEW SOUTH WALES

The top producers are – Allandale, Arrowfield, Bimbadgen, Bloodwood, **De Bortoli (Riverina)**, **Brokenwood**, **Clonakilla**, Keith Tulloch, **Lake's Folly**, Lindemans, **Logan Wines**,

McWilliam's/Mount Pleasant, Meerea Park, Rosemount (Hunter Valley), Rothbury Estate, Simon Gilbert, Tower Estate and Tyrrell's.

VICTORIA
The top producers are – Baileys, Bannockburn, Bass Phillip, Battely, Best's Great Western, Bindi, Bleasdale, De Bortoli (Yarra Valley), Brown Brothers, Campbells, Chambers Rosewood, Cobaw Ridge, Coldstream Hills, Craiglee, Crawford River, Curlewis, Dalwhinnie, David Traeger, Diamond Valley Vineyards, Domaine Chandon (Green Point), Domaine Epis, Dromana, Gembrook Hill, Giaconda £, Heathcote Winery, Jasper Hill, Kooyong, McPherson, Main Ridge, Métier Wines, Mitchelton, Morris, Mount Ida, Mount Langi Ghiran, Mount Mary, Redbank, Savaterre, Scorpo, Scotchmans Hill, Seppelt Great Western, Sorrenberg, Stonier, Tahbilk, Tallarook, Taltarni, Virgin Hills, Wild Duck Creek, Yarra Burn, Yarra Yering, Yeringberg and Yering Station.

TASMANIA
The top producers are – Chatto, Clover Hill, Craigow, Domaine A (Stoney Vineyard), Elsewhere, Freycinet, Grey Sands, Jansz, No Regrets, Pipers Brook (Ninth Island), Providence, Spring Vale, Stefano Lubiana, Tamar Ridge and Touchwood.

AUSTRIA
In contrast to Australia, Austria is flavour of the month in the UK press. The Austrians cannot do a single thing wrong and we are being blessed with waves of funky Riesling and Grüner Veltliner, shipped into the UK in meaningful quantities for the first time. There are only a couple of problems – distribution is poor and prices are terrifying.

If it weren't for these two hitches, we would all be queuing up for their delicious wines. Sadly this will not happen overnight.

The top producers are – Alois Kracher, **Bründlmayer**, **Emmerich Knoll**, **Feiler-Artinger**, **Franz Hirtzberger**, Fred Loimer, Freie Weingärtner Wachau, Graf Hardegg, G & H Heinrich, Helmut Lang, Hiedler, Höpler, Josef Pöckl, Jurtschitsch, **Manfred Tement**, Paul Achs, **F.X. Pichler**, Polz, **Prager**, Salomon, Schloss Gobelsburg, Sepp Moser, Velich, Wieninger, Willi Opitz and Dr Wolfgang Unger.

CANADA

It seems that Canadian wines have stalled in the UK. Nothing at all has happened over the last year. I drink all of my Canadian wines in Canada, which is where I reckon you'll have to go to use this list of fantastic producers.

The best estates are – **Burrowing Owl**, **Cave Springs**, **Château des Charmes**, Daniel Lenko, Henry of Pelham, **Inniskillin**, **Mission Hill**, Paradise Ranch, Quails' Gate, Southbrook Farms, Sumac Ridge and Tinhorn Creek.

CHILE AND ARGENTINA

Things are starting to rumble down in South America. Chile and Argentina are finally girding their collective loins and marshalling a few more serious bottles in our direction. The UK diet of chunky, meaty reds and fresh, simple, vibrant whites was starting to get a little samey, and at last there are some more intriguing wines emerging from this fertile part of the world. Chile's list of estates, in particular, has seen some augmentation and the Top 250 reflects this newfound confidence and pizzazz.

The best Chilean estates are – **Alvaro Espinoza**, **Casa Lapostolle**, **Concha y Toro**, **Cousiño Macul**, J & F Lurton, **Michel Laroche & Jorge Coderch**, **Miguel Torres**, San Pedro, Valdivieso, **Veramonte**,

Viña Errázuriz, **Viña Haras de Pirque**, Viña Leyda, **Viña Montes**, **Viña MontGras**, Viña Morandé, **Viña Pérez Cruz** and **Viñedos Organicos Emiliana**.

The best Argentinean estates are – Argento, **Bodega Noemía de Patagonia**, **Catena Zapata (Catena)**, **Familia Zuccardi (La Agricola)**, **Finca El Retiro**, **Norton**, **Santa Julia**, Terrazas, Valentin Bianchi and Weinert.

FRANCE
BORDEAUX

I realise that most decent red Bordeaux (clarets) fall into the tremblingly scary price bracket and they also usually need ten years under their belts to really start drinking, but there is no getting away from it – this is one of the most important wine regions in the world. When the châteaux get it right (and the weather is kind), the wines are hard to beat. I am brutally tough on this list each year, as I have no time for faddy fashionistas – I am only interested in rock-hard, stellar estates, whose wines are worth every penny. Bordeaux is the home to the majestic red grapes Cabernet Sauvignon, Merlot and Cabernet Franc. The percentages of each grape variety in the final blend vary from château to château, depending on the soil and the plantings. The wines will also have spent eighteen months or so maturing in smart oak barrels. This classic recipe is the model for red wines around the globe. *Bonne chance!*

RED WINES
THE LEFT BANK

Graves Bahans-Haut-Brion £, **Carmes-Haut-Brion**, Chantegrive, **Domaine de Chevalier**, de Fieuzal, Haut-Bailly, **Haut-Brion £**, **La Mission-Haut-Brion £**, **Pape-Clément**, Picque-Caillou and Smith-Haut-Lafitte.

Haut-Médoc and (Bas) Médoc Arnauld, Cambon la Pelouse, de Lamarque, Malescasse, Patache d'Aux, **Potensac**, Rollan de By, **Sociando-Mallet**, Tour du Haut-Moulin and Villegeorge.

Margaux d'Angludet, Brane-Cantenac, Cantemerle, **Durfort-Vivens**, Ferrière, d'Issan, La Lagune, **Margaux £**, **Palmer £**, Pavillon Rouge du Château Margaux and Rausan-Ségla.

Moulis and Listrac Chasse-Spleen, Clarke, Fourcas Loubaney and **Poujeaux**.

Pauillac Batailley, Les Forts de Latour, **Grand-Puy-Lacoste**, **Haut-Bages-Libéral**, Haut-Batailley, **Lafite-Rothschild £**, **Latour £**, **Lynch-Bages**, Mouton-Rothschild **£**, **Pichon-Longueville Baron £**, **Pichon-Longueville-Comtesse de Lalande £** and **Pontet-Canet**.

St-Estèphe Beau-Site, Le Boscq, **Calon-Ségur**, **Cos d'Estournel £**, Cos Labory, Haut-Marbuzet, La Haye, **Lafon-Rochet**, **Montrose £**, Les-Ormes-de-Pez, de Pez and Ségur de Cabanac.

St-Julien Clos du Marquis, **Ducru-Beaucaillou £**, **Gruaud-Larose**, Lagrange, Langoa-Barton, **Léoville-Barton £**, **Léoville-Las-Cases £**, **Léoville-Poyferré £**, St-Pierre and Talbot.

THE RIGHT BANK

Canon-Fronsac and Fronsac Canon-Moueix, **de Carles**, Fontenil, du Gaby, Hervé-Laroque, Mazeris, Moulin-Haut-Laroque and La Vieille-Cure.

Castillon d'Aiguilhe and Puyanché.

Côtes de Bourg and Blaye Haut-Sociando, **Roc des Cambes** and Tayac.

Lalande-de-Pomerol Bel-Air, Belles-Graves, La Fleur de Boüard and Laborde.

Pomerol Beauregard, Bon Pasteur, **Certan Marzelle**, Certan-de-May, **Clinet £**, Clos de Litanies, Clos du Clocher, Clos René, **La Conseillante £**, La Croix-St Georges, Domaine de l'Eglise, **l'Eglise-**

Clinet £, l'Enclos, **l'Evangile £**, La Fleur de Gay, La Fleur-Pétrus, Le Gay, Gazin, **Hosanna**, **Lafleur £**, Lafleur-Gazin, Latour à Pomerol, Petit Village, **Pétrus £**, Le Pin, **Trotanoy £** and Vieux-Château-Certan £. **St-Emilion** Angélus £, **L'Arrosée**, **Ausone £**, Beau-Séjour Bécot, Belair, Canon-La-Gaffelière £, Le Castelot, **Cheval Blanc £**, Clos Fourtet, Dassault, **La Dominique**, **Figeac**, Larmande, **Magdelaine**, Monbousquet, Tertre-Rôteboeuf £, La Tour-du-Pin-Figeac, **Troplong-Mondot £** and Valandraud.

DRY WHITE WINES

Carbonnieux, Clos Floridène, **Domaine de Chevalier £**, de Fieuzal, **Haut-Brion £**, Laville-Haut-Brion £, **Pavillon Blanc de Château Margaux**, **Smith-Haut-Lafitte** and La Tour Martillac.

SWEET WHITE WINES

Sauternes and Barsac d'Arche, Bastor-Lamontagne, Broustet, **Climens £**, **Coutet £**, Doisy-Daëne, Doisy-Dubroca, Doisy-Védrines, de Fargues, Filhot, Gilette, Guiraud, Les Justices, **Lafaurie-Peyraguey £**, de Malle, Nairac, Rabaud-Promis, **Raymond-Lafon £**, Rayne-Vigneau, **Rieussec £**, **Suduiraut £**, La Tour Blanche £ and d'Yquem £.

BURGUNDY

My favourite wine region is home to the most incredible Chardonnay and Pinot Noir in the world. I visit Burgundy several times a year – for work and for pleasure. I adore the wines, the food and the people. But, and this is very important, just because this is the most hallowed turf in the wine world, it doesn't mean that people don't make some dross here! Unless you arm yourself with this failsafe list of top domaines, you could very seriously (and expensively) lose your way. Burgundy is a veritable minefield of tiny vineyards and thousands of producers. Pick very carefully and use my vintage table at the back of this guide, too, and you will be fine. Everyone else in the wine world tries to reach the heights of Pinot and Chardonnay perfection that they achieve here in Burgundy. They can't – this soil and setting are unique. Some come close, but these vineyards are very special – you must visit and you'll see why. You will also find the zippy white grape Aligoté and much-derided red variety Gamay (Beaujolais), ably support the two aforementioned super-grapes. Stick to these and you can eat and drink without busting the bank, but only for lunch, mind you, as it's back to Pinot and Chardonnay for dinner! What follows is worth its weight in Grand Cru Pinot Noir – the ultimate list of Domaines. This will, I hope, unlock the code to the most enigmatic region of all.

CHABLIS
Chablis (white) **Billaud-Simon**, A & F Boudin, Daniel Dampt, des Genèves, Jean Durup, **Jean-Paul Droin**, **Laroche**, Laurent Tribut, Louis Michel, **Raveneau £**, **René & Vincent Dauvissat** and William Fèvre.
St-Bris-le-Vineux and **Chitry** (white) Jean-Hugues Goisot.

CÔTE DE NUITS
Marsannay-la-Côte and **Fixin** (mainly red) Bruno Clair, Charles Audoin, **Fougeray de Beauclair** and René Bouvier.
Gevrey-Chambertin (red) **Armand Rousseau**, Bernard Dugat-Py, **Claude Dugat**, **Denis Mortet**, Drouhin-Laroze, **Fourrier**, **Géantet-Pansiot**, **Joseph Roty** and **Sérafin**.
Morey-St-Denis (red) **Dujac**, Hubert Lignier, **des Lambrays**, **Ponsot** and **Virgile Lignier**.
Chambolle-Musigny & Vougeot (red) **Christian Clerget**, **Comte de Vogüé**, **Ghislaine Barthod**, Jacques-Frédéric Mugnier, Pierre

Bertheau, **G. Roumier** and de la Vougeraie.
Vosne-Romanée and **Flagey-Echézeaux** (red) **Anne Gros, Emanuel Rouget, Jean Grivot**, Lamarche, **Leroy £, Méo-Camuzet**, Mongeard-Mugneret, René Engel, **Robert Arnoux**, de la Romanée-Conti £ and Sylvain Cathiard.
Nuits-St-Georges (red) Alain Michelot, Bertrand Ambroise, J-C Boisset, Daniel Chopin-Groffier, Daniel Rion, **Dominique Laurent,** Faiveley, Jean Chauvenet, Jean-Jacques Confuron, Lécheneaut, **Nicolas Potel** and **Robert Chevillon.**

CÔTE DE BEAUNE
Ladoix (mainly red) Edmond Cornu.
Aloxe-Corton and **Ladoix-Serrigny** (mainly red) Michel Voarick.
Pernand-Vergelesses (red and white) **Bonneau du Martray (Corton-Charlemagne) £**, Dubreuil-Fontaine and Maurice Rollin.
Savigny-lès-Beaune (red and white) **Chandon de Briailles, Jean-Marc Pavelot** and Maurice Ecard.
Chorey-lès-Beaune (red) Germain and **Tollot-Beaut.**
Beaune (mainly red) Bouchard Père et Fils, A-F Gros & François Parent, Joseph Drouhin, **Louis Jadot** and Maison Champy.
Pommard (red) **Comte Armand,** de Courcel, **Jean-Marc Boillot** and Parent.
Volnay (red) Coste Caumartin, **Hubert de Montille,** Marquis d'Angerville, **Michel Lafarge** and Roblet-Monnot.
Monthelie (red and white) **Annick Parent** and Denis Boussey.
Auxey-Duresses (red and white) Claude Maréchal and Jean-Pierre Diconne.
St-Romain (mainly white) d'Auvenay and Christophe Buisson.
Meursault (white) **des Comtes Lafon £, Henri Germain,** Jean-François Coche-Dury £, Jean-Michel Gaunoux, **Jean-Philippe Fichet**, Marc Rougeot, Michel Tessier, **Patrick Javillier, Roulot** and

Vincent Bouzereau.

Puligny-Montrachet (white) Chartron & Trébuchet, **Domaine Leflaive £**, **Etienne Sauzet £**, **Louis Carillon**, Olivier Leflaive and Paul Pernot.

Chassagne-Montrachet (white) **Bernard Morey**, Blain-Gagnard, Fontaine-Gagnard, Gagnard-Delagrange, Guy Amiot, **Jean-Noël Gagnard**, **Marc Morey**, Michel Colin-Deléger, **Michel Niellon** and Ramonet £.

St-Aubin (red and white) Gérard Thomas, Henri Prudhon and Marc Colin.

Santenay (red and white) Vincent Girardin.

CÔTE CHALONNAISE
Rully (red and white) Eric de Suremain, de la Folie and Vincent Dureuil-Janthial.

Montagny (white) Stéphane Aladame.

Mercurey (red and white) Antonin Rodet, **Bruno Lorenzon**, Michel & Laurent Juillot and J. & F. Raquillet.

Givry (red and white) François Lumpp and Joblot.

MÂCONNAIS
Mâcon, **Pouilly-Fuissé**, **St-Véran** and **Viré-Clessé** (mainly white) **André Bonhomme**, **Château de Beauregard**, **Château Fuissé (Jean-Jacques Vincent)**, Daniel Barraud, **des Deux Roches**, Goyard, **Guillemot-Michel**, **Jean Thévenet**, **Michel Forest**, Robert-Denogent, Talmard and Verget (Guffens-Heynen).

BEAUJOLAIS
Producing mainly red, the most highly regarded sub-regions are the ten Cru Villages: Brouilly, Chénas, Chiroubles, Côte de Brouilly, Fleurie, Juliénas, Morgon, Moulin-à-Vent, Régnié and St-Amour.

The top producers are – Alain Passot, André Cologne, Aucoeur, Bernard Mélinand, **F & J Calot**, Champagnon, **Château de Pierreux**, **Coudert**, Georges Duboeuf (domaine-bottled wines only), **J.-L. Dutraive**, J.-F. Echallier (des Pins), Hélène & Denis Barbelet, Henry Fessy, Jacky Janodet, **Jean-Charles Pivot**, **Jean Foillard**, **Louis Jadot (Château des Jacques)**, **Marcel Lapierre**, Maurice Gaget, **Michel Chignard**, Pascal Granger, Patrick Brunet, **Paul Janin** and **Vissoux**.

CHAMPAGNE

I try not to put too many non-vintage Champagnes in my Top 250 as they tend to vary so much in flavour with bottle age and storage conditions. So use this list as a guide to the consistently best suppliers of NV and vintage Champagne. I have also included a stunning list of smaller houses for you to track down when you are on holiday in France or if you are eagled-eyed in the UK. They are all terrific value.

FAMOUS NAMES

Billecart-Salmon *NV* Brut Réserve, Brut Rosé, Blanc de Blancs and Demi-Sec. *Vintage* Blanc de Blancs, Le Clos Saint-Hilaire, Cuvée Nicolas-François Billecart, Elisabeth Salmon Rosé and Grande Cuvée.
Bollinger *NV* Special Cuvée. *Vintage* Grande Année, RD and Vieilles Vignes Françaises Blanc de Noirs.
Deutz *Vintage* Blanc de Blancs and Cuvée William Deutz.
Gosset *NV* Brut Excellence, Grande Réserve Brut and Grand Réserve Rosé. *Vintage* Célébris and Grande Millésime Brut.
Alfred Gratien *Vintage* Brut.
Charles Heidsieck *NV* Mise en Cave and Rosé. *Vintage* Brut Millésime.
Jacquesson *Vintage* Avize Grand Cru Blanc de Blancs, Dégorgement Tardive and Grand Vin Signature.
Krug £ *NV* Grande Cuvée. *Vintage* Vintage and Clos du Mesnil.

Laurent-Perrier *NV* Cuvée Rosé Brut, Grand Siècle 'La Cuvée' and Ultra Brut.

Moët & Chandon *Vintage* Brut Impérial and Cuvée Dom Pérignon Brut.

Pol Roger *NV* Brut 'White Foil'. *Vintage* Brut Chardonnay, Brut Rosé, Brut Vintage and Cuvée Sir Winston Churchill.

Louis Roederer *NV* Brut Premier. *Vintage* Blanc de Blancs, Brut Millésime, Brut Rosé, Cristal and Cristal Rosé.

Ruinart *Vintage* Dom Ruinart Blanc de Blancs and 'R' de Ruinart Brut.

Salon £ *Vintage* Blanc de Blancs.

Taittinger *NV* Brut Réserve. Vintage Comtes de Champagne Blanc de Blancs.

Alain Thiénot *Vintage* Brut and Grande Cuvée.

Veuve Clicquot *NV* Brut 'Yellow Label' and Demi-Sec. *Vintage* La Grande Dame Brut, La Grande Dame Rosé and Vintage Réserve.

SMALLER HOUSES
Albert Beerens, André Jacquart, Bertrand Robert, Château de Boursault, **Claude Carré**, **Delamotte**, Edouard Brun, Egly-Ouriet, **Fernand Thill**, Fleury, **Gatinois**, Gérard Dubois, J-M Gobillard, **D. Henriet-Bazin**, Jacques Selosse, **Larmandier-Bernier,** Leclerc Briant, Legras, **A. Margaine**, Le Mesnil, **Paul Déthune**, **Pertois-Moriset**, Pierre Gimonnet, Pierre Moncuit, **Pierre Vaudon**, **G. Tribaut** and **Vilmart**.

ALSACE
Alsace has had a run of wonderful vintages and now is the time to dive in and locate some of these celestial wines. They are all under-priced and over-performing, and they give us some of the best food-matching, apéritif-style, decadently sweet and casual-glugging

wines in the world. You will have to look to the smaller, independent wine merchants for most of these names as they are all fairly small producers. Grape varieties to seek out are Gewürztraminer, Riesling, Tokay-Pinot Gris, Muscat, Pinot Blanc and Sylvaner. It is worth avoiding the reds and fizzies!

The best producers are – Albert Boxler, Albert Mann, André Thomas, Bott-Geyl, Ernest Burn, Hugel, **Josmeyer**, **Marc Kreydenweiss**, **Marcel Deiss**, Mittnacht-Klack, **Ostertag**, Paul Blanck, Rolly Gassmann, Schlumberger, Schoffit, **Trimbach**, **Weinbach** and **Zind-Humbrecht**.

THE LOIRE VALLEY

This fragmented list of wines follows the Loire river inland from the Atlantic, picking out the greatest estates from the key areas in this elongated, inexpensive region. Sauvignon Blanc and Chenin Blanc are the main white grapes grown here. The Sauvignons are nearly always dry, whereas the Chenins can be fizzy, dry, medium-sweet or full-on sweeties. The majority of serious reds are made from Cabernet Franc, with Gamay and Pinot Noir stepping in for lighter styles.

Muscadet (white) Château de Chasseloir, Chéreau, Luc Choblet, de la Mortaine and **de la Quilla**.

Savennières (white) **des Baumard**, **Clos de la Coulée de Serrant** and La Roche-aux-Moines.

Coteaux du Layon, Coteaux de l'Aubance, Bonnezeaux and **Quarts de Chaume** (white sweeties) **des Baumard**, Château de Fesles, **Château Pierre-Bise**, Didier Richou, de la Roulierie and Vincent Lecointre.

Saumur (sparkling) Bouvet-Ladubay.

Saumur and **Saumur Champigny** (red and white) **du Hureau**, **Filliatreau**, Langlois-Château and **Nerleux**.

Chinon (mainly red) **Bernard Baudry**, **Charles Joguet**, Couly-Dutheil and **Desbourdes**.

St-Nicolas de Bourgueil (red) Jean-Paul Mabileau and Max & Lydie Cognard-Taluau.

Bourgueil (red) Joël Taluau, Lamé-Delille-Boucard, **de la Lande (Delaunay)** and **Pierre-Jacques Druet**.

Vouvray (white) Bourillon-Dorléans, **Gaston Huet** and Philippe Foreau.

Sauvignon de Touraine (white) **Alain Marcadet**.

Gamay de Touraine (red) Henry Marionnet.

Jasnières (white) Jean-Baptiste Pinon and Joël Gigou.

Cheverny (white) Salvard.

Sancerre (white, rosé and red) Alain Gueneau, **Alphonse Mellot**, André Dézat, **André Vatan**, Bailly-Reverdy, Christian Lauverjat, Cotat, Daulny, **Henri Bourgeois**, Henri Natter, Merlin-Cherrier, **Pascal & Nicolas Reverdy**, Philippe de Benoist, **Serge Laloue**, **Sylvain Bailly**, Vacheron and **Vincent Delaporte**.

Pouilly-Fumé (white) André Dézat (Domaine Thibault), Cedrick Bardin, Château du Nozet (de Ladoucette), **Château de Tracy**, **Didier Dagueneau**, Hervé Seguin, Jean-Claude Chatelain, **Michel Redde**, Serge Dagueneau and Tabordet.

Menetou-Salon (mainly white) de Chatenoy, **Henry Pellé** and **Jean Teiller**.

Quincy (white) **Jacques Rouzé**.

THE RHÔNE VALLEY

The Rhône is home to a cornucopia of great French wines. It makes some of the most spectacular reds and whites on the planet, while at the same time giving us amazing bargains. It is here that Syrah, Grenache and Mourvèdre rule the reds. Viognier commands the whites in the north, while Roussanne and Marsanne are in charge in the south. If you take the time to get to know this region well, you can drink very smart wine for very little outlay.

THE NORTHERN RHÔNE
FROM NORTH TO SOUTH

Côte Rôtie (red) Bernard Burgaud, Chapoutier, **Clusel-Roch £**, **E. Guigal (Château d'Ampuis) £**, Guy Bernard, **Jamet**, Jean-Michel Gerin, Marius Gentaz-Dervieux, **Pierre Gaillard**, René Rostaing, Yves Cuilleron and **Yves Gangloff £**.

Condrieu (white) **André Perret**, Christian Facchin, **François Villard £**, **Georges Vernay**, Louis Cheze, Robert Niero and **Yves Cuilleron £**.

St-Joseph (red and white) Bernard Faurie, Delas, **Jean-Louis Chave**, Jean-Louis Grippat and **Pierre Gonon**.

Hermitage (red and white) **Chapoutier £**, Delas, Grippat, **Jean-Louis Chave £**, Michel Ferraton, **Paul Jaboulet Aîné £**, Sorrel and Tardieu-Laurent £.

Crozes-Hermitage (mainly red) **Alain Graillot**, Albert Belle, du Colombier, Domaine Pochon, **Gilles Robin** and Olivier Dumaine.

Cornas (red) **Alain Voge**, **Auguste Clape**, Jean Lionnet, Noël Verset, **Robert Michel**, **Thierry Allemand** and **du Tunnel** (Stéphane Robert).

THE SOUTHERN RHÔNE

Côtes-du-Rhône and **-Villages** (red) **Brusset**, Château du Trignon, **Clos Petite Bellane**, Coudoulet de Beaucastel, **Domaine Gramenon**, E. Guigal, Marcel Richaud, Piaugier, Rayas (Fonsalette) and **Tardieu-Laurent**.

Lirac, Rasteau, Tavel and **Vacqueyras** (red) **Château des Tours**, Clos des Cazaux, des Espiers, **de la Mordorée**, La Soumade and **du Trapadis**.

Gigondas (red) Château du Trignon, Font-Sane, R. & J.-P. Meffre (Saint-Gayan), **Saint-Cosme** and Santa-Duc.

Châteauneuf-du-Pape (red and white) **de Beaucastel**, Les Cailloux, Chapoutier, de la Charbonnière, **Charvin**, **Clos du Caillou**, Clos des

Papes, **de Ferrand**, Fortia, **de la Janasse**, de Marcoux, **de la Mordorée**, du Pegaü, **Rayas**, Versino and Le Vieux Donjon. **Muscat de Beaumes-de-Venise** (sweet white) Chapoutier, **Domaine de Durban** and Paul Jaboulet Aîné.

FRENCH COUNTRY
This may be the most jumpy section in the book to read (Italy is a close second), but take it slowly and you'll find some amazing, handcrafted wines that don't cost a bomb and deliver amazing amounts of flavour. 'French Country' is an old-fashioned term really, as it just means 'the rest of France's southerly wine regions'. Years ago this would be a jumbled mass of funky estates, some of which made passable wines, and others that bumbled along selling their bottles to locals. How things have changed. There is nothing other than exceptionally professional, committed producers in this list, making some of the most remarkable wines in the whole of France.

SOUTHWEST FRANCE
Bergerac (red and white) de la Jaubertie, **Moulin des Dames** and **La Tour des Gendres**.
Cahors (reds) **du Cédre**, **Clos Triguedina**, Lagrezette and **Les Laquets**.
Jurançon (dry and sweet whites) Bellegarde, **Cauhapé**, Charles Hours, Clos Guirouilh, Clos Lapeyre, Clos Uroulat and **de Lahargue**.
Madiran (reds) d'Aydie, **Alain Brumont (Bouscassé and Montus)** and Domaine Pichard.
Monbazillac (sweet white) de l'Ancienne Cure, la Borderie and **Tirecul La Gravière**.
Saussignac (sweet white) Château Richard and Clos d'Yvigne.

LANGUEDOC-ROUSSILLON
Banyuls (fortified) and **Collioure** (red) **de la Casa Blanca**, Château

de Jau, **du Mas Blanc** and de la Rectoire.
La Clape (red and white) Camplazens, **Château de Capitoul**, de l'Hospitalet and Pech-Redon.
Corbières (mainly red) La Baronne, des Chandelles, Château les Palais, Château Vaugélas, **Etang des Colombes**, de Lastours, **Meunier St. Louis** and Pech-Latt.
Costières de Nîmes (red, white and rosé) **des Aveylans**, de Belle-Coste, Grande-Cassagne, **Mourgues-du-Grès** and **de Nages**.
Coteaux du Languedoc (red and white) Abbaye de Valmagne, d'Aupilhac, Les Aurelles, **Mas d'Azelon**, **Mas de Chimères**, Font Caude, **Mas Jullien**, **Mas Mortiès**, **Peyre Rose**, Puech-Haut, **Roc d'Anglade** and La Sauvagéonne.
Faugères (mainly red) **Alquier**, de Ciffre and **des Estanilles**.
Minervois (red and white) **Borie de Maurel**, Le Cazal, **Clos Centeilles**, Fabas, de Gourgazaud, **Lignon** and d'Oupia.
Pic St-Loup (mainly red) Cazeneuve, Ermitage du Pic St-Loup, **de l'Hortus**, **de Lascaux**, Lascours and Mas Bruguière.
St-Chinian (red and white) Canet-Valette, Cazal-Viel, Coujan, des Jougla and Mas Champart.

Miscellaneous estates of excellence (and where to find them):
de l'Aigle – Limoux; **Bégude** – Limoux; **Cazes** – Rivesaltes; **Clos de Fées** – Côtes de Roussillon-Villages; **Domaine de Baruel** – Cévennes; **Domaine Gardiés** – Côtes de Roussillon-Villages; **Domaine des Ravanès** – Coteaux de Murveil; **Elian da Ros** – Côtes du Marmandais; **de la Granges des Pères** – l'Hérault; **Mas Amiel** – Maury; **Mas de Daumas Gassac** – l'Hérault.

PROVENCE
Bandol (red) **de la Bégude**, Château Jean-Pierre Gaussen, **Lafran-Veyrolles**, La Laidière, Mas de la Rouvière, Maubernard, de

Pibarnon, **Pradeaux**, **Ray-Jane**, Souviou, **La Suffrène** and **Tempier**.
Les Baux-de-Provence (mainly red) Hauvette, des Terres Blanches
and **de Trévallon £**.
Bellet (red, white and rosé) Château de Crémat.
Cassis (mainly white) Clos Ste-Madeleine.
Côtes de Provence (mainly red) **de la Courtade**, Gavoty, de
Rimauresq and de St-Baillon.
Palette (red, white and rosé) **Château Simone**.

GERMANY

Germany is making better wines than ever before. The new,
drier styles of Riesling are simply spellbinding. The long-awaited
Riesling revolution is here – join in! What follows is the hit list of
some of the finest exponents of this grape variety on the planet.
All you have to do is find them and drink them.
The best producers are – **J.B. Becker**, Dr Bürklin-Wolf,
J.J. Cristoffel, **Daniel Vollenweider**, Dönnhoff, **Egon Müller**,
Fritz Haag, Koehler-Ruprecht, Künstler, **Josef Leitz**,
Langwerth von Simmern, H. & R. Lingenfelder, **Dr Loosen**,
Müller-Cattoir, **J.J. Prüm**, **Reichsgraf von Kesselstatt**, **Robert Weil**,
Schloss Lieser, Schloss Reinhartshausen, **Selbach-Oster**, von
Schubert-Maximin Grünhaus, Dr H. Thanisch, Weingut Kerpen
and Willi Schaefer

GREAT BRITAIN

After two of the greatest years on record (remember the weather
last summer!), we are starting to make some fantastic wines in
the UK. Even the French are looking to invest in sparkling wine
operations in the south of England. Once the 2002 and 2003
vintages are firmly on the shelves you should start to support
your local English wine producers. If they can't make wine in these

two years, they should give up and go home! So it is a little disappointing that my list of top wineries in the UK has only grown this year by one name. Remember prices are lowest if you buy direct and also almost all UK wineries welcome visitors – see www.englishwineproducers.com.

The chosen few are – Biddenden, **Camel Valley**, **Chapel Down (Curious Grape)**, **Clay Hill**, Coddington, **Davenport**, Nyetimber, RidgeView and Shawsgate.

ITALY

Italy is firing on all cylinders! But, it is still the most complicated wine country of all, so let me guide you with my bang-up-to-date list of the best Italian producers. Italy makes some of the finest value wines on the shelves, and if you are tempted to venture up the price ladder, you'll find they also make some seriously brilliant wines around the ten–fifteen pound mark. You will probably have to go to top-quality independent wine merchants to find the majority of the estates listed below.

NORTHWEST
PIEDMONT

Barolo, Barbaresco, Barbera, Dolcetto and other reds – Aldo **Conterno**, **Angelo Gaja £**, **Ascheri**, **Bruno Rocca**, **Ca' Rossa**, Ceretto, Cigliuti, Conterno Fantino, Domenico Clerico, **Elio Altare**, **Fontanafredda**, Giacomo Conterno, Giuseppe Mascarello, **Luciano Sandrone**, **Paolo Scavino**, **Parusso**, E. Pira, Roberto Voerzio and **La Spinetta**.

Moscato (fizzy, sweet white) **Fontanafredda** and **La Spinetta £**.

Gavi (dry white) **La Giustiniana**, **Nicola Bergaglio** and **La Scolca**.

Arneis (dry white) **Bric Cenciurio** and Carlo Deltetto.

LOMBARDY
Red and white – Bellavista (Franciacorta), Ca' del Bosco (Franciacorta), Ca' dei Frati (Lugana), Fratelli Muratori (Franciacorta) and Nino Negri (Valtellina).

NORTHEAST
TRENTINO
All styles – Bossi Fedrigotti, Endrizzi, **Ferrari**, **Foradori**, Letrari, Pojer & Sandri, **San Leonardo**, Vigneto Dalzocchio and La-Vis.
ALTO ADIGE
All styles – Alois Lageder, **Colterenzio**, **Franz Haas**, Hofstätter and San Michele Appiano.
VENETO
Soave (white) **Ca' Rugate**, Gini, **Pieropan**, Prà and **Roberto Anselmi**.
Valpolicella (red) **Allegrini**, Ca' del Pipa, **Dal Forno**, **Giuseppe Quintarelli £** and Masi.
Miscellaneous estates of excellence – (fizz) **Ruggeri** (Valdobbiadene); (reds and sweeties) Maculan (Breganze).
FRIULI-VENEZIA GIULIA
Mainly white – **Dario Raccaro**, Davide Moschioni, **Giovanni Puiatti**, Girolamo Dorigo, **Lis Neris (Alvararo Pecorari)**, Livio Felluga, Mario Schiopetto, Miani, Ronco del Gnemiz, **Roncùs**, **Tercic**, Villa Russiz and **Vinnaioli Jermann**.

CENTRAL
TUSCANY
Chianti (red) P. Antinori, Carobbio, **Castello di Brolio**, **Castello di Fonterutoli**, Felsina Berardenga, **Le Filigare**, Fontodi, **Isole e Olena**, **La Massa**, Il Molino di Grace, Poggerino, **Querciabella**, Selvapiana and Villa Caffagio.
Brunello di Montalcino (red) Altesino, **Argiano**, Case Basse, Ciacci

Piccolomini d'Aragona, **Collosorbo**, Corte Pavone, **Costanti**, Donatella Cinelli Colmbini, **Fanti San Filippo**, Fuligni, La Gerla, Lisini, **Mastrojanni**, Pietroso, Poggio Antico, **Il Poggione**, Sesti, Silvio Nardi and **Uccelliera**.

Vino Nobile di Montepulciano (red) **Dei**, Il Macchione, **Poliziano** and Villa Sant'Anna.

Carmignano (red) Ambra and **Tenuta di Capezzana**.

Super-Tuscans (red) **Il Borro**, Il Bosco (Manzano), **Brancaia**, Camartina (Querciabella) £, Campora (Falchini), Il Carbonaione (Poggio Scalette), **Casalfero (Barone Ricasoli)**, Cepparello (Isole e Olena) £, Cortaccio (Villa Caffagio), Flaccianello della Pieve (Fontodi), Fontalloro (Felsina Berardenga), Ghiaie della Furba (Capezzana), **Lupicaia (Tenuta del Terricio)** £, **Nambrot (Tenuta di Ghizzano)** £, Ornellaia (Mondavi/L. Antinori) £, Palazzo Altesi (Altesino), Paleo Rosso (Le Macchiole), Le Pergole Torte (Montevertine), Saffredi (Le Pupille) £, Sammarco (Castello dei Rampolla), **Sassicaia (Marchesi Incisa della Rochetta)** £, **Siepi (Fonterutoli)** £, **Solaia (P. Antinori)** £, **Solengo (Argiano)** £, Tassinaia (Tenuta del Terriccio) and Tignanello (P. Antinori).

Maremma and Morellino (mainly red) Costanza Malfatti, **Lohsa (Poliziano)**, Le Pupille and **Tenuta di Belguardo & Poggio Bronzone (Mazzei)**.

Vernaccia di San Gimignano (white) Montenidoli, **Panizzi** and Pietraserena.

Vin Santo (sweetie) **Avignonesi** £, **Isole e Olena** £, Selvapiana and Villa Branca.

MARCHE

Red and white – **Coroncino**, Saladini Pilastri, Le Terrazze and **Umani Ronchi**.

UMBRIA

Red and white –**Arnaldo Caprai**, La Carraia, **Castello della Sala**, La

Fiorita Lamborghini, Luigi Bigi, Lungarotti, **Palazzone** and **Sportoletti**.

LAZIO
Red and white – **Castel De Paolis**, **Falesco** and Pallavincini.

ABRUZZO AND MOLISE
Red and white – Edoardo Valentini, **Di Majo Norante** and **Podere Castorani**.

SOUTHERN AND ISLANDS – (ALL STYLES)
PUGLIA
Angelo Rocca, Apollonio, Botromagno, **Cosimo Taurino**, Francesco Candido, **Tenuta Rubino** and Vallone.

CAMPANIA
Colli di Lapio, Feudi di San Gregorio, **Luigi Maffini**, **Mastroberardino**, **Montevetrano** and **Taburno**.

BASILICATA
D'Angelo, Basilisco and Paternoster.

CALABRIA
Librandi and San Francesco.

SICILY AND PANTELLERIA
Abbazia Santa Anastasia, **Abraxas**, De Bartoli, Cusumano, **Inycon**, **Maurigi**, **Morgante**, **Planeta** and Salvatore Murana.

SARDINIA
Argiolas, **Gallura**, Giovanni Cherchi, **Santadi** and Sella & Mosca.

NEW ZEALAND
Everyone has been waiting in vain for New Zealand to get off its bum and do something. This country, with some superb wines and a massive potential to impress, has been creeping along at a snail's pace of late. The last year has thankfully seen some more exciting estates selling wine in the UK, and also some of the stalwart

operations introducing us to new ranges. But, in truth, I need a lot more action to be satisfied otherwise NZ is in danger of being left behind by the likes of Chile and Argentina (price/quality-wise), South Africa (effort-wise) and Australia (in everything but Sauvignon Blanc). I am heading down to New Zealand in the autumn to do a big tour and I hope to bring back some good news for you for next year's book. Until then, here is my list of serious estates. Not as many as there should be, but at least I can vouch for these guys making top quality wines – Alana Estate, Allan Scott, Alpha Domus, Amisfield, **Ata Rangi**, Cable Bay, **Chard Farm**, **Cloudy Bay**, **Craggy Range**, Dog Point, **Dry River**, Esk Valley, **Felton Road**, **Forrest Estate**, Goldwater Estate, Grove Mill, Hawkesbridge, Huia, **Hunter's**, **Isabel Estate**, **Jackson Estate**, Kath Lynskey, Kim Crawford, **Kumeu River**, Lawson's Dry Hills, Martinborough Vineyards, **Matakana**, Mills Reef, Mt Difficulty, Mount Edward, Mount Michael, **Mountford**, **Murdoch James**, Ollsens, **Palliser Estate**, Pegasus Bay, Peregrine, Rippon, **Saint Clair**, Selaks, **Seresin**, Sleeping Dogs, Stonecroft, **Stonyridge**, Te Mata, Tohu, **Two Paddocks**, Unison, **Valli**, **Vavasour**, Vidal, **Villa Maria**, West Brook and **Wither Hills**.

PORTUGAL

Portugal will always make two of the finest fortified wines in the world – port and Madeira. These two wondrous creations are staggeringly serious in the right hands. I have the definitive list of top producers for you here. In addition to this, I have also compiled a list of the top producers of non-fortified wines. I must admit that I don't drink much Portuguese wine at home, but things are moving forwards smoothly and the future is bright.

PORT

The best special-occasion port houses are – **Dow**, **Fonseca**, **Graham**,

Quinta do Noval Nacional, **Taylor** and **Warre**.
The less famous overachievers are – Churchill, **Niepoort**, Quinta do Portal, **Quinta do Vesuvio, Quinto do Infantado, Ramos-Pinto** and **Senhora da Ribeira**.

MADEIRA
The top producers are – **Blandy's, Cossart Gordon** and **Henriques & Henriques**.

THE REST OF PORTUGAL
Here's a short hit list of fine winemakers in the better regions.
Alentejo Cortes de Cima, Quinta de Cabriz, Quinta do Carmo, **João Portugal Ramos** and Segada.
Bairrada Caves São João and **Luis Pato**.
Beiras Caves Aliança.
Dão Alvaro Castro, Conde de Santar, Quinta da Cabriz, Quinta dos Carvalhais and **Quinta dos Roques**.
Douro Duas Quintas, **Niepoort, Quinta do Crasto**, Quinta da Gaivosa, Quinta do Infantado, **Quinta do Portal**, Quinta de Roriz, **Quinta de la Rosa**, Quinta do Vale da Raposa and **Redoma**.
Estremadura Palha Canas, **Quinta da Boavista** and Quinta de Pancas.
Ribatejo Bright Brothers and **Quinta da Lagoalva**.
Terras do Sado João Pires, José-Maria da Fonseca, Pasmados, Periquita and **Quinta de Camarate**.
Vinho Verde Palácio da Brejoeira and **Quinta do Ameal**.

SOUTH AFRICA
My goodness, South Africa has come a long way in the past few years. On my annual trip to the Cape this year I found loads of new wineries making excellent wines – there must be a new operation starting every day! Everywhere you turn there is another bottle of

remarkable wine. Go for any of the wines made by these estates and you should, I hope, be impressed at not only the taste, but also the value for money. This list is growing at a rate of knots (it has doubled in three years) – South Africa is on the warpath and the New World should watch out.

The top producers are – **Avondale**, Beaumont, Beyerskloof, **Boekenhoutskloof (Porcupine Ridge)**, **Bouchard Finlayson**, Brahms, Coleraine, **Columella (Sadie Family)**, **De Toren**, De Trafford, De Wetshof, **Diemersfontein**, **Dornier (Donatus in the UK)**, **Fairview**, Flagstone, **Glen Carlou**, **Graham Beck**, Grangehurst, **Hamilton Russell**, Hartenberg, **Iona**, Jean Daneel, **Jordan**, Kanonkop, **Ken Forrester**, Klein Constantia, Lammershoek, Land's End, Lindhorst, Linton Park, Longridge, **Luddite**, **Meinert**, Mischa, Mont Rochelle, **Mont du Toit**, Morgenhof, La Motte, Nabygelegen, Neil Ellis, Nelson's Creek, Newton Johnson, L'Ormarins, Paul Cluver, Phileo, **Raats**, Remhoogte, **Rijk's**, Rudera, Rupert & Rothschild, **Rustenberg (Brampton)**, Rust en Vrede, **Scali**, Signal Hill, Simonsig, Southern Right, Spice Route, **Springfield**, Stark-Condé, Stellenzicht, **Thelema**, **Veenwouden**, **Vergelegen**, Viljoensdrift, Villiera, Warwick Estate, Waterford (**Kevin Arnold**) and Wildekrans.

SPAIN

I have listed my Spanish wines by region first and then by producer. Spain is still woefully under represented in the UK at the top end but, bit by bit, Spanish companies are encouraging us to understand and accept their new wines. There is so much development and modernisation going that I think, in the next ten years, it will become a real force to be reckoned with worldwide.

ANDALUCÍA

Jerez (sherry) **Emilio Lustau**, **Fernando de Castilla**, **González Byass**, Hidalgo, Osborne and **Valdespino**.

ARAGÓN
Calatayud Marqués de Aragón and San Gregorio.
Campo de Borja Bodegas Borsao.
Somontano Blecua (Viñas del Vero) and Enate.

CASTILLA Y LEÓN
Bierzo Descendientes de J. Palacios.
Ribera del Duero Alión, Cillar de Silos, Condado de Haza, Dominio de Pingus, Pago de Carraovejas, **Pesquera**, Tarsus, Valduero and **Vega Sicilia £.**
Valladolid Mauro.
Rueda Agrícola Castellana and **Bodegas Dos Victorias.**
Toro Alquiriz (Vega Sicilia) and Viña Bajoz.
Arribes del Duero Durius Alto Duero (Marqués de Griñon).

CATALUÑA
Conca de Barberá Josep Foraster and Miguel Torres.
Empordà-Costa Brava Mas Estela.
Penedès Albet I Noya, Can Ràfols dels Caus, **Jean Léon**, Marquès de Monistrol, **Miguel Torres** and Puig i Roca.
Tarragona-Montsant and **Priorat** Celler de Capçanes, Clos Mogador £, Clos de L'Obac, Dits Del Terra, L'Ermita and Finca Dofi (Alvaro Palacios), **Laurona**, Mas d'en Compte, Mas Igneus, **Mas Martinet** and Scala Dei.
Terra Alta Bàrbara Forés and Xavier Clua.

EXTREMADURA, CASTILLA-LA MANCHA AND MADRID
Almansa Piqueras.
Castilla-La Mancha Dominio de Valdepusa.
Valdepeñas Los Llanos.

ISLANDS
Mallorca Anima Negra.

LEVANTE
Jumilla Casa de la Ermita.
Valencia Dominio Los Pinos.

NORTHERN COASTAL SPAIN
Rías Baixas Fillaboa, **Lagar de Cervera**, Lagar de Fornelos, Martín Codax, **Pazo de Barrantes**, **Pazo de Señorans**, Valdamor and Valmiñor.
Bizkaiko and **Getariako Txacolina** Bodegas Ametzoi and **Txomín Etaniz**.

RIOJA AND NAVARRA
Rioja Artadi, Barón de Ley, **Contino**, **CVNE**, Lopez de Heredia, **Marqués de Griñon**, **Marqués de Murrieta**, **Marqués de Vargas**, Muga, Navajas, Remelluri, La Rioja Alta, Roda, Urbina and Viña Salceda.
Navarra Agramont, Guelbenzu, Julián Chivite, Ochoa, Príncipe de Viana and **Vega del Castillo**.

USA
CALIFORNIA
A recent trip to California showed me that, while there is a band of ridiculously silly micro-boutiques flogging their wine at astronomical prices, the majority of winemakers are actually looking at the world with a level business head and this means there are plenty of wines for us to choose from, at fair prices. The main problem is that this huge, diverse industry has no trouble in selling its wines locally and so is lazy about what we, overseas, think about them (value-wise

and in global quality terms). Comparing like for like in the New World arena, California has many wines to be very proud of, but value for money is still an issue. Australia is the place that takes chunks out of it at the ten pound mark, but as you drift upwards, California has some real gems worth tracking down, and they taste like nothing else in the world. Also, whenever you need a hit of Zinfandel (and we all do), this is the place to come.

I have arranged the wineries in order of style of wine rather than by region as most producers source grapes from far and wide, and it is also easier for me to get my head around!

Cabernet Sauvignon/Merlot/Cabernet Franc Araujo, **Arietta £**, Beringer, **Bryant Family £**, Cain, **Caymus £**, Clos LaChance, **Corison**, **Dalle Valle £**, **Diamond Creek £**, Dominus, **Duckhorn**, Dunn, **Etude**, Flora Springs, **Forman**, **Frog's Leap**, Gallo Estate, **Harlan Estate £**, Havens, Hess Collection, **Joseph Phelps £**, Justin Vineyards, Lail Vineyards, Matanzas Creek, **Moraga**, Niebaum Coppola, **Newton £**, **Opus One**, Pahlmeyer, **Paradigm £**, Paul Hobbs, **Peter Michael £**, Philip Togni, **Quintessa £**, **Ridge £**, **Robert Mondavi**, St Francis, **Shafer £**, Silver Oak, **Spottswoode £**, **Stag's Leap Wine Cellars £** and **Viader £**.

Chardonnay Arrowood, **Au Bon Climat**, Beringer, Clos LaChance, **David Ramey**, **Frog's Leap**, Gallo Estate, **Hanzell £**, **Kistler £**, **Kongsgaard £**, **Landmark £**, **Lymar £**, Morgan, Paul Hobbs, Peter Michael, **Shafer £** and Sinskey.

Sauvignon Blanc Beringer, Carmenet, **Frog's Leap**, **Matanzas Creek** and **Robert Mondavi**.

Pinot Noir Au Bon Climat, **Calera £**, Cinnabar, **Etude £**, Gary Farrell, **Hanzell**, **Kistler £**, Marimar Torres, **J. Rochioli £**, Sinskey and Talley Vineyards.

Rhône Rangers Alban, Au Bon Climat, Bonny Doon, **Cline**, Jade

Mountain, **Qupé**, **Sean Thackrey**, **Tablas Creek £**, **Turley £** and **Wild Hog**.

Zinfandel Biale, Cline, **Elyse**, **Doug Nalle**, De Loach, **Ravenswood**, Renwood, **Ridge £**, Rosenblum, Seghesio and **Turley £**.

Sparkling **Domaine Carneros**, **Domaine Chandon**, Mumm Napa, Roedere Estate and **Schramsberg**.

Inexpensive estates: **Avila**, **Bogle**, **Fetzer Bonterra**, J. Lohr, Marietta Cellars, **Ramsay**, Seventh Moon and Wente.

PACIFIC NORTHWEST

Wines from Oregon and Washington State are still very hard to get hold of in the UK and, therefore, are expensive. Good luck with your search – these producers make sensational wines.

Oregon's best estates – **Adelsheim**, Archery Summit, Beaux Frères, Bethel Heights, **Cristom**, **Domaine Drouhin £**, Duck Pond, **Evesham Wood**, King Estate, Ponzi and Rex Hill.

Washington State's best estates – **Andrew Will £**, Château Ste-Michelle, DiStefano, **L'Ecole No 41**, **Leonetti Cellar £**, **Pepper Bridge**, **Quilceda Creek £**, Snoqualmie, **Woodward Canyon** and **Zefina**.

THE REST OF THE WORLD

Once again, I have skipped a load of (what I would call) less interesting winemaking countries and regions in the main body of the text, in order to give them a small shout in this paragraph. I know that the Jura, Savoie and Corsica were missed out of the French bit, but I haven't drunk any bottles from these regions this year. How important can they be? I am also peeved that I haven't made it out to the Alps for a spot of skiing for ages, so maybe this is my own private protest! Having said that, they always taste better out there anyway. While Austria gatecrashes into our wine psyche,

Switzerland's fine produce fails to register on the palate. If the Swiss will drink all of their wine in their own country we'll never see what they can do. Eastern Europe still fails to get me excited, although Nagyréde and Riverview from Hungary are good operations, and, despite the silly bottle and preposterous adverts, Blueridge from Bulgaria manages to make passable wine. If you know of any better please tell me. Tokaji from Hungary is widely regarded as the greatest wine from these parts and if you haven't experienced this incredible burst of honeyed, luxurious, tropical fruit before you should find a bottle immediately. They are all expensive, but look out for these producers – Disznókö, Oremus and the Royal Tokaji Wine Company. Château Musar is still the Lebanon's one great wine. Greek wines are improving and Boutari, Gaia Estate, Gerovassiliou and Tsantali are my favourite estates. I have managed to avoid Cypriot wine and, unlike last year, the charms of Tenerife's finest. North African wines, from Tunisia and Morocco, are seen on UK shelves occasionally. There are some pretty chunky Carignans around, but nothing that can't be trumped by Sicilian Nero d'Avola or Primitivo from Puglia. Mexican, Bolivian and Peruvian wines are still a mystery to me (thank goodness), and I have not repeated last year's near fatal brush with Chinese wine. The Hatten winery in Bali is still looking good, as are the Monsoon Valley wines from Thailand and the Sula Vineyard projects in India. It will not be long before these wines are going strong in the UK and, perhaps, we will be able to drink truly authentic, indigenous wines with our Asian and Indian cuisine – that would be a real treat.

That about covers it – anything else?

DIRECTORY
OF UK WINE
MERCHANTS

I have had so many wine merchants writing in this year in the hope of being included in this illustrious list of the UK's best wine companies that this is the longest list we have ever published. If, however, your favourite wine shop is still not listed, or you are a brand new wine merchant and you want the world to know, then drop me a line for next year's book. The following pages contain the vital contact details for the merchants responsible for selling nearly all of the finest bottles of wine in the UK. If you find a wine you like the sound of in the Top 250 (there are bound to be a few that take your fancy!), don't delay as some of the wines are in very short supply. Make sure you use this directory – get speed dialling and reserve a few bottles today. The following list of merchants is arranged in alphabetical and regional order to help you access as wide a choice of shops as possible. Remember that every outlet mentioned delivers wine around the country, so take advantage of this service if you are pushed for time, not in the locale or feel like placing a particularly weighty order. Many of these companies also have newsletters and offers (either sent via e-mail or post), so ask to be put on their mailing list and you will be the first to hear about new releases and bin end sales. Most importantly of all, if you find an independent wine merchant near you, do your best to give them as much business as you can. These hardworking companies are the lifeblood of the wine trade. Each year the supermarkets and the big wine chains invariably increase their selections and source better and better wine but their orders are usually many hundreds, if not thousands, of cases. The smaller outfits sniff out individual parcels, sometimes a case at a time, and you want to be the first to know about these rare gems. In the same way that your local butcher or fishmonger knows your likes and dislikes, your local wine merchant will get to know your taste. There is nothing better than this calibre of personal service.

RECOMMENDED LARGER CHAIN STORES AND SUPERMARKETS (PLUS ABBREVIATIONS)

Asda (**Asd**) 265 stores 0500 100055 www.asda.co.uk ✪

E.H. Booth & Co., of Lancashire, Cheshire, Cumbria and Yorkshire (**Boo**) 25 stores 01772 251701 www.booths-supermarkets.co.uk ✪

Co-operative Group CWS (**Coo**) 1,756 stores 0800 068 6727 www.co-op.co.uk

Majestic Wine Warehouses (**Maj**) 115 stores 01923 298200 www.majestic.co.uk ✪C

Marks & Spencer (**M&S**) 332 stores 020 7935 4422 www.marksandspencer.com ✪

Wm Morrison (**Mor**) 128 stores 01924 870000 www.morereasons.co.uk

Oddbins (**Odd**) 230 stores and **Oddbins Fine Wine shops** (**OFW**) 8 stores 020 8944 4400 www.oddbins.com ✪

Safeway (**Saf**) 480 stores 020 8848 8744 www.safeway.co.uk ✪

Sainsbury's (**Sai**) 551 stores 0800 636262 www.sainsburys.co.uk ✪

Somerfield Stores (**Som**) 550 stores 0117 935 6669 www.somerfield.co.uk

Tesco Stores (**Tes**) 742 stores 0800 505555 www.tesco.com ✪

Thresher Group – including **Thresher** (**Thr**) and **Wine Rack** (**WRa**) 1,400 stores 01707 387200 www.threshergroup.com ✪

Unwins Ltd (**Unw**) 388 stores 01322 272711 www.unwins.co.uk

Waitrose (**Wai**) 144 stores 01344 825232 www.waitrose.com ✪

Wine Cellar (**WCe**) 50 stores 0800 838251 www.winecellar.co.uk

○ = Jukesy-rated wine merchant worthy of particular note
C = Wine sold by the case (often mixed) of twelve bottles

RECOMMENDED INDEPENDENT RETAIL SPECIALISTS, SMALL CHAINS, WINE BROKERS AND MAIL ORDER WINE COMPANIES SORTED ALPHABETICALLY

A & A Wines, Cranleigh, Surrey 01483 274666 aawines@aol.com **C**

A & B Vintners, Brenchley, Kent 01892 724977 info@abvintners.co.uk **○MC**

Adnams Wine Merchants, Southwold, Suffolk 01502 727200 wines@adnams.co.uk **○**

Ameys Wines, Sudbury, Suffolk 01787 377144 **○**

Amps Fine Wines of Oundle, near Peterborough, Northamptonshire 01832 273502 info@ampsfinewines.co.uk

Arkell Vintners, Swindon, Wiltshire 01793 823026 wines@arkells.com

John Armit Wines, London 020 7908 0600 web@armit.co.uk **○MCF**

W.J. Armstrong, East Grinstead, West Sussex 01342 321478 www.wjarmstrong.com

Arnolds, Broadway, Worcestershire 01386 852427

Arriba Kettle & Co., Honeybourne, Worcestershire 01386 833024 arriba.kettle@btopenworld.com **C**

Australian Wine Club, Slough, Berkshire 0800 8562004 orders@australianwine.co.uk **○MC**

Averys, Bristol 0117 921 4146 **○**

Bacchanalia, Cambridge 01223 576292 **○**

Bacchus Fine Wines, Warrington, Buckinghamshire 01234 711140 wine@bacchus.co.uk **○C**

Bakers & Larners, Holt, Norfolk 01263 712323 ctbaker@cwcom.net

Stanley Ball, Crawley, West Sussex 01293 525777 stanley_ball@msn.com

Ballantynes, Cowbridge, Vale of Glamorgan 01446 774840 enq@ballantynes.co.uk **○**

Balls Brothers, London 020 7739 1642 wine@ballsbrothers.co.uk **MC**

Georges Barbier, London 020 8852 5801 georgesbarbier@f2s.com ✪MC

Barrels & Bottles, Sheffield 0114 255 6611 sales@barrelsandbottles.co.uk

Bat & Bottle, Oakham, Rutland 0845 108 4407 post@batwine.com ✪

Beaconsfield Wine Cellar, Beaconsfield, Buckinghamshire
01494 675545 thecellars@btinternet.com

Bedales, London 020 7403 8853 info@bedalestreet.com

Bella Wines, Newmarket, Suffolk 01638 604899
sales@bellawines.co.uk ✪M

Bennetts Fine Wines, Chipping Campden, Gloucestershire 01386 840392
enquiries@bennettsfinewines.com ✪

Bentalls, Kingston-upon-Thames, Surrey 020 8546 1001

Bergerac Wine Cellar, St Helier, Jersey 01534 870756

Berkmann Wine Cellars, London 020 7609 4711 info@berkmann.co.uk
✪M

Berry Bros. & Rudd, London 0870 900 4300 www.bbr.com ✪F

Best Cellars, Ashburton, Devon 01364 652546 sales@bestcellars.co.uk

Bibendum Wine Ltd, London 020 7449 4120
sales@bibendum-wine.co.uk ✪MCF

Bideford Wines, Bideford, Devon 01237 470507

Bintwo, Padstow, Cornwall 01841 532022 david@bintwo.com ✪

Le Bon Vin, Sheffield 0114 2560090 sales@lebonvin.co.uk

Bonhote Foster, Bumpstead, Suffolk 01440 730779
bonhote.info@corkexpress.co.uk **M**

Booths of Stockport, Heaton Moor, Stockport 0161 432 3309
johnbooth@lineone.net

Bordeaux Index, London 020 7253 2110 sales@bordeauxindex.com ✪MF

The Bottleneck, Broadstairs, Kent 01843 861095
sales@thebottleneck.co.uk

Bowland Forest Vintners, Clitheroe, Lancashire 01200 448688
milescorish@aol.com

Brinkleys Wines, London 020 7351 1683 www.brinkleys.com

UK wine merchants 203

Burgundy Shuttle, London 07771 630826 **MC**
Burgundy Wines, Brighton, East Sussex 01273 330012
md@BurgundyWines.co.uk
Butlers Wine Cellar, Brighton, East Sussex 01273 698724
henry@butlers-winecellar.co.uk ✪
Anthony Byrne Fine Wines, Ramsey, Cambridgeshire 01487 814555
sales@abfw.co.uk **MC**
D. Byrne & Co., Clitheroe, Lancashire 01200 423152 ✪

Cairns & Hickey, Bramhope, Leeds 0113 267 3746 pcairns@c-
hwines.fsnet.co.uk
Cape Wine & Food, Staines, Middlesex 01784 451860
capewineandfood@aol.com
Carley & Webb, Framlingham, Suffolk 01728 723503
Carringtons, Manchester 0161 466 2546
Castang Wine Shippers, Pelynt, Cornwall 01503 220359 sales@castang-
wines.co.uk **MC**
Cave Cru Classé, London 020 7378 8579 enquiries@ccc.co.uk **MCF**
Les Caves du Patron, Stoneygate, Leicester 0116 221 8221
wines@lescavesdupatron.com
Les Caves de Pyrene, Guildford, Surrey 01483 538820
sales@lescaves.co.uk ✪
Ceci Paolo, Ledbury, Herefordshire 01531 632976 www.cecipaolo.com
The Cellar Door, Overton, Hampshire 01256 770 397
info@thecellardoor.co.uk
Cellar Door Wines, St Albans, Hertfordshire 01727 854488
sales@cellardoorwines.co.uk
Champagne & Wine Cellar, Winchcombe, Gloucestershire 01242 603514
grape.expectations@btinternet.com
Andrew Chapman Fine Wines, Abingdon, Oxfordshire 0845 458 0707
info@surf4wine.co.uk ✪

Simon Charles Vintners, London 020 7228 3409
  wine@scvintners.f9.co.uk ✪
The Charterhouse Wine Co., Spalding, Lincolnshire 01775 720 300
  info@charterhousewine.co.uk
Cheers Wine Merchants, Swansea 01792 403895
  andrewcheers@hotmail.com
Cheshire Smokehouse, Wilmslow, Cheshire 01625 540123
  sales@cheshiresmokehouselimited.co.uk
Chiltern Cellars, High Wycombe, Buckinghamshire 01494 526212
Chippendale Fine Wines, Bradford, West Yorkshire 01274 582424
  mikepoll@chippendalewine.free-online.co.uk **MC**
Church House Vintners, Compton, Berkshire 01635 579 327
  chv@saqnet.co.uk **MC**
Clifton Cellars, Bristol 0117 973 0287 admin@cliftoncellars.co.uk
Brian Coad Fine Wines, Plympton, Devon 01752 334970
  brian.coad@berkmann.co.uk ✪**MC**
Cockburns of Leith, Edinburgh 0131 346 1113 sales@winelist.co.uk
Colombier Vins Fins, Swadlincote, Derbyshire 01283 552552
  ju@colombierwines.co.uk **MC**
Compendium, Belfast 028 9079 1197 info@compendiumwines.com
Connolly's, Birmingham 0121 236 9269 chris@connollyswine.co.uk ✪
Constantine Stores, Falmouth, Cornwall 01326 340226
  andrew@drinkfinder.co.uk
Cooden Cellars, Eastbourne, East Sussex 01323 649663
  cooden@lineone.net ✪
Corks, Cotham, Bristol 0117 973 1620 sales@corksof.com
Corkscrew Wines, Carlisle, Cumbria 01228 543033
  corkscrewwines@aol.com
Corney & Barrow, London 020 7265 2400 wine@corbar.co.uk ✪**F**
Crane River Fine Wines, Middlesex 020 8891 4343
  craneriviera@aol.com **MC**

○ = Jukesy-rated wine merchant worthy of particular note
C = Wine sold by the case (often mixed) of twelve bottles

Creber's, Tavistock, Devon 01822 612266
Croque-en-Bouche, Malvern Wells, Worcestershire
01684 565612 mail@croque.co.uk ○MC

Dartmouth Vintners, Dartmouth, Devon 01803 832602
bill@dartmouthvintners.fsnet.co.uk
Andrew Darwin Fine Wines, Kington, Herefordshire 01544 230534
darwin@kc3.co.uk
Davy's Wine Merchants, London 020 7407 9670 jdavy@davy.co.uk
Decorum Vintners, London 020 8969 6581 admin@decvin.com ○MC
deFINE Food and Wine, Sandiway, Cheshire 01606 882101
office@definefoodandwine.com ○
Rodney Densem Wines, Nantwich, Cheshire 01270 626999
sales@rdwines.com
F.L. Dickins, Rickmansworth, Hertfordshire 01923 773636
Direct Wine Shipments, Belfast 028 9050 8000
enquiry@directwine.co.uk ○
Direct Wines, Theale, Reading 0870 444 8383
orders@laithwaites.co.uk MF
Domaine Direct, London 020 7837 1142 mail@domainedirect.co.uk ○C
The Dorchester Wine Centre at Eldridge Pope, Dorchester, Dorset
01305 258266 wineshopdorchester@eldridge.pope.co.uk ○
Dunells Premier Wines Ltd, St Peter, Jersey 01534 736418
dunells.wines@jerseymail.co.uk ○

Eagle's Wines, London 020 7223 7209
East Coast Wines, Grimsby, South Humberside 01472 827207
sales@eastcoastwinewarehouse.com
Edencroft Fine Wines, Nantwich, Cheshire 01270 629975
sales@edencroft.co.uk
Ells Fine Wines, Portadown 028 3833 2306 rrwines@hotmail.com

El Vino, London 020 7353 5384 www.elvino.co.uk
English Wine Centre, Alfriston Roundabout, East Sussex 01323 870164
  bottles@englishwine.co.uk
Eton Vintners, Windsor 01753 790188 sales@etonvintners.co.uk **M**
Evertons, Ombersley, Worcestershire 01905 620282 sales@evertons.co.uk
Evingtons Wine Merchants, Leicester 0116 254 2702
  evingtonwine@fsbdial.co.uk
Execellars, Kennford, Exeter, Devon 0800 0838075 andy@execellars.co.uk

Farr Vintners, London 020 7821 2000 sales@farr-vintners.com ✪MF
Fine & Rare Wines, London 020 8960 1995 wine@frw.co.uk ✪MF
Fine Cheese Co., Bath 01225 483407 sales@finecheese.co.uk
Fine Wines of New Zealand, London 020 7482 0093 info@fwnz.co.uk ✪M
Irma Fingal-Rock, Monmouth, Monmouthshire 01600 712372
  tom@pinotnoir.co.uk
Le Fleming Wines, Harpenden, Hertfordshire 01582 760125 **MC**
The Flying Corkscrew, Hemel Hempstead, Hertfordshire 01442 412311
  sales@flyingcorkscrew.com ✪
La Forge Wines, Marksbury, Bath 01761 472349
  kevin@laforgewines.com **MF**
Fortnum & Mason, London 020 7734 8040
  info@fortnumandmason.co.uk ✪
Four Walls Wine Company, Chilgrove, West Sussex 01243 535360
  fourwallswine@aol.com ✪MF
Friarwood, London 020 7736 2628 sales@friarwood.com
FWW Wines, London 020 8567 3731 sales@fwwwines.demon.co.uk ✪MC

Gallery Wines, Gomshall, Surrey 01483 203795
  info@thegomshallgallery.net
Garland Wine Cellar, Ashtead, Surrey 01372 275247
  stephen@garlandwines.co.uk

Garrards, Cockermouth, Cumbria 01900 823592
admin@garrards-wine.co.uk

Gauntleys, Nottingham 0115 911 0555 rhone@gauntleywine.com ✪

General Wine Company, Liphook, Hampshire 01428 727744
sales@thegeneralwine.co.uk ✪

Goedhuis & Co., London 020 7793 7900 sales@goedhuis.com ✪MCF

Gourmet Vintners, Billingshurst, West Sussex 01403 784128
sales@gourmetvintners.co.uk

The Grape Shop, London 020 7924 3638 dp@thegrapeshop.com ✪

Peter Graham Wines, Norwich, Norfolk 01603 625657
louisa@petergrahamwines.com

Richard Granger Fine Wine Merchants, Newcastle upon Tyne 0191 281
5000 sales@richardgrangerwines.co.uk

The Great Grog Wine Co., Edinburgh 0131 662 4777 www.greatgrog.co.uk

Great Northern Wine Company, Ripon, North Yorkshire 01765 606767
info@greatnorthernwine.com M

Great Western Wine Company, Bath 01225 322800
post@greatwesternwine.co.uk ✪

Peter Green, Edinburgh 0131 229 5925 shop@petergreenwines.com

The Grogblossom, London 020 7794 7808

Patrick Grubb Selections, Oxford 01869 340229
patrickgrubbselections@btinternet.com ✪

Gunson Fine Wines, South Godstone, Surrey 01342 843974
gunsonfinewines@aol.com ✪MC

H & H Bancroft, London 020 7232 5450
sales@handhbancroftwines.com ✪MC

Hailsham Cellars, Hailsham, East Sussex 01323 441212
wine@hailshamcellars.com

Halifax Wine Company, Halifax, West Yorkshire 01422 256333
andy@halifaxwinecompany.com

Hall and Woodhouse Ltd, Blandford, Dorset 01258 452 141
admin@hall-woodhouse.co.uk
Handford Wines, London 020 7221 9614 wine@handford.net ✪F
Hanslope Wines, Milton Keynes, Buckinghamshire 01908 510262
charles@hanslopewines.co.uk
Roger Harris Wines, Weston Longville, Norfolk 01603 880171
sales@rogerharriswines.co.uk ✪MC
Harrods, London 020 7730 1234 ✪F
Harrogate Fine Wine, Harrogate, North Yorkshire 01423 522270
enquiries@harrogatefinewine.co.uk
Harvey Nichols & Co., London 020 7201 8537
wineshop@harveynichols.com ✪
Richard Harvey Wines, Wareham, Dorset 01929 481437
harvey@lds.co.uk **MC**
The Haslemere Cellar, Haslemere, Surrey 01428 645081
info@haslemerecellar.co.uk ✪
Hayman Barwell Jones, Ipswich, Suffolk 01473 232322 ✪MC
Haynes, Hanson & Clark, London 020 7259 0102
london@hhandc.co.uk and Stow-on-the-Wold,
Gloucestershire 01451 870808 stow@hhandc.co.uk ✪
Hedley Wright, Bishop's Stortford, Hertfordshire 01279 465818
sales@hedleywright.co.uk **C**
Pierre Henck, Walsall, West Midlands 01543 377 111
birm1@morgenrot.co.uk **MC**
Henderson Wines, Edinburgh 0131 447 8580
hendersonwines@btconnect.com
Charles Hennings Vintners, Pulborough, West Sussex 01798 872671
sales@chv-wine.co.uk
Hicks & Don, Edington, Wiltshire 01380 831234
mailbox@hicksanddon.co.uk **M**
George Hill, Loughborough, Leicestershire 01509 212717

andrewh@georgehill.co.uk
Hills Drinks and Oasis Wines, Benfleet, Essex 01268 772611
hillsdrinks@btconnect.com
Hopton Wines, Kidderminster, Shropshire 01299 270734
chris@hoptoncourt.fsnet.co.uk **MC**
Hoults Wine Merchants, Huddersfield, West Yorkshire 01484 510700
bobwine@hotmail.com
House of Townend, Kingston upon Hull, East Yorkshire 01482 586582
info@houseoftownend.co.uk ❂
Ian G. Howe, Newark, Nottinghamshire 01636 704366
howe@chablis-burgundy.co.uk
Victor Hugo Wines, St Saviour, Jersey 01534 507977 sales@victor-hugo-
wines.com

Inspired Wines, Cleobury Mortimer, Shropshire 01299 270064
info@inspired-wines.co.uk
Inverarity Vaults, Biggar 01899 308000 info@inverarity-vaults.com
Irvine Robertson, Edinburgh 0131 553 3521 irviner@nildram.co.uk **C**

Jeroboams (incorporating **Laytons Wine Merchants**), London
020 7259 6716 sales@jeroboams.co.uk ❂
Michael Jobling, Newcastle-upon-Tyne 0191 378 4554 **MC**
N.D. John, Swansea 01792 644688 nj@ndjohnwinemerchants.co.uk
The Jolly Vintner, Tiverton, Devon 01884 255644
L & F Jones, Radstock near Bath 01761 417117
buying.buying@lfjones.aclm.co.uk
S.H. Jones, Banbury, Oxfordshire 01295 251179 shj@shjones.com ❂
Justerini & Brooks, London 020 7208 2507 ❂**F**
Just in Case Wine Merchants, Bishop's Waltham, Hampshire 01489
892969 justincase@bishopswaltham9.fsnet.co.uk

Joseph Keegan & Sons Ltd, Holyhead, Isle of Anglesey 01407 762333
  enquiries@josephkeegan.co.uk
Christopher Keiller, Redruth, Cornwall 01209 215706
  ghost@gladys.demon.co.uk
John Kelly Wines, Boston Spa, West Yorkshire 01937 842965
  john@kellywines.co.uk **MC**
Kelly of Cults Ltd, Aberdeen 0845 456 1902
Kendalls, Manchester 0161 8323414
Kendrick Wines, Bromley, Kent 020 8467 7524 kmcclem@aol.com
David Kibble Wines, Fontwell, West Sussex 01243 544111
Richard Kihl, Aldeburgh, Suffolk 01728 454455
  sales@richardkihl.ltd.uk ✪**CF**

Laithwaites, Reading, Berkshire 0870 444 8282
  orders@laithwaites.co.uk **MC**
Lay & Wheeler, Holton St Mary, Suffolk 0845 330 1855
  sales@laywheeler.com ✪
Laymont & Shaw, Truro, Cornwall 01872 270545 info@laymont-
  shaw.co.uk ✪**MC**
Lea & Sandeman, London 020 7244 0522 sales@leaandsandeman.co.uk ✪
Liberty Wine, London 020 7720 5350 info@libertywine.co.uk ✪**MC**
O.W. Loeb & Co. Ltd, London 020 7234 0385 finewine@owloeb.com
  ✪**MC**
J & H Logan, Edinburgh 0131 667 2855
Longford Wines, Lewes, East Sussex 01273 400012
  longfordwines@aol.com **MC**
Love Saves the Day, Manchester 0161 832 0777
  chris@lovesavestheday.co.uk ✪
Luckins Wine Store, Great Dunmow, Essex 01371 872839
  andyfiltness@winebuffs.net
Luvian's Bottle Shop, Cupar, Fife 01334 654820 info@luvians.com

Magnum Wine Company, Swindon, Wiltshire 01793 642569 ✪
Map Wines, Bridgewater, Somerset 01278 459 622 davidpreece@map-wines.freeserve.co.uk
Martinez Wines, Ilkley, West Yorkshire 01943 603241 editor@martinez.co.uk ✪MC
Mason & Mason, West Stoke, West Sussex 01243 575821 sales@masonandmasonwines.co.uk ✪MC
Mayfair Cellars, London 020 7386 7999 sales@mayfaircellars.co.uk MC
Mill Hill Wines, London 020 8959 6754 millhillwines@aol.com
Mille Gusti, London 020 8997 3932 millegusti@hotmail.com ✪MC
Mills Whitcombe, Peterchurch, Herefordshire 01981 550028 info@millswhitcombe.co.uk ✪C
Milton Sandford Wines, Knowl Hill, Berkshire 01628 829449 sales@miltonsandfordwines.com ✪MC
Mitchells Wines, Sheffield 0114 274 5587 info@mitchellsdirect.com
Montrachet Fine Wines, London 020 7928 1990 charles@montrachetwine.com ✪MC
Moonshine, Bourne, Lincolnshire 01778 421050 andy@moonshine.fsbusiness.co.uk
Moreno Wines, London 020 7286 0678 sales@moreno-wines.co.uk ✪
Moriarty Vintners, Cardiff 029 2022 9996 sales@moriarty-vintners.com
Morris & Verdin, London 020 7921 5300 sales@m-v.co.uk ✪MC

Nectarous Wines, Cheltenham, Gloucestershire 01242 224466 taste@nectarous.co.uk
The New Pantry, London 020 7602 6964
James Nicholson, Crossgar, Co. Down, Northern Ireland 028 4483 0091 shop@jnwine.com ✪
Nickolls & Perks, Stourbridge, West Midlands 01384 394518 sales@nickollsandperks.co.uk
Nicolas UK of London 20+ stores 020 8944 7514 www.nicolas.co.uk

Nidderdale Fine Wines, Harrogate, North Yorkshire 01423 711703
info@southaustralianwines.com ✪
Noble Rot Wine Warehouse, Bromsgrove, Worcestershire
01527 575606 info@noble-rot.co.uk ✪
The Nobody Inn, Doddiscombsleigh, Devon 01647 252394
info@nobodyinn.co.uk ✪
Novum Wines, London 020 7820 6720 info@novumwines.com ✪

Off the Vine, St Albans, Hertfordshire 01727 898290
The Old Forge Wine Cellar, Storrington, West Sussex 01903 744246
chris@worldofwine.co.uk
Oxford Wine Company, Witney, Oxfordshire 01865 301144
info@oxfordwine.co.uk ✪
Oz Wines, London 0845 450 1261 sales@ozwinesonline.co.uk ✪

Page & Sons, Ramsgate, Kent 01843 591214 mail@pageandsons.co.uk
Thomas Panton, Tetbury, Gloucestershire 01666 503088
info@wineimporter.co.uk **M**
Parfrements, Coventry, West Midlands 024 7650 3646
Paxton & Whitfield, London 020 7930 0259 sales@cheesemongers.co.uk
Peake Wine Associates, Fareham, Hampshire 01329 822733
roy@farehamwinecellar.co.uk
Thos Peatling, Bury St Edmunds, Suffolk 01284 714285
sales@thospeatling.co.uk
Peckham & Rye, Glasgow 0141 445 4555 alan.rose@peckhams.co.uk ✪
Penistone Court Wine Cellars, Penistone, Sheffield 01226 766037
pcwc@dircon.co.uk ✪**MC**
Philglas & Swiggot, London 020 7924 4494 wine@philglas-
swiggot.co.uk ✪
Laurence Philippe Wines, Chelmsford, Essex 01245 475454
lpwines@lineone.net

Christopher Piper Wines, Ottery St Mary, Devon 01404 814139
sales@christopherpiperwines.co.uk ❂
Terry Platt Wine Merchants, Llandudno, Conwy 01492 874099
info@terryplattwines.co.uk ❂MC
Planet Wine Ltd, Sale, Cheshire 0161 973 1122
sales@planetwine.co.uk MC
Playford Ros, Thirsk, North Yorkshire 01845 526777
sales@playfordros.com MC
Portal, Dingwall & Norris, Emsworth, Hampshire 01243 370280
angela@pdnagencies.com
Portland Wine Co., Sale, Manchester 0161 962 8752
portwineco@aol.com
Premier Cru Fine Wine, Guiseley, Leeds 01943 877004
enquiries@premiercrufinewine.co.uk

Quay West Wines, Stoke Canon, Exeter 01392 841833
sales@quaywestwines.co.uk C
Quellyn Roberts, Chester, Cheshire 01244 310455
sales@qrwines.co.uk

R.S. Wines, Winford, Bath and Northeast Somerset 01275 331 444
sales@rswines.co.uk MC
Arthur Rackham Emporia, Guildford, Surrey 0870 870 1110 C
Raeburn Fine Wines, Edinburgh 0131 343 1159
sales@raeburnfinewines.com ❂
Ravensbourne Wine, London 020 8692 9655
sales@ravensbournewine.co.uk C
Regency Wines, Exeter, Devon 01392 444123
Reid Wines, Hallatrow, Bristol 01761 452645 reidwines@aol.com ❂MF
La Réserve, London 020 7589 2020 realwine@la-reserve.co.uk ❂
Revelstoke Wines, London 020 8545 0077 sales@revelstoke.co.uk ❂MC

Richardson & Sons, Whitehaven, Cumbria 01946 65334
  richardsonandsons@btconnect.com
Howard Ripley Ltd, London 020 8877 3065 info@howardripley.com
  ✿MC
Roberson, London 020 7371 2121 retail@roberson.co.uk ✿
Roberts & Speight, Beverley, East Yorkshire 01482 870717
  sales@foodbites.karoo.co.uk
Robert Rolls, London 020 7606 1166 mail@rollswine.com ✿MCF
R & R Fine Wines, Bury, Lancashire 0161 762 0022
  fine.wines@btconnect.com ✿

St Martin Vintners, Brighton, East Sussex 01273 777788
  sales@stmartinvintners.co.uk
Sandhams Wine Merchants Ltd, Caistor, Lincolnshire
  01472 852118 sales@sandhamswine.co.uk
Scatchard, Liverpool 0151 236 6468 jon@scatchards.com
Seckford Wines, Woodbridge, Suffolk 01394 446622
  sales@seckfordwines.co.uk ✿MCF
Selfridges, London 020 7318 3730 and Manchester 0161 838 0659
  wine.club@selfridges.co.uk ✿
Shaftesbury Fine Wines, Shaftesbury, Dorset 01747 850059
  prb@shafwine.freeserve.co.uk
Shaws of Beaumaris, Isle of Anglesey 01248 810328
  wines@shaws.sagehost.co.uk
Edward Sheldon, Shipston-on-Stour, Warwickshire 01608 661409
  finewine@edward-sheldon.co.uk
H. Smith, Ashbourne, Derbyshire 01335 342150
  horace.smith@tiscali.co.uk
Laurence Smith, Edinburgh 0131 667 3327 vintnersmith@aol.com MC
Soho Wine Supply, London 020 7636 8490 info@sohowine.co.uk
Sommelier Wine Co. Ltd, St Peter Port, Guernsey 01481 721677 ✿

Springfield Wines, near Huddersfield, West Yorkshire 01484 864929
springfieldwines@aol.com

Frank Stainton Wines, Kendal, Cumbria 01539 731886
admin@stainton-wines.co.uk

Stanton Wine Co., Broadway, Worcestershire 01386 852501
sales@stantonwineco.co.uk

William Stedman, Caerleon, Newport 01633 430055
info@wmstedman.co.uk

Charles Steevenson, Tavistock, Devon 01822 616272
sales@steevensonwines.co.uk MC

Stevens Garnier, Oxford 01865 263303 info@stevensgarnier.co.uk ○

Stokes Fine Wines, London 020 8944 5979
sales@stokesfinewines.com ○MC

Stone, Vine & Sun, Winchester, Hampshire 0845 061 4604
sales@stonevine.co.uk ○

Stratford's Wine Agencies Ltd, Cookham-on-Thames, Berkshire 01628
810606 sales@stratfordwine.co.uk ○MC

SWIG, London 020 7903 8311 imbibe@swig.co.uk ○MC

T & W Wines, Brandon, Suffolk 01842 814414 contact@tw-wines.com

Tanners, Shrewsbury, Shropshire 01743 234455
sales@tanners-wines.co.uk ○

Taurus Wines, Bramley, Surrey 01483 548484
sales@tauruswines.co.uk

ten-acre wines, London 020 7431 2930 info@ten-acre.co.uk ○

Theatre of Wine, London 020 8858 6363

Totnes Wine Co., Totnes, Devon 01803 866357 info@totneswine.co.uk

Trenchermans, Sherborne, Dorset 01935 432857
info@trenchermans.com

Turville Valley Wines, Great Missenden, Buckinghamshire
01494 868818 info@turville-valley-wines.com ○MCF

Uncorked, London 020 7638 5998 drink@uncorked.co.uk ✪
Unwined Ltd, Sedgebrook, Nottinghamshire 01949 844324
  enquiries@unwined.biz

Valvona & Crolla, Edinburgh 0131 556 6066 sales@valvonacrolla.co.uk ✪
Helen Verdcourt, Maidenhead, Berkshire 01628 625577 **MC**
Veritas Wines, Cambridge 01223 212500 info@veritaswines.co.uk
Vicki's Wine Merchants, Chobham, Surrey 01276 858374
Les Vignerons de St Georges, Windlesham, Surrey 01276 850136
Villeneuve Wines, Peebles, Haddington and Edinburgh
  01721 722500 wines@villeneuvewines.com ✪
Vin du Van, Appledore, Kent 01233 758727 ✪**MC**
Vinceremos, Leeds 0113 2440002 info@vinceremos.co.uk **MC**
The Vine Trail, Hotwells, Bristol 0117 921 1770
  enquiries@vinetrail.co.uk ✪**MC**
The Vineyard, Dorking, Surrey 01306 876828
The Vineyard Cellars, Hungerford, Berkshire 01488 681313
  jamesfreebody@vineyardcellars.com ✪**MC**
Vino Vino, New Malden, Surrey 07703 436949
  vinovino@macunlimited.net **MC**
The Vintage House, London 020 7437 2592 vintagehouse.co@virgin.net
Vintage Roots, Arborfield, Berkshire 0118 976 1999
  info@vintageroots.co.uk ✪**M**
Vintage Wine Cellars, Luton, Bedfordshire 01582 455068
  sales@vintagewinecellars.co.uk

Wadebridge Wines, Wadebridge, Cornwall 01208 812692
  enquiries@wwrw.co.uk
Waterloo Wine, London 020 7403 7967 sales@waterloowine.co.uk
Waters of Coventry, Heathcote, Warwick 01926 888889
  info@waters-wine-merchants.co.uk

UK wine merchants 217

T.B. Watson Ltd, Dumfries, Dumfriesshire 01387 256601
karen@tbwatson.co.uk

David J. Watt Fine Wines, Ashby-de-la-Zouch, Leicestershire
01530 413953 fwatt@lineone.net **M**

Wattisfield Wines, Bury St Edmunds, Suffolk 01359 251260

Weavers of Nottingham, Nottingham 0115 958 0922
weavers@weaverswines.com ○

Welshpool Wine, Powys 01938 553243 info@welshpoolwine.com ○

Wessex Wines, Bridport, Dorset 01308 427177
wessexwines@amserve.com **C**

Whitebridge Wines, Stone, Staffordshire 01785 817229
sales@whitebridgewines.co.uk

Whitesides, Clitheroe, Lancashire 01200 422281
wine@whitesideswine.co.uk

Whittalls Wines, Walsall, West Midlands 01922 636161 www@efb.co.uk **C**

Wicked Wines, Pockthorpe, Kilham, East Yorkshire 01377 255725

Wilkinson Vintners Ltd, London 020 7616 0404
wilkinson@finewine.co.uk ○**MCF**

James Williams, Narberth, Pembrokeshire 01834 862200

Wimbledon Wine Cellar, London 020 8540 9979
enquiries@wimbledonwinecellar.com ○

Winchcombe Wine Merchants, Winchcombe, Gloucestershire
01451 850686

The WineBarn, Winchester, Hampshire 01962 774102
info@thewinebarn.co.uk

Wine Barrels, London 020 7228 3306 edwood@scvintners.f9.co.uk

The Wine Cellar, South Croydon, Surrey 020 8657 6936
winecellarsnd@aol.com

Winecellars, London 020 8963 4816 www.winecellars.co.uk ○**MC**

Wine in Cornwall, Falmouth/Penryn, Cornwall 01326 379426
sales@wineincornwall.co.uk

The Wine Library, London 020 7481 0415
  wine.library@virgin.net

The Wine Man, Streatley-on-Thames, West Berkshire
  01635 203050 sales@wine-man.com **MC**

The Wine Mill, Nelson, Lancashire 01282 614618
  enquiries@thewinemill.co.uk

Wine Society, Stevenage, Hertfordshire 01438 741177
  memberservices@thewinesociety.com ✪**MCF**

The Wine Treasury, London 020 7793 9999
  bottled@winetreasury.com ✪**MC**

The Winery, London 020 7286 6475 info@thewineryuk.com ✪**F**

Wines of Interest, Ipswich, Suffolk 0870 224 5640
  sales@winesofinterest.co.uk

Wine Raks, Aberdeen 01224 311460 mike@wineraks.co.uk

The Winesmith, Peterborough, Cambridgeshire 01780 783102
  cases@winesmith.co.uk

WineTime, Milnthorpe, Cumbria 01539 562030 **MC**

T. Wright, Bolton, Greater Manchester 01204 697805
  wayne.t.wright@fsmill.net

The Wright Wine Company, Skipton, North Yorkshire 01756 700886
  www.wineandwhisky.co.uk ✪

Wrightson & Co. Wine Merchants, Manfield, Darlington 01325 374134
  simon@wrightsonwines.co.uk **MC**

Wycombe Wines, High Wycombe, Buckinghamshire 01494 437228

Peter Wylie Fine Wines, Plymtree, Devon 01884 277555
  peter@wylie-fine-wines.demon.co.uk ✪**F**

Yapp Brothers, Mere, Wiltshire 01747 860423
  sales@yapp.co.uk ✪**MC**

Noel Young Wines, Trumpington, Cambridgeshire 01223 844744
  admin@nywines.co.uk ✪ **F**

✪ = Jukesy-rated wine merchant worthy of particular note
C = Wine sold by the case (often mixed) of twelve bottles

RECOMMENDED INDEPENDENT RETAIL SPECIALISTS, SMALL CHAINS, WINE BROKERS AND MAIL ORDER WINE COMPANIES SORTED REGIONALLY (For contact details see alphabetical list)

LONDON

John Armit Wines, W11 ✪MCF
Balls Brothers, E2 MC
Georges Barbier, SE12 ✪MC
Bedales, SE1
Berkmann Wine Cellars, N7 ✪M
Berry Bros. & Rudd, SW1 ✪F
Bibendum Wine Ltd, NW1 ✪MCF
Bordeaux Index, EC1 ✪MF
Brinkleys Wines, SW10
Burgundy Shuttle, EC3 MC
Cape Food & Wine, Staines
Cave Cru Classé, SE1 MCF
Simon Charles Vintners, SW11 ✪
Corney & Barrow, E1 ✪F
Crane River Fine Wines, Middlesex MC
Davy's Wine Merchants, SE1
Decorum Vintners, W10 ✪MC
Domaine Direct, N1 ✪C
Eagle's Wines, SW11
El Vino, EC4
Farr Vintners, SW11 ✪MF
Fine & Rare Wines, W10 ✪MF
Fine Wines of New Zealand, NW1 ✪M

Fortnum & Mason, W1 ✪
Friarwood, SW6
FWW Wines, W5 ✪MC
Goedhuis & Co., SW8 ✪MCF
The Grape Shop, SW11 ✪
The Grogblossom, NW6
H & H Bancroft, SW8 ✪MC
Handford Wines, W11 ✪F
Harrods, SW1 ✪F
Harvey Nichols & Co., SW1 ✪
Haynes, Hanson & Clark, SW1 ✪
Jeroboams (incorporating Laytons Wine Merchants), W1 ✪
Justerini & Brooks, SW1 ✪F
Lea & Sandeman, SW10 ✪
Liberty Wines, SW8 ✪MC
O.W. Loeb & Co. Ltd, SE1 ✪MC
Mayfair Cellars, SW6 MC
Mill Hill Wines, NW7
Mille Gusti, W13 ✪MC
Montrachet Fine Wines, SE1 ✪MC
Moreno Wines, W9 ✪
Morris & Verdin, SE1 ✪MC
The New Pantry, W14
Nicolas UK of London 20+ stores
Novum Wines, SE11 ✪

Oz Wines, SW18 ✪
Paxton & Whitfield, SW1
Philglas & Swiggot, SW11 ✪
Ravensbourne Wine, SE10 C
La Réserve, SW3 ✪
Revelstoke Wines, SW19 ✪MC
Howard Ripley Ltd, N21 ✪MC
Roberson, W14 ✪
Robert Rolls, EC1 ✪MCF
Selfridges, W1 ✪
Soho Wine Supply, W1
Stokes Fine Wines, SW18 ✪MC
SWIG, SW6 ✪MC
ten-acre wines, NW3 ✪
Theatre of Wine, SE10
Uncorked, EC2 ✪
The Vintage House, W1
Waterloo Wine, SE1
Wilkinson Vintners Ltd, N19 ✪MCF
Wimbledon Wine Cellar, SW19 ✪
Wine Barrels, SW11
Winecellars, NW10 ✪MC
The Wine Library, EC3
The Wine Treasury, SW8 ✪MC
The Winery, W9 ✪F

SOUTH EAST
A & A Wines, Cranleigh, Surrey C
A & B Vintners, Brenchley, Kent ✪MC

W.J. Armstrong, East Grinstead, West Sussex
Australian Wine Club, Slough, Berkshire ✪MC
Bacchus Fine Wines, Warrington, Buckinghamshire ✪C
Stanley Ball, Crawley, West Sussex
Beaconsfield Wine Cellar, Beaconsfield, Buckinghamshire
Bentalls, Kingston-upon-Thames, Surrey
The Bottleneck, Broadstairs, Kent
Burgundy Wines, Brighton, East Sussex
Butlers Wine Cellar, Brighton, East Sussex ✪
Les Caves de Pyrene, Guildford, Surrey ✪
Cellar Door, Overton, Hampshire
Cellar Door Wines, St Albans, Hertfordshire
Chiltern Cellars, High Wycombe, Buckinghamshire
Church House Vintners, Compton, Berkshire MC
Cooden Cellars, Eastbourne, East Sussex ✪
F.L. Dickins, Rickmansworth, Hertfordshire
Direct Wines, Theale, Reading MC

English Wine Centre, Alfriston,
East Sussex

Eton Vintners, Windsor M

Le Fleming Wines, Harpenden,
Hertfordshire MC

The Flying Corkscrew, Hemel
Hempstead, Hertfordshire ❂

Four Walls Wine Company,
Chilgrove, West Sussex ❂MF

Gallery Wines, Gomshall, Surrey

Garland Wine Cellar,
Ashtead, Surrey

General Wine Company,
Liphook, Hampshire ❂

Gourmet Vintners,
Billingshurst, West Sussex

Gunson Fine Wines, South
Godstone, Surrey ❂MC

Hailsham Cellars, Hailsham,
East Sussex

Hanslope Wines, Milton Keynes,
Buckinghamshire

The Haslemere Cellar,
Haslemere, Surrey ❂

Hedley Wright, Bishop's Stortford,
Hertfordshire C

Charles Hennings Vintners,
Pulborough, West Sussex

Just in Case Wine Merchants,
Bishop's Waltham,
Hampshire

Kendrick Wines, Bromley, Kent

David Kibble Wines, Fontwell,
West Sussex

Laithwaites, Reading MC

Longford Wines, Lewes,
East Sussex MC

Mason & Mason, West Stoke,
West Sussex ❂MC

Milton Sandford Wines,
Knowl Hill, Berkshire ❂MC

Off the Vine, St Albans,
Hertfordshire

The Old Forge Wine Cellar,
Storrington, West Sussex

Page & Sons, Ramsgate, Kent

Peake Wine Associates,
Fareham, Hampshire

Portal, Dingwall & Norris,
Emsworth, Hampshire

Arthur Purchase, Chichester,
West Sussex

Arthur Rackham Emporia,
Guildford, Surrey C

St Martin Vintners, Brighton,
East Sussex

Stone, Vine & Sun, Winchester,
Hampshire ❂

Stratford's Wine Agencies Ltd,
Cookham-on-Thames, Berkshire
❂MC

Taurus Wines, Bramley, Surrey

Turville Valley Wines, Great
  Missenden, Buckinghamshire
  ✪MCF
Helen Verdcourt, Maidenhead,
  Berkshire MC
Veritas Wines, Cambridge
Vicki's Wine Merchants,
  Chobham, Surrey
Les Vignerons de St Georges,
  Windlesham, Surrey
Vin du Van, Appledore,
  Kent ✪MC
The Vineyard, Dorking, Surrey
The Vineyard Cellars, Hungerford,
  Berkshire ✪MC
Vino Vino, New Malden,
  Surrey MC
Vintage Roots, Arborfield,
  Berkshire ✪M
Vintage Wine Cellars, Luton,
  Bedfordshire
The WineBarn, Winchester,
  Hampshire
The Wine Cellar, Croydon,
  Surrey
The Wine Man, Streatley-on-
  Thames, West Berkshire MC
Wine Society, Stevenage,
  Hertfordshire ✪MCF
Wycombe Wines, High Wycombe,
  Buckinghamshire

SOUTH WEST

Arkell Vintners, Swindon, Wiltshire
Averys, Bristol ✪
Best Cellars, Ashburton, Devon
Bideford Wines, Bideford, Devon
Bintwo, Padstow, Cornwall ✪
Castang Wine Shippers, Pelynt,
  Cornwall MC
Clifton Cellars, Bristol
Brian Coad Fine Wines,
  Plympton, Devon ✪MC
Constantine Stores, near Falmouth,
  Cornwall
Corks, Cotham, Bristol
Creber's, Tavistock, Devon
Dartmouth Vintners,
  Dartmouth, Devon
The Dorchester Wine Centre
  at Eldridge Pope, Dorchester,
  Dorset ✪
Execellars, Kennford, Exeter,
  Devon
Fine Cheese Co., Bath
La Forge Wines, Marksbury,
  Bath MF
Great Western Wine Company,
  Bath ✪
Hall and Woodhouse Ltd,
  Blandford, Dorset
Richard Harvey Wines, Wareham,
  Dorset MC

Hicks & Don, Edington,
  Wiltshire M
The Jolly Vintner, Tiverton, Devon
L & F Jones, Radstock near Bath
Christopher Keiller, Redruth,
  Cornwall
Laymont & Shaw, Truro,
  Cornwall ✪MC
Magnum Wine Company,
  Swindon, Wiltshire ✪
Map Wines, Bridgewater,
  Somerset
The Nobody Inn,
  Doddiscombsleigh, Devon ✪
Christopher Piper Wines,
  Ottery St Mary, Devon ✪
Quay West Wines,
  Stoke Canon, Exeter C
R.S. Wines, Winford, Bath and
  Northeast Somerset MC
Regency Wines, Exeter, Devon
Reid Wines, Hallatrow,
  Bristol ✪MF
Shaftesbury Fine Wines,
  Shaftesbury, Dorset
Charles Steevenson, Tavistock,
  Devon MC
Totnes Wine Co., Totnes, Devon
Trenchermans, Sherborne, Dorset
The Vine Trail, Hotwells,
  Bristol ✪MC

Wadebridge Wines,
  Wadebridge, Cornwall
Wessex Wines, Bridport, Dorset C
Wine in Cornwall,
  Falmouth/Penryn, Cornwall
Peter Wylie Fine Wines, Plymtree,
  Devon ✪F
Yapp Brothers, Mere, Wiltshire
  ✪MC

MIDLANDS

Amps Fine Wines of Oundle,
  near Peterborough,
  Northamptonshire
Arnolds, Broadway,
  Worcestershire
Arriba Kettle & Co., Honeybourne,
  Worcestershire C
Bat & Bottle, Oakham, Rutland ✪
Bennetts Fine Wines, Chipping
  Campden, Gloucestershire ✪
Les Caves du Patron, Stoneygate,
  Leicestershire
Ceci Paolo, Ledbury, Herefordshire
Champagne & Wine Cellar,
  Winchcombe, Gloucestershire
Andrew Chapman Fine Wines,
  Abingdon, Oxfordshire ✪
Colombier Vins Fins, Swadlincote,
  Derbyshire MC
Connolly's, Birmingham ✪

M = Mail order company, usually with no retail premises
F = Fine wine sales/wine broker/good range of expensive stuff!

Croque-en-Bouche, Malvern Wells, Worcestershire ✪MC

Andrew Darwin Fine Wines, Kington, Herefordshire

Evertons, Ombersley, Worcestershire

Evingtons Wine Merchants, Leicester

Gauntleys, Nottingham ✪

Patrick Grubb Selections, Oxford ✪

Haynes, Hanson & Clark, Stow-on-the-Wold, Gloucestershire ✪

Pierre Henck, Walsall, West Midlands MC

George Hill, Loughborough, Leicestershire

Hopton Wines, Kidderminster, Shropshire MC

Ian G. Howe, Newark, Nottinghamshire

Inspired Wines, Cleobury Mortimer, Shropshire

S.H. Jones, Banbury, Oxfordshire ✪

Mills Whitcombe, Peterchurch, Herefordshire ✪C

Nectarous Wines, Cheltenham, Gloucestershire

Nickolls & Perks, Stourbridge, West Midlands

Noble Rot Wine Warehouse, Bromsgrove, Worcestershire ✪

Oxford Wine Company, Witney, Oxfordshire ✪

Thomas Panton, Tetbury, Gloucestershire M

Parfrements, Coventry, West Midlands

Edward Sheldon, Shipston-on-Stour, Warwickshire

H. Smith, Ashbourne, Derbyshire

Stanton Wine Co., Broadway, Worcestershire

Stevens Garnier, Oxford ✪

Tanners, Shrewsbury, Shropshire ✪

Waters of Coventry, Heathcote, Warwick

David J. Watt Fine Wines, Ashby-de-la-Zouch, Leicestershire M

Weavers of Nottingham, Nottingham ✪

Whitebridge Wines, Stone, Staffordshire

Whittalls Wines, Walsall, West Midlands C

Winchcombe Wine Merchants, Winchcombe, Gloucestershire

EASTERN COUNTIES

Adnams Wine Merchants, Southwold, Suffolk ☼

Ameys Wines, Sudbury, Suffolk

Bacchanalia, Cambridge ☼

Bakers & Larners, Holt, Norfolk

Bella Wines, Newmarket, Suffolk ☼M

Bonhote Foster, Bumpstead, Suffolk M

Anthony Byrne Fine Wines, Ramsey, Cambridgeshire MC

Carley & Webb, Framlingham, Suffolk

The Charterhouse Wine Co., Spalding, Lincolnshire

East Coast Wines, Grimsby, South Humberside

Peter Graham Wines, Norwich, Norfolk

Roger Harris Wines, Weston Longville, Norfolk ☼MC

Hayman Barwell Jones, Ipswich, Suffolk ☼MC

Hills Drinks and Oasis Wines, Benfleet, Essex

Richard Kihl, Aldeburgh, Suffolk ☼FC

Lay & Wheeler, Holton St Mary, Suffolk ☼

Luckins Wine Store, Great Dunmow, Essex

Moonshine, Bourne, Lincolnshire

Thos Peatling, Bury St Edmunds, Suffolk

Laurence Philippe Wines, Chelmsford, Essex

Sandhams Wine Merchants Ltd, Caistor, Lincolnshire

Seckford Wines, Woodbridge, Suffolk ☼MCF

T & W Wines, Brandon, Suffolk

Unwined, Sedgebrook, Nottinghamshire

Wattisfield Wines, Bury St Edmunds, Suffolk

Wines of Interest, Ipswich, Suffolk

The Winesmith, Peterborough, Cambridgeshire

Noel Young Wines, Trumpington, Cambridgeshire ☼F

NORTH WEST

Booths of Stockport, Heaton Moor, Stockport

Bowland Forest Vintners, Clitheroe, Lancashire

D. Byrne & Co., Clitheroe, Lancashire ☼

Carringtons, Manchester

M = Mail order company, usually with no retail premises
F = Fine wine sales/wine broker/good range of expensive stuff!

Cheshire Smokehouse, Wilmslow,
   Cheshire
Corkscrew Wines, Carlisle, Cumbria
deFINE Food and Wine, Sandiway,
   Cheshire ✪
Rodney Densem Wines, Nantwich,
   Cheshire
Edencroft Fine Wines, Nantwich,
   Cheshire
Garrards, Cockermouth, Cumbria
Kendalls, Manchester
Love Saves the Day, Manchester ✪
Planet Wine Ltd, Sale, Cheshire MC
Portland Wine Co., Sale,
   Manchester
Quellyn Roberts, Chester, Cheshire
Richardson & Sons,
   Whitehaven, Cumbria
R & R Fine Wines, Bury,
   Lancashire ✪
Scatchard, Liverpool
Selfridges, Manchester ✪
Frank Stainton Wines,
   Kendal, Cumbria
Whitesides, Clitheroe,
   Lancashire
The Wine Mill, Nelson, Lancashire
WineTime, Milnthorpe,
   Cumbria MC
T. Wright, Bolton,
   Greater Manchester

NORTH EAST

Barrels & Bottles, Sheffield
Le Bon Vin, Sheffield
Cairns & Hickey,
   Bramhope, Leeds
Chippendale Fine Wines,
   Bradford, West Yorkshire
   MC
Great Northern Wine Company,
   Ripon, North Yorkshire M
Richard Granger Fine Wine
   Merchants, Newcastle upon Tyne
Halifax Wine Company,
   Halifax, West Yorkshire
Harrogate Fine Wine,
   Harrogate, North Yorkshire
Hoults Wine Merchants,
   Huddersfield, West Yorkshire
House of Townend, Kingston upon
   Hull, East Yorkshire ✪
Michael Jobling, Newcastle upon
   Tyne MC
John Kelly Wines, Boston Spa,
   West Yorkshire MC
Martinez Wines, Ilkley,
   West Yorkshire ✪MC
Mitchells Wines, Sheffield
Nidderdale Fine Wines, Harrogate,
   North Yorkshire ✪
Penistone Court, Penistone,
   Sheffield ✪MC

✪ = Jukesy-rated wine merchant worthy of particular note
C = Wine sold by the case (often mixed) of twelve bottles

Playford Ros, Thirsk, North Yorkshire **MC**
Premier Cru Fine Wine, Guiseley, Leeds
Roberts & Speight, Beverley, East Yorkshire
Springfield Wines, near Huddersfield, West Yorkshire
Vinceremos, Leeds **MC**
Wicked Wines, Pockthorpe, Kilham, East Yorkshire
The Wright Wine Company, Skipton, North Yorkshire ✪
Wrightson & Co. Wine Merchants, Manfield, Darlington **MC**

SCOTLAND
Cockburns of Leith, Edinburgh
The Great Grog Wine Co., Edinburgh
Peter Green, Edinburgh
Henderson Wines, Edinburgh
Inverarity Vaults, Biggar
Irvine Robertson, Edinburgh **C**
Kelly of Cults Ltd, Aberdeen
J & H Logan, Edinburgh
Luvian's Bottle Shop, Cupar, Fife
Peckham & Rye, Glasgow ✪
Raeburn Fine Wines, Edinburgh ✪
Laurence Smith, Edinburgh **MC**
Valvona & Crolla, Edinburgh ✪

Villeneuve Wines, Peebles, Haddington and Edinburgh ✪
T.B. Watson Ltd, Dumfries
Wine Raks, Aberdeen

WALES
Ballantynes, Cowbridge, Vale of Glamorgan ✪
Cheers Wine Merchants, Swansea
Irma Fingal-Rock, Monmouth, Monmouthshire
N.D. John, Swansea
Joseph Keegan & Sons Ltd, Holyhead, Isle of Anglesey
Moriarty Vintners, Cardiff
Terry Platt Wine Merchants, Llandudno, Conwy ✪**MC**
Shaws of Beaumaris, Isle of Anglesey
William Stedman, Caerleon, Newport
Welshpool Wine, Powys ✪
James Williams, Narberth, Pembrokeshire

NORTHERN IRELAND
Compendium, Belfast
Direct Wine Shipments, Belfast ✪
Ells Fine Wines, Portadown
James Nicholson, Crossgar, Co. Down ✪

CHANNEL ISLANDS

Bergerac Wine Cellar,
  St Helier, Jersey
Dunells Premier Wines Ltd,
  St Peter, Jersey ✪

Victor Hugo Wines,
  St Saviour, Jersey
Sommelier Wine Co. Ltd,
  St Peter Port, Guernsey ✪

If you are a wine merchant in the UK and would like to be
mentioned on this list, or if your details are listed incorrectly, the
author and publisher will be delighted to amend later editions.
We have tried to make The Wine List as helpful as possible but if
you have any ideas as to how we could improve it then write to
The Wine List, c/o Headline Book Publishing, 338 Euston Road,
London, NW1 3BH.

AUSTRALIA

| Margaret River, WA | 2003 2002 2001 2000 1999 1997 1996 1995 1994 1993 1991 1990 |

| Barossa Valley, SA | 2003 2002 2001 1999 1998 1997 1996 1995 1994 1991 1990 1986 |

| Clare Valley, SA | 2003 2002 2001 2000 1999 1998 1997 1996 1995 1994 1991 1990 |

| Coonawarra, SA | 2003 2002 2001 2000 1999 1998 1996 1994 1993 1992 1991 1990 |

| Yarra Valley, VIC | 2003 2002 2001 2000 1999 1998 1997 1995 1994 1993 1992 1991 1990 |

| Hunter Valley, NSW | 2003 2002 2001 1999 1998 1996 1995 1994 1993 1991 |

FRANCE

| Alsace | | 2003 2002 2001 2000 1999 1998 1997 1996 1995 1990 1989 1988 1986 1985 1983 |

Burgundy	Chablis	2003 2002 2000 1999 1998 1997 1996 1995 1992 1990 1989 1988 1986
	Côte d'Or	2003 2002 2001 2000 1999 1998 1997 1996 1995 1992 1990 1989 1988 1986 1985 1983
	Beaujolais	2003 2002 2000 1999 1998 1997 1995 1990 1989 1988

Bordeaux	Left Bank	2003 2001 2000 1999 1998 1996 1995 1990
		1989 1988 1986 1985 1983 1982
	Right Bank	2003 2001 2000 1999 1998 1996 1995 1990
		1989 1988 1986 1985 1983 1982
	Sauternes	2003 2001 1999 1998 1997 1996 1995 1990
		1989 1988 1986 1985 1983
Rhône	Northern	2003 2001 2000 1999 1998 1997 1996 1995
		1994 1991 1990 1989 1988 1985 1983
	Southern	2003 2001 2000 1999 1998 1995 1990 1989
		1988 1985 1983 1981
Loire	Sweeties	2003 2002 2001 2000 1999 1997 1996 1995
		1993 1990 1989 1988 1985 1983 1982
Champagne		2003 2002 2000 1999 1998 1997 1996 1995
		1990 1989 1988 1985 1983 1982
Languedoc/ Roussillon		2003 2001 2000 1999 1998 1996 1995 1994
		1993 1990 1989 1988 1986 1985
Provence		2003 2001 2000 1999 1998 1997 1996 1995
		1993 1991 1990 1989 1988 1985 1982

GERMANY
Mosel

2003 2002 2001 1999 1997 1996 1995 1994
1993 1991 1990 1989 1988 1985 1983

Rheingau	2003 2002 2001 1999 1998 1997 1996 1995 1993 1990 1989 1988 1985 1983

ITALY
Piedmont	2001 2000 1999 1998 1997 1996 1995 1990 1989 1988 1985
Tuscany	2003 2001 2000 1999 1997 1996 1995 1993 1990 1988 1986 1985 1982
Veneto	2003 2002 2001 2000 1997 1995 1993 1990 1988 1985

NEW ZEALAND
North Island Hawkes Bay, (reds)	2003 2001 2000 1999 1998 1996 1995 1994 1991
South Island Marlborough, (whites)	2003 2002 2001 2000 1999 1998 1997

PORTUGAL
Vintage Port	2003 2002 2001 2000 1997 1995 1994 1992 1985 1983 1980 1977 1970 1966 1963

SOUTH AFRICA
SOUTH AFRICA	2003 2002 2001 2000 1997 1995 1994 1993 1992 1991

SOUTH AMERICA
Chile   2004 2003 2002 2001 1999 1996 1995

Argentina   2004 2002 2001 1999 1997 1996 1995

SPAIN
Rioja   2003 2002 2001 2000 1999 1998 1996 1995
                       1994 1991 1990 1987 1982 1981

Ribera del Duero   2003 2001 1999 1998 1997 1996 1995 1994
                       1991 1990 1987 1986 1983 1982 1981

Penedès/Priorat   2003 2001 2000 1999 1998 1996 1995 1994
                       1993 1992 1985

USA
North Coast   2003 2002 2001 1999 1998 1997 1996 1995
                       1994 1993 1992 1991 1990 1987 1985 1984

Napa and Carneros   2003 2002 2001 2000 1999 1997 1996 1995
                       1994 1993 1992 1991 1990 1987 1986 1985
                       1984

Central Coast   2003 2002 2001 2000 1999 1998 1997 1996
                       1995 1994 1993 1992 1991 1990

Oregon/Washington   2003 2002 2001 2000 1999 1998 1996 1994
                       1992 1991 1990 1989

notes

index 237

238   index

ACKNOWLEDGEMENTS

Once again, I would like to thank everyone I have met over the last year, both in the UK wine trade and on my travels abroad – your time, energy, enthusiasm and, crucially, willingness to open thousands of bottles of wine for me is both phenomenally generous and very humbling. There are far too many of you to name individually but you have all helped enormously, and without you I would never be able to put this book together. The Wine List is an immensely enjoyable book to work on and I look forward to doing it all again next year. Special thanks must go to Nathalie for her incredible support, Isadora and Elspeth for their extraordinarily perceptive tasting notes (they are three and four years old!), Ma and Pa for their stoicism, Robert Kirby for his quiet guidance, and the team at Headline – Bryone, Emily, Fiona, George, Kerr, Nicci, Val and especially Jo for her amazing eye for detail and unerring encouragement, and James for his exceptional powers of persuasion.